Steven J. McShe

∴ April '86.

Saint-Germain-des-Prés

Jean-Paul Sartre, philosopher and writer

Paul Webster and Nicholas Powell

Saint-Germain-des-Prés

Constable · London

First published in Great Britain 1984
by Constable and Company Limited
10 Orange Street London WC2H 7EG
Copyright © 1984 by Paul Webster and Nicholas Powell
ISBN 0 09 465480 8
Set in Linotron Plantin 11pt by
Rowland Phototypesetting Limited
Bury St Edmunds, Suffolk
Printed in Great Britain by
St Edmundsbury Press
Bury St Edmunds, Suffolk

Contents

List of Illustrations

Acknowledgements

The authors would like to thank the many people who gave advice, guidance or administrative help for this book which is based more on original conversations than written material. Some people gave up a considerable amount of working time to point out new sources, following the progress of the book like worried relatives. As it is impossible to mention individual kindnesses in detail, the authors have to fall back on an alphabetical list to express their gratitude. They would particularly like to mention Raymond Aron, Alexandre Astruc, Serge Barcellini, Jean-Louis Barrault, Nicolas Bataille, Claude and Ida Bourdet, Jean Bruller (Vercors), Jacques Canetti, Jean Cau, Anne-Marie Cazalis, Jacques Doniol-Valcroze, Guy Dumur, Marguerite Duras, Léo Ferré, Antoine Gallimard, Juliette Gréco, Roger Grenier, André Halimi, Robert Hossein, Eugène Ionesco, Francis Jeanson, Eartha Kitt, Dionys Mascolo, Helen Moran, Laurence Morel, Marcel Mouloudji, Jean-Jacques Pauvert, Alain Resnais, Nathalie Sarraute, Catherine Sauvage, Robert Scipion, Simone Signoret, Philippe Sollers, Marcelle Tiraboschi, Alain Vian, Claire Webster and Timothy Webster. Habie Schwarz researched the cinema chapter. Caroline Moorehead of *The Times* supplied the reaction of Simone de Beauvoir to the publication of *Le Deuxième Sexe*. The authors would also like to note the kindness of the library staffs at *La Croix*, *L'Express*, *L'Humanité*, *Le Matin*, *Paris Match* and the Photothèque of the Ministry of Culture. The book was edited by Elfreda Powell.

Introduction

J'irai cracher sur vos tombes

The Broussais General Hospital where Jean-Paul Sartre died in 1980 is set at the southern extreme of Paris's fourteenth arrondissement in grey, urban architecture. More than a mile of narrow streets and congested main roads separate the hospital, with its aspect of a northern textile mill, from Montparnasse cemetery where he is buried.

Sartre died in exile from his intellectual homeland in the cultural heart of the Left Bank, an introverted square of streets caught between the elegant nineteenth-century buildings and literary cafés of the boulevard Montparnasse and the banks of the Seine along Saint-Germain-des-Prés and the Quartier Latin. In a sense, his body had to be reclaimed from alien country for burial in the academic and literary atmosphere where he had spent all his adult life until his death at seventy-four on April 15.

The escort that brought him back among his own was to develop into the most impressive spontaneous homage given to any cultural figure since the war; a gathering that became both a pageant of contemporary French social history and a demonstration of Sartre's power to stir controversy even in death.

Several hours before the funeral procession got under way at 2.35 pm on April 19, four days after he died of pulmonary oedema, an anonymous black-clad woman carrying a red rose wrapped in silver paper had begun a long wait at the hospital gates. By the time the hearse emerged she was surrounded by 20,000 people. The procession swelled to more than 50,000, bringing traffic to a halt as thousands of others watched from their windows or on television screens.

However, it was not a solemn occasion. Sartre's funeral, like his life, was marked by passion and chaos. The crowd literally fought over his body once they had swarmed into Montparnasse cemetery where many of France's great men and women are buried. For days, newspapers had stirred up a national fervour over the Sartrian heritage, publishing hundreds of pages of tributes.

Even the Right, which had vilified his calls for moral, social and political reform during the past three decades tried to make amends. President Valéry Giscard d'Estaing, whose conservative supporters were the most virulent opponents of Sartre's Left-wing philosophy, went to the Broussais Hospital to bow over the corpse.

The verbal mêlée inspired by attempts to claim a part of the Sartrian legacy developed into physical clashes at the funeral. In scuffles, as people pushed towards the grave, trampling over Baudelaire's tomb and breaking memorial crosses, a man fell head first into the newly-dug pit. Another was taken to hospital after being beaten to the ground while men and women had to be treated by first aid volunteers. Sartre's last minutes under a grim, drizzly sky were marked by screams, insults, tears of pain and cries of triumph or dismay. One word was heard over and over again: 'Indecent, indecent.' It had been repeated hundreds of times since the hearse had emerged from the hospital to be surrounded by flocks of professional and amateur photographers.

The crowd seemed to have little unity either in age or cause.

What might be called the family mourners were few in number, a handful of people who had remained friends with Sartre over the years despite his deliberately quarrelsome nature. But most people had come because the diminutive, podgy philosopher and author had marked their lives in different ways during his uneven political course along the edges of the Communist Party until he announced his total disillusion with the movement two years before his death.

Among the oldest were former pupils at Paris lycées who remembered Sartre as a fascinating philosophy teacher before and during the war who encouraged rebellion against family and national values. A bigger group had been affected by Sartre's two decades in Saint-Germain-des-Prés after the war when the quartier's existentialist vigour caused a cultural exodus from Montparnasse. Others had fought alongside Sartre in his opposition to the Algerian war, crucible of the French post-war conscience, while the youngest had formed an attachment through his backing of the extreme Left in his last years and foundation of the newspaper, *Libération*.

But the mass of mourners was broken into other fractions as Sartre had been in the forefront of the major battles for minority groups for more than thirty years, a role that followed the swerves of his bewildering political zig-zags and survived both savagely expressed contempt from his enemies and a horrifying last decade of crippling illness. During these struggles, Sartre had often claimed to be a fundamental anarchist. It was hardly surprising that his funeral obeyed no known rules, that it resembled the disordered political marches against authority that he had so often led.

In this turbulent and sometimes violent atmosphere, the only person who seemed to have come expecting a conventional burial was his lifelong companion, Simone de Beauvoir. She had long feared that the philosopher would die before her – 'the worst thing that could happen to me' – and she seemed numbed with shock. Their last decade had united them in a miserable fight to give Sartre's life some meaning as he fought against appalling health and blindness. When he died, she was at the

Broussais Hospital, which used to be known as La Charité. She lay down beside his cold body and slept with him for some hours until a nurse came to cover Sartre with a sheet.

At the funeral, where she was easily recognisable by her tangerine-coloured turban, she was jostled and pushed by a crowd unable to comprehend that the burial meant more to her than other intimate memories she had shared in her autobiography and novels. She, above all, had made Sartre public property, handing on analysis of his personal, moral and philosophical struggles to an avid public as if the great man should be read like a newspaper. She had refused to marry him and would not live with him, despite their close relationship, and no one yet knew of the curious post-mortem ceremony at the Broussais Hospital when she had lain beside the corpse. At the Montparnasse cemetery, she was just one more component in a grey fiesta until a gatekeeper went to get a chair from his lodge and set her apart as a half riot swirled around her.

A few days later, De Beauvoir, whose flat overlooks the cemetery, returned there with a few friends, including Simone Signoret, Yves Montand and Juliette Gréco, for a private reflection on Sartre's life. By then, she was preparing to write the harrowing account of the philosopher's last years, *La Cérémonie des Adieux*. In the next two years, she also released his incomplete Phony War diaries and his love letters.

The enormous success of these books showed how deeply Sartre had entered the national conscience. Philosophical, literary and moral guerilla wars, awakened by Sartre, were to be refought with undimmed passion. Two of France's main literary magazines, *Lire* and *Les Nouvelles*, in 1982 and 1984, both decided that no French intellectual had filled the vacuum left by the philosopher. As the fifth anniversary of his death approached in 1985, the Sartre cult was being reassessed with as much excitement as during the post-war years, the period when he lived in the picturesque quartier of Saint-Germain-des-Prés.

It is still impossible to trace any political or social progress in post-war France without finding lines directly linking argument and counter-argument to the atmosphere created around

Sartre during the years of the Liberation and the Fourth Republic to its demise in 1958. These were the Saint-Germain years when an economically desperate and militarily humiliated France displayed a cultural vigour unmatched in Europe, an intellectual renaissance that has not yet run its course.

Political controversy stirred by Sartre's attachment to revolutionary Marxism would alone justify a study of the area during the post-war years as it was to draw in all the most honoured writers of the day including Albert Camus, André Malraux, Louis Aragon and François Mauriac who were either attracted or repelled by the philosopher's argument or personality. The long-term significance of this debate can still be seen in the make-up of François Mitterrand's Socialist administration of 1981.

But Sartre, with his insistence on an atheistic, free-conscience philosophy of existentialism was also to release forces that created a middle-class youth movement that broke down France's strict moral traditions. The movement produced some of the most fascinating youth leaders of the Forties and Fifties – Boris Vian, Juliette Gréco, Françoise Sagan and Brigitte Bardot – whose mode of life was to find its adepts all over the Western world.

The determined campaigns for women's independence by Simone de Beauvoir contributed to moral liberalism that, linked with the youth cult, shook the rigidity of Europe's most conventional bourgeoisie. Pressure for a personal choice of life-style created a dynamic of its own that led indirectly to the creation of the Absurdist Theatre of Eugène Ionesco and Samuel Beckett and the cinéma Nouvelle Vague of François Truffaut and Alain Resnais. Neither Jacques Brel nor Georges Brassens, nor a host of other poet singers, would have had such an impact without the atmosphere of Saint-Germain-des-Prés and the legend of its most famous cellar club, Le Tabou.

This rebellion across many fronts had great difficulty emerging from the square kilometre of streets between the church of Saint Sulpice and the Seine, which make up the parish, or in crossing the class lines from the young Parisian middle class which provided its main following.

The area was considered a refuge for free thought, an escape from the rest of the capital still preoccupied with trying to reconstruct a version of the feeble, divided Third Republic that had been dismantled during the Vichy period and largely resurrected in 1945 as the Fourth Republic. Parliament, Church and Army behaved as if the most disastrous event in French history, the Second World War, owed nothing to the inherent flaws in the fabric of national institutions and the outdated character of social attitudes.

Intellectual leaders in Saint-Germain, including those who rejected existentialism and sought a progressive form of Christian-based Socialism, felt under siege. For some years after the war there was a feeling that the Resistance movement, which had a strong base in Saint-Germain, had not been fully dismantled, particularly as the Vichy influence was still powerful in national politics.

To cross the boundary into Saint-Germain in the late Forties was often considered a political or moral statement as both the Catholic Church and the Communist Party considered that the area represented a descent into evil and heresy. Although it was to attract a stream of foreign intellectual visitors like William Faulkner, Ezra Pound, Carson McCullers, Richard Wright or Arthur Koestler, fascinated by its stimulating debating atmosphere among its literary cafés and cellar bars, there were many French writers who refused to set foot there at all except to see their publishers.

Even now, there are some who prefer to believe that the Saint-Germain era was a fleeting accident or a highly-successful publicity operation, although its rise and fall can be traced as easily as its international influence. They argue that Saint-Germain existed as an intellectual centre before and after Sartre, particularly because most publishing houses were there and the industry itself had its joint headquarters on the boulevard Saint-Germain. But without Sartre's presence from 1942 until he moved back to Montparnasse twenty years later,

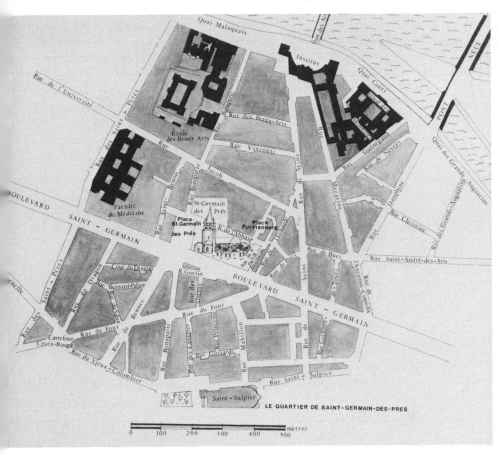

Map of Saint-Germain-des-Prés

Café de Flore is on the corner of Saint-Benoît and Saint-Germain. Les Deux Magots is on the corner of the Place and boulevard Saint-Germain. Sartre's flat is on the corner of the Place and rue Bonaparte. Le Tabou is on the corner of rue Christine and rue Dauphine

Saint-Germain would have probably been no more than a cultural annexe to the geographically wider idea of the Left Bank.

Sartre's influence, however, would have been considerably less without the élitist, highly-concentrated French tertiary education system, a factor unlikely to recur since the opening out of university education following the May 1968 student riots. Until higher learning institutions were spread throughout Paris and the nation, after these riots, all advanced educational influence was exercised within a narrow band of territory on the Left Bank where only a few thousand students, handpicked in the provinces and Paris, were prepared for national leadership. For several years, they were destined to live on an enlarged campus, forming clans based on the traditions of their learning institutions, repeatedly told to revere the eminent academics who guided them. Among the art, medical, law, political science and literature students, the élite of the élite, like Sartre, came from the Ecole Normale Supérieure, which supplied lycée professeurs with the vocation of educating a new generation of leaders.

To maintain influence after graduation, it was necessary to keep strong links with the Left Bank where even the National Assembly and Senate were situated. The intellectual star system, with its jealousies and friendships, depended on the instant access to a very restricted network. The centre often shifted and the geographical terms to describe ideas were not always simple. The first movement to seize on the term Rive Gauche to give an illusion of progressive politics was a Thirties' fascist movement.

Even the geographical limits of Saint-Germain-des-Prés, Montparnasse or the Quartier Latin are often elastic as they can suggest cultural or political ideals rather than clearly defined boundaries. Left Bank itself, is often used to describe a state of mind rather than a strict reference to the fifth, sixth and seventh arrondissements running along the Seine opposite the supposedly more bourgeois districts on the Right Bank. As an image of progressive thought, Left Bank obviously includes much of the fourteenth arrondissement and the boulevard Montparnasse with its literary cafés, La Rotonde, La Coupole and Le Sélect as well as the nearby Closerie des Lilas.

Scattered around this area of the fourteenth are artists' ateliers, including Jean Dubuffet's, and some 'fringe' theatres and clubs. Eugène Ionesco and Simone de Beauvoir are among its best-known residents, but the peak of Montparnasse's fame was in the Twenties and Thirties with the influx of American, British and Irish writers at a time when André Malraux and André Gide dominated a militant French Left-wing conscience.

Learning institutions are concentrated nearer the river. Hardly two kilometres separate France's élite at the Sorbonne, the medical faculty, the Beaux Arts, the Political Science Institute, the Ecole Normale Supérieure, the city's most-prized lycées and, until recently, the Polytechnique. L'Institut de France, overlooking the Seine at the Pont Neuf, shelters France's leading cultural and scientific associations, including the Académie Française.

In the Thirties, Montparnasse's main rival as an intellectual gathering point was Montmartre, way across to the north of the river. The Surrealists, a rebellious group of young bourgeoisie attracted by anarchy linked to earlier Dadaism, met at the café Cyrano in the place Blanche under Montmartre itself, the turn-of-the-century gathering point for Impressionists.

Saint-Germain-des-Prés, however, is barely five minutes' walk from the place Montparnasse, now dominated by Europe's biggest office block. The rue de Rennes is a direct link with Saint-Germain which, in the Thirties, had the attraction of a rural backwater. Its square kilometre of territory, split in two by the boulevard Saint-Germain, built for Napoléon III by Baron Haussmann, covers hardly thirty streets, many of them with picturesque names evoking a period of commercial and ecclesiastical prosperity in the middle ages. The enclosed, village atmosphere of Saint-Germain, which became so important after the war in creating an introverted society, is enhanced by the beautiful Abbaye de Saint-Germain on the central square. The Abbey, dedicated to an early Christian Parisian Bishop, has an eleventh-century tower, the oldest in Paris.

In the Thirties and Forties, the medieval atmosphere was almost untouched. What little traffic there was avoided the narrow streets where the walls of the ancient houses appeared to lean dangerously into the cobbled alleys. Some roads were still

Saint-Germain-des-Prés

The Abbey of Saint-Germain with the terrace of the Deux Magots in front

The junction between the rue de Seine and rue de l'Echaudé

The offices of Les Editions de Minuit, home of the Nouveau Roman

Le Tabou cellar bar in the rue Dauphine as it is today

Place Saint-Germain with the 11th-century Abbey. Sartre lived in the block of flats on the left of the picture

The Café de Flore on the corner of the rue Saint-Benoît and the boulevard Saint-Germain

The fountain and church of Saint-Sulpice at the southern limit of Saint-Germain

paved with slippery woodblocks well into the Fifties. It was a
pleasant place to walk in, particularly in the summer, when the
narrowness of the streets provided shade absent along the wide
pavements of the boulevard Saint-Germain. Historians were
particularly attracted to the quartier, one of the last remnants of
old Paris which evoked the lush fields and the monastic rhythm
on the Left Bank before Saint-Germain developed haphazardly
into a prosperous commercial centre. Patronage from influential cardinals, including De Bourbons, had attracted the quartier's share of famous residents over the centuries. Among them
were Bernard Palissy, an artist who developed the French
ceramics industry in the sixteenth century, the playwright Jean
Racine who died there in 1699 and the nineteenth-century
painter, Eugène Delacroix, who painted a chapel in Saint
Sulpice. Later, Honoré de Balzac established his printing
works in Saint-Germain.

By the twentieth century, the quartier was considered something of a slum in comparison to the spacious nineteenth-
century apartments in Montparnasse. Most of its residents were
working class, except for students, mainly from the Beaux-
Arts, who were prepared to put up with lodgings made damp by
the closeness to the Seine and the rats which infested the cheap
hotels and boarding houses that depended on a shifting population of young tenants.

However, the place Saint-Germain-des-Prés with its chest-
nut trees, handsome church tower and the sunny terrace of the
Café des Deux Magots made a pleasant detour for Montparnasse residents, some of whom would be making their way to
the main publishing houses, including the dominant Gallimard,
or the Académie Française on the Quai Conti, overlooking
the Pont Neuf. Nowhere in Paris was there a scene more
reminiscent of a rural parish.

The Deux Magots, which had once been a wholesale textile
depot, had two rival cafés, the Brasserie Lipp across the
boulevard Saint-Germain and the prosaic Café de Flore on the
same pavement on the corner of rue Saint-Benoît. The Deux
Magots had its most interesting period before the first World

War when literary links were established, notably with the Italian-born poet Guillaume Apollinaire. But its clientèle was considered somewhat bourgeois, booksellers, lawyers and other professional career men. In the Twenties and Thirties, the Brasserie Lipp was more popular with intellectuals. It had also established its role as a politicians' meeting ground as both the National Assembly and the Senate were short bus rides away. It was there in 1935 that the extreme Right-wing Action Française, which recruited much of its strength from the law students in the Quartier Latin, tried to lynch the Socialist leader, Léon Blum.

The novelist, Boris Vian, who inspired the post-war youth movement, considered reference to the high days of the Lipp and the Deux Magots as much part of Saint-Germain's 'pre-history' as the links with Racine or Delacroix. The modern Saint-Germain era began with the sudden popularity of the Flore in 1938, but several people who were to play a leading role after the war had made Saint-Germain their centre well before that.

Marguerite Duras, then a secretary in the Colonial Office after coming to Paris from Indo-China in her early twenties, had moved into the flat in the rue Saint-Benoît that would be a centre of unorthodox Communist debate in the Forties. Pierre Bost, a well-established novelist whose screen adaptations after the war were to make him a contemptuous figure for the cinema Nouvelle Vague of the Fifties, lived in the rue de l'Abbaye. As a schoolboy Alain Resnais moved into the rue de l'Université, on the edge of Saint-Germain in 1938, a year that saw the publication of Sartre's *La Nausée*.

By that time, a group of dissident Surrealists had broken away from the Montmartre clan, and were meeting regularly in the Café de Flore because there was an easy Métro link with the Montmartre area. Among them were Jacques Prévert, the group's leader, who would write what amounted to Saint-Germain's post-war anthem, 'Je suis comme je suis', and the actor-director Roger Blin who launched Samuel Beckett as a playwright.

Gaston Gallimard, the publisher who sponsored the post-war generation of authors who concentrated around Sartre, was a regular at the Lipp while Raymond Queneau, a Gallimard author, whose influence on Boris Vian was immense, won the Deux Magots literary prize for a novel, *Chiendent*, in 1933. Queneau, another former Surrealist, celebrated his prize at the Flore and abandoned the Deux Magots for ever in 1938 when André Breton, the disputed Surrealist overlord, decided to make his headquarters there.

Unconsciously, Gallimard and Queneau established a post-war pattern in which Gallimard's publishing offices in the rue Sébastien-Bottin next to the church of Saint-Thomas-d'Aquin became a sort of colonial outpost of Saint-Germain where writers would gather before visiting the area's ever-growing number of literary cafés and cellar bars. Foreign authors were often taken on guided group tours to see the main gathering places. In the Thirties, though, there was little to suggest that cafés like the Old Navy on the boulevard Saint-Germain would become a meeting place for the theatre's avant-garde, that the Montana hotel bar would be a base for progressive film-makers or that Le Village bar would become associated with a publishing phenomenon called 'Saganism'.

No café has had so much influence on French cultural life in so short a time as the Café de Flore, whose heyday lasted only between 1938 and 1946. Before Prévert's group began meeting there, attracting a young gang of future cinema and stage stars, Saint-Germain's most generally recognised contribution to contemporary culture was the office of the *Cahiers des Arts* on the other side of the boulevard in the rue du Dragon. The magazine provided a focal point for expatriate artists like the Swiss, Alberto Giacometti, who was closely involved with Sartre's entourage after the war, even modelling some of his thimble-sized sculptures on the tables of the Café de Flore while the philosopher wrote nearby.

But an even greater attraction for expatriates than *Les Cahiers des Arts* was the presence of Pablo Picasso's atelier in the rue des

Grands Augustins often visited by his friend, Georges Braque. Picasso's own following included many of the Spanish refugees of the Franco era who frequently met him at the Flore during the war. The rue des Grands-Augustins, where the actor-director Jean-Louis Barrault and his actress wife, Madeleine Renaud, lived was just outside the boundary of Saint-Germain in the Quartier de la Monnaie.

But, like many other small 'islands' of influence such as the rue du Vieux Colombier, the southern end of the rue de Rennes or the rue de l'Université, it was so strongly associated with the life of Saint-Germain that Grands Augustins residents were considered part of the family centred on the Flore. The café had been taken over in 1938 by its often irascible but fatherly proprietor, Paul Boubal, an exile from the central French region of the Auvergne like the owners of the Lipp and the Deux Magots.

On his arrival, the café was totally renovated, breaking a link with its clientèle of local tradesmen and shop assistants and its last memory of a brief period when an all-woman orchestra used to play there at the turn of the century.

Boubal's functional décor, which is still unchanged, was the setting Sartre and De Beauvoir discovered when they took refuge there during the war to write their books. It was the starting point for the establishment of two currents of a post-war controversy both linked to the writers' influence. The more serious current pursued a struggle for political commitment in culture, a campaign for a liberal form of Marxism. The other, refusing the austerity of the period or the temptation to look back over France's defeat, chased an easy-going hedonism that grew from innocent egotism to a much-attacked youth rebellion.

The fusion of these two currents, their identification with Sartre's philosophy of existentialism and the attraction they formed for astute commercial exploitation are the essential elements of the Saint-Germain period. Some of the results were dubious, some of the characters involved were detestable. Much of what was written or said about Saint-Germain, particularly in the first decade after the war, was myth. But even in trying to separate the legend from the lies, the attractive personalities from the contemptible, the honest innovation from the commercial invention, there is no escape from the fact that the activists of Saint-Germain forced France to modernise its ideas and institutions. An already diminished France might well have dwindled to insignificance after the war without the interplay of personalities mobilised either in favour of or against the turbulent philosophy of the tiny quartier.

Sartre made his entrance onto this narrow stage when he escaped from prisoner-of-war camp in 1941. The German Army were in occupation. France was cut off from the world. There could have been no better time to judge the abasement of a proud nation; no better time for one of the greatest thinkers of the century to assess his own power to change history.

1

L'Etre et le Néant

The Paris which Jean-Paul Sartre discovered in March 1941 on his escape from a German PoW camp was only a travesty of a capital. The presidential palace, the National Assembly and the Senate were empty. Laws were made in the distant Auvergne spa town of Vichy. The French nation was no longer a Republic of Liberty, Equality and Fraternity. In its place was a State with the dour appeal to Work, Family and Fatherland. Not only was the country unevenly split between two military bureaucracies, both obsessed with order and racial purity, but parts had been torn away and attached to Germany or put under Italian Fascist rule.

There were no clear lines of loyalty. Militarily, France belonged to Germany. Legally, it belonged to the French State. Morally, it belonged to an overseas-run Resistance. Paris belonged to no one.

Sartre was confronted by a 'flat and useless agglomeration' when he stepped from the train at the Gare de l'Est. It was not merely the lack of motorised traffic that made Paris seem empty. There was no pride nor purpose. The two million inhabitants lived through the war years with a sense of resignation rather than defeat.

The only resistance to the Nazis when their troops marched down the streets around the Arc de Triomphe in June 1940 was from the crippled guardian of the unknown soldier's tomb and the chairman of a First War veterans' association. Together, the two old men symbolically lit the flame, sang the Marseillaise and wept.

Until a French-crewed Sherman tank of Leclerc's Second Armoured Division stood near the same spot in August 1944 and destroyed a Panzer on the Place de la Concorde, Paris was left on the sidelines of the war, governed like no other territory in Occupied Europe. Only the echoes of bombs on the distant industrial periphery and the furtive murders of resistants by the Nazi occupier punctuated an atmosphere approaching peacetime normality.

The capital was a special territory, subject to Vichy laws, but with its own German military ambassador, Otto Abetz, a pre-war envoy to the French government. A man of considerable charm and intelligence, Abetz was sent to Paris with his own cultural commando, a group of German academics, philosophers and writers, including Ernst Junger, whose job was to flatter the French intelligentsia into believing they had a role in a European-wide cultural empire. Goebbels wanted him to crush French intellectual independence. Abetz, whose wife was French, preferred to seduce and domesticate French culture like the many mistresses he attracted among leading French actresses.

As neither French nor Germans were concerned that Jews were excluded from this uneven union, cooperation under the auspices of the Institut Allemand became a way of life with many Parisian writers, artists and entertainers attending Nazi receptions and joining organised visits to Berlin. Their collaboration, reported in a wholly pro-Nazi Press, dulled public reaction to the Occupiers.

To all except those brave men and women who had reason to fear the Gestapo, Paris became the symbol to the outside world of Nazi tolerance. In his prison cell after the war, Abetz claimed that more plays, films and books had been produced during the war than in peacetime and that 'even an ideological adversary like Jean-Paul Sartre' had been encouraged to publish and stage plays.

Despite this broadmindedness, little of the progeny of the German-French cultural marriage of ideas remains alive today. Most of it was hysterical racial propaganda. One work, however, was to be at the core of a moral rebellion against bourgeois values in post-war France. Sartre's *L'Etre et le Néant*, the book which provided the social and political coherence to Saint-Germain-des-Prés, was largely a development of the existential theories of the pro-Nazi philosopher, Martin Heidegger, who died in 1976. The same atheistic ideas were vulgarised in existential plays and books by Sartre and his companion, Simone de Beauvoir.

The rebellion, with its Marxist and anarchist overtones, was not one which either the Nazis or the French Right wanted and it was not Sartre's intention to give them encouragement. But the book serves to illustrate the complications of judging personal behaviour during a period in which the masters of abnegation and discipline nurtured a guru of personal freedom and anarchy.

Sartre did not explain why he chose the Occupation, one of his most productive literary periods, to draw French attention to Heidegger. The war years were 'so ambiguous that the memory I keep of them is confused', he was to say later. In that confusion, though, Sartre felt a sensation of liberty that he was never to feel in his life again.

'Because the Nazi poison slid right into our thoughts, each rightful thought was a conquest. Will it be understood if I say that, at the same time, it was intolerable but that it suited us perfectly well?'

The paradox sums up the most equivocal period of French history when the dividing line between resistance and treason was as narrow as that between genius and madness. It was a paradox bespoke for Sartre who saw himself in his autobi-

ographical study, *Les Mots*, as being made up of 'all men and
who is worth all and any of them'. He was also made up of all the
contradictions of his time; worth all and any of them.

Sartre's decision to escape from Stalag XII on the Luxembourg
border where he was interned after being rounded up with his
meteorological unit in the Lorraine, was not an easy one. The
period of camp life was among the most reassuring of his adult
life. He rediscovered much of the warmth and easy companionship of his student days at the Ecole Normale Supérieure in
Paris's Left Bank fifth arrondissement where he spent his four
happiest years before graduating as a philosophy teacher.

Remnants of Sartre's war diaries show how much he enjoyed
his period as a private, testing wind levels behind the front
lines. The other privates – he called them 'acolytes' – showed
him the respect due to a man of 35 already on the edge of fame
after publishing his self-analysing novel, *La Nausée*. In return,
they offered him access to a sense of working-class solidarity
that he was to idealise and envy all his life.

Obsessed by what his friends called his 'mongrelism', a facet
of which was the conflict between his bourgeois background
and an unconditional, sentimental admiration for the proletariat, Sartre revelled in the easy-going defiance of the van-
quished in the PoW camp which broke down rank, physical
difference and class structure.

'What I liked in the camp was the sensation of being part of a
mass,' Sartre said, a statement which clashes with his life-long
preoccupation of the impact of 'The Other'.

The feeling that he was part of a group of social outcasts
developed during the Phony War when the French people made
it clear to their soldiers that they were opposed to another fight
with Germany. He was hurt at not being fêted like a First War
poilu and struck by the remark of one of his companions who
said that while on leave he was treated with contempt 'like one
of the unemployed'.

In the camp, Sartre experienced the thrill of joint resistance
to the Occupier. On July 13, at midnight, all 1.8 million French

soldiers in captivity joined in the *Marseillaise*, an enormous chorus that echoed across frontiers. By Christmas, Sartre was sure that intellectuals could contribute to encouraging action against the Nazis and wrote a play recalling Jewish resistance to the Romans at the time of the Nativity.

'It is the coward who makes himself a coward and the hero who makes himself a hero', Sartre was to write five years later in 'L'Existentialisme est-il un humanisme?' 'What counts is total commitment.'

The first real test of that theory was his escape. Sartre obtained false medical papers from a priest who had been at the centre of many of Sartre's discussions on Heidegger's existential theories while the French philosopher was attached to the camp infirmary. The papers indicated that Sartre was a civilian rounded up by mistake. German doctors were easily convinced that the French Army was unlikely to have called up a man with genuinely weak and painful eyes, approaching blindness because of a divergent squint.

As only 70,000 French prisoners were to escape during the war, Sartre's action was worthy even if it lacked the courage of another escape that year, a daring leap over the wire by Sergeant François Mitterrand, only recently recovered from battlefield wounds after two previous attempts.

The philosopher, however, was inspired by a dream of action like that of the future President of the Republic, who founded an intelligence network among returning prisoners that recruited among the intellectuals of the Left Bank. 'Any other attitude would be a flight, a hollow pretension, a masquerade founded on bad faith', Sartre wrote in January 1940 in another reference to 'commitment'. His aim as he took the train to Paris from Luxembourg was to ensure that if the Germans won the war, they would lose the peace. What he failed to take into account was the appalling lethargy which had overtaken France in the presence of the invader.

On his first night in the capital after so many months of overcrowded camp life, Sartre was shaken by a sense of agoraphobia.

He was made dizzy by the sensation that customers in cafés had so much space that they seemed 'scattered like stars'. With an open regret for the simplicity of the prisoner-of-war's life, he was also seized with sudden anger that he had re-discovered the complications of 'bourgeois society'.

As a prisoner, Sartre was not fully aware of the significance of Hitler's victory. Not only was resistance negligible, but all traditional points of moral leadership which could have rallied the French had disappeared in the terms he had known before capture. Political parties no longer existed, having dumped all responsibility on the Vichy régime in a shameful, common resignation. The Church was committed to Maréchal Pétain who, after meeting Hitler, convinced the French that Collaboration was a 'matter of honour'. What was left of the Army buried its weapons. Young conscripts, who had never reached the Front, were transferred to rural, civilian worksites and put under the charge of a former Chief Scout.

The familiar names of popular entertainment heroes still appeared on cinema posters and theatre announcements in the streets. A few months later, the first Resistance movements were to condemn publicly dozens of people who seemed so much at the heart of that solid, everyday France that repre-sented a reassuring link with the pre-war years. Personalities like the boxer Georges Carpentier, singer Maurice Chevalier and actor-director Sacha Guitry were treated as traitors because they had seen no point in altering their way of life.

Even more striking for Sartre was the way the publishing industry had overcome its scruples over providing indirect moral support for the invader. His own publisher, Gaston Gallimard, launched a collection of German Classics. The publisher also placed the unbalanced collaborationist author, Pierre Drieu la Rochelle, in charge of the literary magazine, *La Nouvelle Revue Française*. This last decision particularly pleased the Germans, who, absurd as it seems, rated the influential Revue alongside the big banks and the Communist Party as a fundamental force of the nation.

Having been handed the task of censoring itself, the publishing industry, in general, complied with Nazi priorities. No moral disapproval was shown when the Jewish firm of Calmann-Lévy, which published Flaubert, Dumas and Sand, was forcibly baptised Les Editions Balzac. Meanwhile, the publisher Robert Denoël released a book on *How to Recognise a Jew* and Mercure de France pressed hard to bring out *Mein Kampf* with a new preface by Hitler. Eventually, more than a thousand books and seven hundred authors were banned with little pressure from German censors.

The scarcity of motorised traffic, replaced by bicycles and bicycle taxis, and the general discretion of the occupiers added to an illusion of provincial tranquillity and common-sense compromise that needed courage to disturb. Like every would-be resistant, Sartre was faced with inventing his own form of defiance while accepting a life style little different from that of peace time except for the highly organised rationing system for food, clothes and fuel.

In one of the most inspired phrases of the war, the pro-Nazi magazine, *La France au travail*, remarked that the 'French were not up to the catastrophe they had so minutely prepared'. The slogan of the early period was coined by the poet and author Jean Cocteau, who plunged with enthusiasm into the murky waters of Collaboration saying: 'Long live the shameful peace.'

Sartre pulled hard the other way, but commitment through intuition or reason was not enough. No one hurried to welcome the returning prophet of action. Sartre had no background of political activism. He was not a celebrity and his physical appearance, which seriously undermined his self-confidence, made him an unlikely recruit for spontaneous militant movements forming around him. To all intents and purposes, Sartre had turned up at a party without an invitation and no one was ready to give him one.

Many years later, Sartre said that when he wrote *La Nausée*, whose title was changed from *Melancholia* for commercial reasons, he was unaware that he was already an anarchist before the war. Few of his friends would have realised that at the time either, as Sartre was a man of habit who needed a feeling of security represented by familiar surroundings.

After the first shock of a return to a 'hollow and empty' Paris with its 'sad and miserable festivals', Sartre settled down in the Hotel Mistral in Montparnasse where he kept a room near to that of his lifetime companion, Simone de Beauvoir, three years younger than him. He was aware that the war had 'cut his life in two'. But he was not yet aware that the central role of Montparnasse in French cultural life which made the position of his living quarters so important, was already compromised by a heavy German presence that would contribute to the intellectual drift towards the narrow streets of Saint-Germain-des-Prés hardly a kilometre away.

It was in this same hotel room that Sartre had often discussed his programme for life in which he saw himself at the age of fifty, with a solid body of literary work behind him, ready to take on great causes similar to André Gide's campaign against colonialism. The day of reckoning came fifteen years too early and he was still only a teacher of philosophy with one reasonably successful novel and a collection of short stories, *Le Mur*, behind him.

His only choice was to take up his job again at the Lycée Pasteur in Neuilly, Paris's richest outer suburb. He taught the younger brothers and sisters of those who had laughed at him on his first appearance in 1938 after leaving his first teaching post in Le Havre. Sartre disliked the atmosphere of the lycée with its hierarchy and conservatism, and despised the other teachers for their intellectual inferiority. But he was totally at ease in the classroom despite the fact, as the actress Simone Signoret recalled, the boys at Pasteur at first thought he 'was off his nut'.

Signoret, who went to Pasteur's girls' associated lycée remembers Sartre's arrival at the school as something of a legend which spread rapidly among the closed circle of the capital's élite teaching establishments. Sartre's bizarre look – one eye seemingly unconnected to the rest of his face – was added to by his clothes, a turtle-neck sweater and a crumpled, camel-hair overcoat.

The casual style was provocative to children from the most convention-ridden bourgeoisie in western Europe who were further taken aback when Sartre puffed his pipe in class and sat on the desk. His teaching methods and their impact were the first indication of the role he was later to play in Saint-Germain-des-Prés as the moral liberator of young people suffocating from a strict upbringing. It was due as much to his personality as his sudden rise to fame.

At Pasteur, a deliberate iconoclasm spilled over outside the classroom with Sartre taking his pupils to a local café and spending hours demolishing French literary style and praising American authors unknown or even forbidden in Neuilly homes like Hemingway, Dos Passos, Steinbeck and Faulkner. He left a marked impression on his pupils. More than forty years later, many still have a vivid memory of his readiness to listen, his kindness and, above all, his persuasive voice and the eloquent, lively and funny way he talked.

Whatever the hatred with which Sartre was attacked after the war for his effect on youthful morality, parents who sent their children to him for a conventional education seem to have been disarmed by his gentle appearance. One of his pupils, who became a psychiatrist, made a study of the 'powerful transference effect' that Sartre was able to induce in his pupils by the almost theatrical atmosphere of his lectures, an effect which adults felt when they flocked to his post-war conferences at the Sorbonne.

This confident, classroom Sartre contrasts with his own recollections of an appalling lack of 'self-coincidence' that resulted from an arrogant feeling of intellectual superiority and a sentiment of hopeless inadequacy in almost every other field. Writing—from the start it was a religion, he said—was a raft in a turbulent inner life.

Sartre's father, a naval officer, died when he was six months old and he was brought up in the home of his Alsatian grandfather, a language teacher and uncle of the missionary Albert Schweitzer. The grandfather, 'a stale God' as Sartre described him, treated Sartre and his widowed mother on equal terms as 'the children'. Sartre said later in talks with his biographer and confidant, Francis Jeanson, that the absence of his real father followed by the 'treachery' of his mother in remarrying when he was twelve years old, made it easier for him to lose his religious faith at an early age. A family split over rival allegiances to Catholicism and Protestantism is cited as another reason for his 'mongrelism'.

Iris Murdoch, the British novelist whose interpretation of Sartre's philosophy played an important part in increasing his impact overseas, wrote that the philosopher's works 'described very exactly, the situation of a being who, deprived of general truths, is tormented by an absolute aspiration'.

Sartre was to turn savagely against his childhood as well as religion – 'I detest my childhood and everything surviving from it' – and searched during the rest of his life for a place where he fitted. His ugliness – he compared himself to a toad – his lack of inherited wealth and his inability to exert influence through power, all helped to exile him from what should have been his natural milieu, the bourgeoisie.

At the Ecole Normale Supérieure he renewed a friendship with his high-school companion Paul Nizan. While they agreed that they were both supermen intellectually, Nizan was worshipped by Sartre as a social and physical superior.

In an appreciation of his friend written when Nizan's books began to re-emerge after the war, Sartre was obsessed both by the fact that his friend had a direct line into the proletariat through his working-class father and by Nizan's ability to assume, with elegance, all changes in masculine fashion which 'turned to rags' when Sartre wore them.

Nizan was much taller than Sartre. Worse, he too had a squint which Sartre saw as handsome because it was convergent while his own divergent squint made his face look like 'un-ploughed land'. This admission of a haunting disability was also recorded in his diaries, where Sartre said he sought the company of beautiful women in the hope of 'unloading' some of his ugliness on them.

Nizan was one of the few people who could have guided

Sartre on his return from prison camp. He had been a member of the Communist Party for twelve years before resigning after the German-Soviet Pact in 1939, walking out of his job as a journalist on the Communist paper, *Ce Soir*, edited by the novelist and poet, Louis Aragon.

The Communists took their revenge by blocking the distribution of Nizan's sizable literary output. Aragon refused to speak of him again except in insulting terms. Nizan would nevertheless have had the influence and the political experience to convince resistance leaders of Sartre's sincerity or point out to Sartre where his talents could best be used. Nizan was killed by a stray bullet during the retreat, leaving an enormous vacuum in Sartre's life.

Sartre's political naïveté during this period was staggering for a man who was to have so much influence in Left-wing circles after the war. He did not even vote in 1936 when the Socialist-led Popular Front came to power and his interest in the Spanish Civil War was confined to admiring André Malraux's virile commitment to the Republican cause. By his own admission, his mobilisation in September 1939 was the first time he felt aware he was a 'social being'. The long gestation period that Sartre needed to sort out his ideas is illustrated by an analysis by Francis Jeanson who believed that Sartre's most important political work, *La Critique de la Raison dialectique*, published in 1960, was fomented by his early war-time sense of powerlessness. It was a message of commitment which, for many, came far too late and was too incomplete to influence the main currents of post-war political thinking.

But the development of Sartre on his return from PoW camp would be meaningless without reference to his relationship with Simone de Beauvoir, a friendship which she described as a 'morganatic marriage' and 'necessary love'. Her own view of this affair which started more than a decade earlier when Sartre was first and she second in the final teaching examinations is disturbingly clinical as far as emotion is concerned, if the non-fictional and fictional stream is followed through her books like *La Force de l'age*, *L'Invitée* or *Les Mandarins*.

Jean Cau, a prize-winning novelist who became an enemy of Sartre's political views after working as his personal assistant for a decade, says the friendship was, first and foremost, 'terribly intellectual'.

'She was his first disciple and a sort of possessive, very constricting mother. Sartre was much more of a poet, more of an artist than her – more naïve, less sectarian, a more open person who loved life. Simone de Beauvoir was his mirror, his adviser, his police force in every sense of the term – for his writing and his personal relations. Her vocation was to be a super prof.'

Perhaps because she is afraid of being saddled with even an echo of stereotyped feminine role, De Beauvoir reinforces this message in her memoirs, fictional and non-fictional. She herself records that one of her pupils called her a 'clock in a refrigerator' while her fascination with 'spinsterish' gossip caused one American writer, Nelson Algren, to call her 'Madame Yackety-yack', after she used their love affair in one of her books. Even women who admire her for her pioneering work for women's rights through *Le Deuxième Sexe* which brought her insults from many men whom she thought were friends have been disturbed by her cold eyes and lack of humour.

For Sartre she always represented a student *copine* – chum – although they spoke to each other with exaggerated middle-class formality all their lives. Sartre was not a person to reinforce her confidence in femininity – his view of love was that it was 'to make oneself loved'. In his books, his lovers are constantly living out a selfish drama in which they wonder about their partners' reaction towards themselves. As De Beauvoir deliberately reduced her physical attractiveness from her student days wearing what Henriette Nizan, Paul's widow, described as 'mourning clothes', she found it difficult to accept Sartre as a male, finally coming to terms with him as an 'intellectual superior'.

Sartre certainly felt tenderness for her as he records that she used to call him her 'doting knight' and that he told her 'everything, more than everything'. And there can be no doubt

A gathering around Simone de Beauvoir's tea-pot at the Café de Flore. Jean-Paul Sartre is on her right, Jean Cau his secretary on her left. On Sartre's right the novelist, Jacques-Laurent Bost

as to the importance of her influence on Sartre's work-rate and dedication, even forbidding him to watch television which she thought bad for him.

Sartre received a tremendous blow to his pride when *La Nausée* was first turned down by the publisher Gaston Gallimard, but De Beauvoir pulled the tearful writer out of a depression by repeating her conviction that the book he had written and rewritten over more than five years was a great work. She had been his most ardent motivator since student days when she admired his first failed novel: *J'apporte l'ennui, j'apporte l'oubli.*

The daughter of a strict Parisian bourgeois family, Simone de Beauvoir's personal rebellion against her background was itself too convention-bound to be much of an inspiration in the war years. As a High School teacher, deliberately living a materially sparse life in hotel rooms just around the corner from where she was born, her main fascination was in encouraging other people to write, finally becoming infected with the passion herself. Her political commitment at the time amounted to little more than the vague feeling that 'the more people were odd or lost, the more we had sympathy with them'.

Between them, Sartre and De Beauvoir had a poor basis for launching a Resistance network, grandly entitled Socialism and Liberty, with its headquarters in the Hotel Mistral. Its members were to include Sartre's former pupils and another graduate of the Ecole Normale Supérieure, the existentialist philosopher, Maurice Merleau-Ponty, the same age as De Beauvoir, who helped found the philosophical and literary review, *Les Temps modernes*, with Sartre after the war.

The group was no less ineffectual than several other intellectual movements set up both by the Left and the Right at this time and, despite its imprudence, the Germans showed no interest in clumsy attempts to distribute anti-Nazi tracts. Sartre soon began to appreciate the tremendous difference between putting heart into a few soldier prisoners surrounded by their guards and trying to rally a city of two million people who gradually became as indifferent to the sight of occasional German soldiers as they were to French policemen.

When writing of Paris under the Occupation for *France Libre* in 1945, Sartre went as far as recognising that a 'sort of shameful and indefinable solidarity was established between Parisians and these [German] soldiers who, deep down, were so similar to our French soldiers'.

Since the average Parisian was also aware that resistance would result in a tightening of rationing Sartre was placed in the intellectual equivalent of the railwayman's dilemma: the largely Communist run railways were ferociously anti-Nazi but the railwaymen knew that sabotaging a train would just as readily cut food supplies to Paris as to the German Army.

No one came to offer Sartre advice, least of all the Communists who were suspicious of his friendship with Nizan and were circulating rumours that Sartre had been sprung from PoW camp in exchange for collaboration. The literary establishment of which he felt part was scattered and divided. Even the most superficial census showed the impossibility of joint action. André Malraux, four years older than Sartre, was living on the Mediterranean coast. André Gide, 72, was also in the south along with Louis Aragon whom Sartre detested for the part he had played in ostracising Nizan after the break with the Party.

Raymond Aron, who awakened Sartre's interest in phenomenology and was his sergeant-instructor when he was called up for National Service in 1929 was in London. Many authors, like Julian Green and André Maurois, were in exile in the United States where they were later joined by Antoine de Saint-Exupéry. François Mauriac, who eventually became one of the most vigorous literary resistants, was at the time suspect as a Catholic bourgeois. Apart from that, he and Sartre were literary enemies. National cultural monuments like the ageing Paul Claudel were in the Free Zone and associated with the Vichy régime, Claudel even writing an ode to the Maréchal, one of four hundred written for him by recognised writers during the war. Worse, writers like Drieu la Rochelle, Louis-Ferdinand

Céline and Robert Brasillach, another brilliant graduate of the
Ecole Normale Supérieure, had sold out to the enemy.

The man who held the key to the inner counsels of intellectual
resistance was the burly former director of Gallimard's *La
Nouvelle Revue Française* for fifteen years, Jean Paulhan. Gide
and other literary pacemakers founded the review in 1911 and
its *NRF* symbol was of such towering prestige that the Germans
issued a priority order for its takeover on invading Paris.

The magazine was the literary hallmark of the publishing
company founded by Gaston Gallimard, a man who exercised
enormous influence on French literature. Gallimard was a
businessman with a shrewd ability to delegate responsibility
while effacing himself behind his ponderous manner and way of
thinking.

A good marriage had inflated the family fortune and turned
Gallimard's offices into a family gathering with brothers, sons
and nephews running the business side. Gallimard entered the
war as the dominant French publishing firm able to attract first
refusal on almost any literary work. It was to emerge from the
war, after a policy of astute balancing between Collaboration
and Resistance, with its writing stable reinforced by the avant-
garde of post-war talent including Sartre, De Beauvoir and
Albert Camus.

The link between pre-war and post-war glory was the novelist, essayist and linguist Jean Paulhan who could make or break
writers through the influence of *La Nouvelle Revue Française*,
which depended on his instinct as a talent scout.

But to appease the invader the magazine was taken from
Paulhan, then 56, in 1940 and put under the direction of Pierre
Drieu la Rochelle, three years older, a renegade Surrealist and
confirmed novelist who was fascinated by the 'bodily revolution' of Nazism. Obsessed by the theme of decadence, he said
he loved strength so much that he desperately wanted to see its
renaissance in his own country where he welcomed Nazism as
'virile socialism'. Drieu, whose incipient madness was to turn
increasingly against himself, intended using the magazine to

gain revenge on the 'heap of Jews, paederasts and surrealists' whom he saw as his personal enemies in a long struggle for intellectual influence. The first of those enemies was Paulhan whom Drieu saw as 'pusillanimous and cunning, swinging between hysterical surrealism and the senile rationalism of the republic of high school teachers'.

Paulhan, who came from the warmth of Nîmes in the south and who had taught Latin in a Madagascar High School was impervious to insults from the unbalanced Drieu who intended to make him 'creep along the walls, his tail between his legs'. But there is no better indication of Drieu's disarray, traceable to an unhappy bourgeois childhood, than the fact he engineered Paulhan's release after the latter was arrested by the Nazis in 1941. Drieu, whose literary career had reached its peak with the publication in 1939 of *Gilles* an autobiographical, pro-Fascist novel, also secretly asked the more liberal-minded members of Ambassador Abetz's cultural commando to protect Sartre and Malraux when they were prisoners.

Paulhan had been given control of the pre-war review partly because his provincial temperament made him an arbitrator in the incestuous literary world where birth in a bourgeois Paris arrondissement, an education in an élitist lycée and conse-cration at a Grande Ecole were as important as basic talent. A realistic judge of his own literary output, Paulhan was able to ride above the incessant quarrels, spite, arrogance and bitter-ness of the mainly Paris-bred intellectual circus. In handing over to Drieu to protect the dominant publishing position of Gallimard, Paulhan lost none of his influence or originality.

He kept an office in Gallimard's headquarters in the rue Sébastien Bottin on the fringes of Saint-Germain-des-Prés while Drieu – 'a long sad fellow with an enormous bumpy skull', according to Sartre – ran the Review just down the corridor. Paulhan's little room became the most important gathering place for intellectual resistance with so many people coming to see him that there was rarely enough room to sit.

Paulhan and Drieu assumed roles similar to managers of rival sporting clubs, gathering around them teams that represented

Left and Right, Communism and Fascism, Liberty and
Domination. While Drieu hosted uniformed Nazis or French
Collaborators, Paulhan recruited for underground publishing
houses like Les Editions de Minuit.

Drieu was too fragile, too prone to nervous crises, too full of
self-hatred to survive the confrontation with the solid, often
mischievous Paulhan. The latter destroyed Drieu's takeover of
the *NRF* by convincing writers to boycott the publication or at
best 'collaborate badly' by offering 'inept non-fiction and stupid
novels'.

The struggle was brief and merciless. Drieu's *NRF* closed
for want of talent, starting a process of increasing isolation that
led to his miserable, lonely suicide at the Liberation. Paulhan's
stature as the inspiration of intellectual resistance soared. It
would have needed only a nod from him for Sartre to have been
absorbed into the ranks in 1941. Paulhan, however, was still
attached to the vestiges of Surrealism with its intense relationship with Marxism. He was still sensitive to Communist
reports, not least from Aragon hiding in the south, that the little
schoolmaster was either politically compromised or incompetent.

Paulhan was not the only Left Bank figure who could have
helped Sartre. One of those who saw Sartre fairly frequently at
the Café de Flore was an underground writer, Vercors, who
went to the café 'because it was in my quartier', against the
advice of Resistance leaders. Vercors, whose real name was Jean
Bruller, was supposedly scraping a living at the time as a
carpenter and not even his wife knew he was the author of the
most famous of Resistance novels *Le Silence de la Mer*.

A book illustrator before the war, Bruller instinctively felt
that any sort of public cultural effort during the war was playing
the Nazis' game which he saw as intended to destroy French
individuality. *Le Silence de la Mer* in which a German officer
(inspired by Abetz) discovers the awful truth of the Nazi
campaign was also a moving love story, making the warning
pass easily.

The RAF parachuted hundreds of copies of the book into

'Vercors' (Jean Bruller), author of *Le Silence de la mer*, the most famous book of the French Resistance movement

France to raise Resistance morale. *Le Silence de la Mer* was also the first work to be published by the underground Editions de Minuit that produced twenty-four volumes by various underground authors, including François Mauriac and Louis Aragon, from its presses in Paris.

Bruller had received training from British Intelligence which helped to conceal one of the most daring operations of the war, as thousands of books were secretly distributed by hand. He was not involved in recruiting writers – that was another of Paulhan's secret activities – but he made it clear that he disapproved of employing writers who sought official publication in the Occupied Zone.

'I was a bad carpenter and did not earn much money,' he said. 'All the same, I think that writers could have earned their living from other jobs, teaching for instance.'

Vercors-Bruller was one of the most active in trying to save Collaborationist writers after the war, but there were others who felt more strongly that intellectuals were not trustworthy unless they were silent.

Saint-Germain-des-Prés was one of the most active areas of Paris Resistance during the war, with the offices of *Les Cahiers des Arts* in the rue du Dragon, just opposite the Café de Flore, a main contact and meeting point. Just across the road, in the rue Saint-Benoît, François Mitterrand visited the author Marguerite Duras to recruit intellectuals for his espionage network.

The most important Resistance event from a strategic point of view also took place in Saint-Germain-des-Prés. On May 27 1943, four days before Sartre presented his first play, *Les Mouches*, the Conseil National de la Résistance met in the rue du Four under the presidency of De Gaulle's delegate, Jean Moulin, tortured and murdered by the Nazis soon afterwards. It was the Council's first meeting, unifying underground groups on the Left and Right, combining the best of the militant and intellectual movements.

Sartre's name was not mentioned although one of those present was the Socialist representative Daniel Mayer, the first man the writer was to ask to find him a Resistance role.

Both Sartre and De Beauvoir led a disordered life in their bare hotel rooms. Dirty plates, half-used toilet articles, unwashed clothes and scattered books had to be hurriedly tidied away to make room for secret meetings. But in their work schedules they kept to the strict demands of a student timetable with the school holidays playing an important part in the ritual.

Not even the war and all the frustrations of a divided country broke their routine. In 1941 the three-month summer vacation was allied to the ambition to 'do something for France' and obtain the clearance of two men who might nail lies about Sartre's escape and supposed Collaborationist role. It was decided to cycle in the Unoccupied Zone and see Malraux and Gide.

Sartre returned from the war impressing De Beauvoir with a sense of moral rigidity he had acquired as a prisoner. He nevertheless accepted the offer of a stolen bicycle from one of De Beauvoir's pupils, perhaps feeling that bicycle stealing was a game as about 7,000 a month were illegally changing hands.

Pre-war holidays with De Beauvoir had more than proved the limits of Sartre's physical capacities. De Beauvoir showed her superior stamina during crippling walks in foreign countries which left Sartre—'the little man', she called him – broken with fatigue and on the verge of despair. The cycling trip was as bad. Neither, they discovered, knew how to repair a puncture and Sartre could barely manage twenty-five miles a day. He was already so involved in the preparation of his philosophical study, *L'Etre et le Néant*, and his play *Les Mouches* that he would go into reveries and swerve into roadside ditches.

Like hundreds of people every day, they crossed the supposedly uncrossable demarcation line between Nazi and Vichy France by following a regular guide, thus bypassing the German Ausweiss centre in Paris which gave out only fifty passes a day. Had the story of the rest of the journey got back to Resistance movements in the capital, it would not have encouraged them to recruit the couple. At first Sartre could not find Gide's address in the south because he could not read his own handwriting. De Beauvoir drank too much and knocked herself unconscious in a spill, losing a tooth.

They first visited Daniel Mayer, who friends had indicated might be recruiting for Left-wing movements. He could do no more than suggest that they could send a birthday card to the imprisoned Socialist, Léon Blum.

There were even more depressing moments in the meetings

with the two intellectual giants. Gide was, even for Sartre with his superiority complex, a literary god whose regularly published *Carnets* were the Left-wing conscience of an entire generation. But he was too old to believe in a French recovery. He had written the year before that 'compromising with the enemy was not cowardly but wise' and that there was no sense in beating against the bars of the cage. He gave Sartre no encouragement whatsoever to continue the fight.

He must also have been suspicious of this emissary from what looked like the inaccessible Nazi-controlled north and the 'unpassable' demarcation line. He tried to persuade Sartre not to visit Malraux, warning the couple that the Spanish Civil war hero thought little of either Sartre's political ideas or the way he wrote.

The warning fed resentment already smouldering in Sartre's mind which was to burst into a spectacular quarrel after the war. Malraux's past revolutionary activities fascinated him, but he wrote patronisingly in his war diaries that Malraux's texts were like his own first drafts and that his style was sloppy.

Malraux had already told friends that he was 'fed up fighting lost causes'. He was also in the middle of a painful break with his first wife, Clara, and was living in Roquebrune on the Riviera with Josette Clotis who was to give him two children.

His own 'derisory' war against Germany in a tank unit whose engines broke down and which was rounded up in its entirety after a brief skirmish depressed him even further. For the next two years he did little except concentrate on his philosophical novel, *La Lutte avec l'ange*.

The meeting with Sartre and De Beauvoir was not helped by Malraux's permanent irritating sniff which sounded like contemptuous sneering as he asked Sartre how many weapons and how much money he had. The war, he said, would be won by the big British and American battalions, a reply he was also to make when approached by the underground Combat movement.

The Sartre-De Beauvoir tandem, however, was charged with moral righteousness. The visit is recorded in De Beauvoir's

André Gide in the mid-fifties, a literary god whose Left-wing writings
inspired an entire generation

minutely detailed autobiography, *La Force de l'age*, in a way
that sounds like a rebuke to Malraux for enjoying the delights of
a villa looking across the bay of Monte Carlo. The meal of
chicken Maryland served by a white-gloved butler was particularly shocking to De Beauvoir, who rarely let a meal go by
without drawing an historical lesson from it.

Malraux was perfectly happy in the villa, which he had
borrowed from Lytton Strachey's sister, Dorothy Bussy. It
provided an idyllic retreat with orange trees, magnolias and a
calm blue sea in an area of France much freer than any other.

The indignation of Simone de Beauvoir was later fed by reports that Malraux travelled up to Paris to see Drieu la Rochelle, who became godfather to Malraux's second child before Malraux joined the Maquis after the Allied invasion of North Africa.

There seems little doubt that Sartre was deeply hurt by the reception he received during the 800-mile bicycle trip and the general lack of interest in his ideas of resistance. Sartre took rebuffs badly, recalling with bitterness all his life the ragging he had at school during a three-year period at La Rochelle and the dirty trick his friends played on him when they convinced him a pretty girl had taken to him. The joke hurt even more as Sartre believed he had bought friendship by stealing from his mother's handbag to buy pastries for his tormentors.

De Beauvoir gave rational reasons for the rapid disbanding of Socialism and Liberty – Sartre had heard of some arrests – but the physical risks of resistance were part of the attraction and it is more likely that Sartre reacted in much the same way as he would have done as a child. When rebuffs became too hard to bear, when his stepfather irritated him with his Right-wing views, Sartre indulged himself in an orgy of writing to win back his self-respect, a habit traceable to the age of eight when he wrote a short story called *The Banana Seller*.

The attraction of a half-lit room, a desk and an apparently intolerable workload was a lifetime's therapy for Sartre, an 'eternal and colossal student', according to a friend's description. His exclusion from other childhood playgroups because of his shyness or his over-protective mother made him yearn from an early age for a posthumous revenge on humanity, the discovery after his death of a monumental manuscript that would make his surviving detractors repent their actions and revere a misunderstood genius.

Two months before Sartre returned from his PoW camp, the best known of contemporary French philosophers, Henri Bergson, a 1927 Nobel prizewinner, died after a long illness. His end was accelerated when the Nazis, backed by Vichy, told all Jews in the Occupied Zone to register in order to exclude

André Malraux, with whom Sartre was to have a spectacular
quarrel after the war

them from academic and business life.

Bergson, whose work on consciousness first aroused Sartre's
interest in philosophy, went from his sick bed in pyjamas and
slippers to the commissariat at Passy, in the sixteenth arrondissement, a few streets from where Sartre was born. It was an
act of solidarity as Bergson, who was eighty-two, had converted
to Catholicism although he kept the secret until just before his
death.

The stiff, moralising philosopher who looked so much a
representative of the nineteenth century would have been excused the census: special orders were drawn up to allow him to
return to his birthplace in Paris after a brief exile in the south
and the Germans agreed to let him die in peace. His humiliating

final weeks are part of that troublesome footnote surrounding
the roundup and murder of thousands of French Jews, the
first of whom were at the centre of Paris's intellectual life.
The silence of their non-Jewish academic friends, including
De Beauvoir, who hurriedly signed documents denying any
Jewish parentage, is still a sensitive subject more than forty
years later.

At the time of Bergson's death, French philosophy was stuck
in a rut, unable to add much to the long stream of ethical
thought stretching back to Descartes. Moral leaders looked for
inspiration outside French frontiers and, particularly, outside
the constraints of Christianity. The philosophical idea which
became so closely associated with Sartre – existentialism – was
in itself a well-worn label based on concepts of essence and
existence dating back to Aquinas and was being propagated at
the time of Bergson's death by the philosopher and playwright
Gabriel Marcel.

Sartre, aware that Bergson's death would relaunch a debate
on the state of French philosophy set out to provide a new basis
of reflection on atheistic existential thought in *L'Etre et le
Néant*, a title which acknowledges the influence of Martin
Heidegger's *Sein und Zeit* (*Being and Time*). Sartre had been
turning over existentialist ideas since 1932 when he studied
Heidegger and his mainly German influences at the Institut
Français in Berlin, taking over a scholarship from Raymond
Aron who, like Sartre, respected Bergson as another old boy of
the Ecole Normale Supérieure.

There is little indication that Sartre saw *L'Etre et le Néant* as
part of his burning ambition to become a full-time professional
writer. The book was aimed at a limited audience as there was
little chance in wartime Paris of finding enough paper to publish
the 350,000-word work. By the time it reached Gallimard in
1943 the paper available for commercial purposes was barely
ten per cent of pre-war supplies. By spreading the quota thin
and using poor quality paper the number of titles was maintained by publishers but print orders were minimal. As a result,
only 2,000 copies of *L'Etre et le Néant* – dedicated to 'Castor',

Sartre's pet name for Simone de Beauvoir – were published and the book was not reviewed.

There is an element of spring-cleaning about the work, as if Sartre wanted to sum up his frustrating years trying to widen the narrow horizons of the children of the detested bourgeoisie. Despite the fact that it was later treated as a moral guide, its message being that the only sense in life is the one you give it, *L'Etre et le Néant* poses a multitude of questions on life without a Supreme Being. The promised follow-up with some of the answers came only in 1960 with *Critique de la Raison dialectique*. The rushed attempt to answer critics immediately after the war in 'L'Existentialisme est-il un Humanisme?' was sufficiently slapdash to embarrass even Sartre.

In writing *L'Etre et le Néant*, Sartre was also sending out a personal signal, that he was cutting through the brushwood of ideas to rediscover the route that would lead to the realisation of his ambition to dedicate himself wholly to literature. Philosophy, he explained later, was 'a means to this end', leaving no doubt that the discipline was a poor second in this hierarchy after literature. In Parisian terms, sending out signals meant putting yourself on display, preferably in a literary café, where it would soon be known that the author of *La Nausée* was writing again.

A clue to where much of the book was written, other than in depressingly underfurnished hotel rooms, is a long passage on how a café waiter assumes his identity through determinedly acting out the flourishes and traditions of his job. The inspiration came in the Café de Flore on the boulevard Saint-Germain which became Sartre and De Beauvoir's headquarters.

Before the war, Montparnasse's literary cafés with stalls that sheltered so many famous authors had served the same purpose. But these cafés were now too conspicuously occupied by German soldiers lapping up a cultural tradition that would also fascinate the liberating Americans three years later.

The Saint-Germain quartier of 7,000 people, stretching down to the banks of the Seine, dominated by the eleventh-century abbey tower in the central Place, was well-established when Sartre and De Beauvoir moved their lodging to the Hotel de la Louisiane with its Thirties style front on the rue de Seine. The working-class district, with its little shops, sawdust cafés and artisans' workshops, was a refuge of dissident pre-war Surrealists who shunned the conventional Montparnasse intellectual rendezvous by establishing a rebellious end of the Left Bank around the Beaux Arts college. Guillaume Apollinaire, the Italian-born poet and precursor of Surrealism, was one of the area's twentieth-century pioneers and he attracted his disciple, the massive André Breton, who became a solid regular at the Flore's rival establishment, Les Deux Magots, whose terrace looks across to the abbey.

The student population from the Fifth arrondissement's Sorbonne and the lycées in the adjoining Latin Quarter where Sartre was a pupil, provided a continual replenishment for Saint-Germain's youthful population attracted by low prices in backstreet cafés and boarding houses. The Flore was enlivened in the mid-Thirties by the '*bande à Prévert*', followers of the witty poet and script writer Jacques Prévert whose table, usually engulfed with laughter, was one of the few the often disagreeable *patron*, Paul Boubal, liked to join.

Many descriptions of the Flore stress its provincial character although it had been redecorated in modern, urban style with red leather seating as the war broke out. Other descriptions portray the place as a club which needed courage to enter, a feeling so strong that uniformed Germans kept away. The Collaborationist Press put it on the blacklist as a smoke-filled alcoholic hide-out for Jews and homosexuals. The Resistance put the café out of bounds saying the Gestapo went there. Neither verdict stopped the Flore attracting both leading Collaborationists and Resistants who kept to their corners while exchanging ideas through the channels of the non-committed who treated the Flore as a no-man's-land.

One of its functions was as an informal recruiting centre for the theatre and cinema. Simone Signoret, whose acting career can be traced directly to her first visit to the Flore in March 1941 when she was invited as an outsider from the bourgeois eighth arrondissement, described the café as the equivalent of Cinderella's pumpkin.

In addition to the obvious attraction of meeting interesting people, not least Picasso who spent his war years in Paris, the Flore was usefully situated near many cheap restaurants where it was often possible to get a snack without food coupons. The importance for Sartre and De Beauvoir, at the time awaiting publication of *L'Invitée*, her first *roman à clef* on their relationship, was that the Flore was at the centre of the gossip network. It was very quickly known that Sartre, now teaching at the Lycée Condorcet near the Gare St. Lazare was in a hurry to quit his job while De Beauvoir's novel was causing speculation on who, among Flore regulars, would be central characters.

Sartre was able to get across the message that he was making progress on *Les Chemins de la Liberté* – the first volume, *L'age de raison* was nearly completed during the Phony War – and he was planning two important plays, *Les Mouches* and *Huis clos*.

In 1943, perhaps because they had received reports that the supposed agent provocateur, Sartre, was doing nothing more than methodically writing and rewriting a philosophical work, Communists overcame their distrust for the little philosopher and invited him to join the Comité National des Ecrivains, the Communist controlled contact group that was to make or break literary reputations after the war. At about the same time Sartre began negotiating a contract for film scripts while Simone de Beauvoir, after losing her teaching job at the Camille Sée girls' lycée embarked on a series of programmes about the Middle Ages with Radio Paris – the official Collaborationist radio station which fought a continual propaganda war with the BBC and daily condemned Britain, Bolshevism, democracy, Jews and Free Masons. The moral condemnation of writers published in the Occupied Zone eased as the war progressed, partly because it went on longer than expected and partly because it was recognised that even writers had to eat.

Once the corner towards a full-time writing career had been turned, Sartre probably did not think to glance back over his shoulder at the marathon *L'Etre et le Néant* which prepared the ground for Saint-Germain-des-Prés's post-war transformation by providing it with a mystical context. The book itself was to become a living example of that process towards self-fulfilment that Sartre first sketched out in his diaries.

The emergence of Saint-Germain-des Prés as a cultural battlefield can safely be dated to June 1943, when another event of immense importance occurred, one which can be added to the existentialist claim that 'consciousness (*"pour soi"*) emerges only in liaison with the wholeness of the *"en soi"* which surrounds it.'

Saint-Germain, like Sartre, needed the regard of 'The Other' to waken its consciousness. The Other was Albert Camus, an out-of-work journalist from Algeria who was to condemn existentialism as a philosophical suicide. On June 1, the day before Sartre's *Les Mouches* was staged for the first time, Camus arrived in Paris.

Sixteen months before, on the recommendation of André Malraux, Gallimard had given Camus a 5,000-franc advance for a novel that was as sparse and concise as Sartre's *L'Etre et le Néant* was thick and heavy. Now, l'Etranger himself was in Paris to disturb the certainties of the cultural élite.

2

L'Etranger

Little is recorded about the meeting between the two men who would contribute so much to the image of post-war France and eventually represent the crippling divisions of the Left. They first shook hands in the crowded foyer of the theatre on the first night of *Les Mouches*. Sartre was said to have found the young, dark-haired Camus, then aged 29, '*sympathique*', the most banal and non-committal of French compliments. The schoolmaster was fully occupied by a play that had taken more than two years to prepare while Camus must have felt as awkward as a new boy in his class.

Other people who met Camus during this period remarked on the unhealthy yellow colour of his skin and his furtive, reticent manner which made them assume he was already part of the Resistance movement. Only when he became more confident of his place in the Paris literary circus did descriptions mention his good looks and charm.

Sartre knew Camus by reputation. In 1942, he had reviewed *L'Etranger* for *Les Cahiers du Sud*, the leading Free Zone arts magazine which Camus read while recovering from tuberculosis in the Massif Central. The review had irritated Camus as Sartre had insisted on the consciousness of gratuitous violence in *L'Etranger*, although Camus had intended to show it as intuitive. This was an early indication of Sartre drawing on another author to support his existential theories, an operation so successful that, despite continual protests, Camus was numbered among post-war 'existentialists'.

Camus was nevertheless flattered by the first handshake. Sartre, who was eight years older, was an important introduction into the Parisian intellectual world that the Algerian journalist had admired only from afar except for three brief stays in Paris. Even in June 1943, it seemed improbable that Camus would ever become part of it himself. His priority was returning to Algiers to join his wife, Francine, and to escape enforced, poverty-stricken exile in central France.

Camus's propulsion to the peak of that establishment barely fifteen months later as an exemplary Resistant entrusted with drawing moral consequences of both Collaboration and Liberation was the result of a series of chances, his brilliant use of language, his skill as an experienced actor and a popular search for new national heroes. It was a position that Camus never planned. Unlike Sartre he had no long-term programme for life or immortality.

On that first meeting, Camus had only a confused idea of resistance to the Nazis. He had told friends that he would be useless as he suffered from an 'enormous torpor'. He was in a miserable state of health and had not worked for a newspaper for two years. His life had been thrown into confusion by the sudden invasion of Southern France in November 1942 after the Allies' attack on North Africa. The ferry service he intended to take to Algeria was cancelled and he was cut off from home. Far from being any use to resistance movements, he was living on handouts arranged by friends inside underground networks.

Because of his tuberculosis and with no prospect of a job, Camus was not to settle in Paris until November 1943, but his visit in June coincided with one of the greater ironic moments of French wartime literature. *Les Mouches* was staged in the nineteenth-century Théâtre de la Cité, previously le Théâtre Sarah-Bernhardt whose name disappeared on orders from Vichy because she was a Jewess.

The unfortunate choice of theatre for what was called a Resistance play received no comment at the time. Nor did it seem strange that the play was much praised by German theatre critics and became a popular outing for uniformed German officers. After the war, when relationships were strained, Malraux used to make a point of the fact that Sartre 'entertained Germans' while he himself was being interrogated by the Gestapo after entering the Maquis in the Dordogne.

Resistance rules on not publishing or producing in the Occupied Zone had been worn down by the indifference of the theatre, film and publishing worlds who accepted routine submission of all possibly controversial texts to the German censors. *Les Mouches*, with its redrawing of the classical Orestes-Electra themes, had passed through the Propagandastaffel offices at 52, Champs Elysées, were it was cleared by Sonderfuhrer Gerhard Heller, the chief censor.

Heller was a francophile, proud of his Huguenot descent. Several books were dedicated to him by Resistance authors during and after the war. He saw his first duty as protecting the Arts, persuading his superiors that it would be a mistake to persecute French cultural leaders. An academic and broadcaster who studied at Toulouse University and never underwent military training, Heller openly admired Paulhan. He must have known that he was a Resistant. He befriended other opponents, including Mauriac, and made no enemies on either side in the French literary world. The Collaborator, Louis-Ferdinand Céline, a qualified general practitioner, diagnosed and treated Heller's incipient Parkinson's disease during the war.

Heller's benign censorship removes little of the ambiguity from *Les Mouches* which the cofounder of the sabotage and spy network, Combat, journalist Claude Bourdet, says was not recognised at the time as being a call to resistance. In fact, the German propaganda magazine, *Signal*, praised the work as that of a 'young novelist full of personal talent' and the play was recommended to German soldiers by the German-language newspaper, *Pariser Zeitung*.

Sartre maintained that the play was a call to French people to resist Vichy pressure to repent over terrorist acts even when they brought reprisals to innocent people. The Germans either missed the heavily coded message or thought the debate was worth raising and served their cause. But as there were no protests from the Germans or hurrahs from the Resistance, Sartre's ethical discussion must have been pitched too high. *Les Mouches* was submerged into the generally healthy theatre scene of wartime Paris.

Camus was to have no second thoughts about staging his own plays in occupied Paris after his early visit to the capital. Thirty-five theatres and five opera houses were in full production, most of them playing to packed houses of mixed French and German audiences. On June 10, 1940, the last theatre to remain open, L'Oeuvre, refunded the entrance fee to its last, lonely client. Ten days later, with the Germans installed in the capital, theatres were already appealing for actors to report for duty as the stage prepared for a golden age. Apart from their entertainment role in a city desperate for distraction, theatres offered warmth and, as dancing was banned, a social gathering place to rival cafés. Because of the curfew, the final curtain had to be timed for the audience to catch the last Métro, turning that humble form of transport into a social event of its own.

Despite his growing reputation, Sartre was lucky to find a theatre and had to rely on a veteran director, Charles Dullin, an habitué of the Café de Flore. Dullin had already used his influence on Sartre's behalf in 1938 by persuading Gallimard to change his mind about rejecting *La Nausée*. The competition for a stage was fierce, not only from a flow of new talent, but also from established writers like Jean Anouilh, Jean Giono, Jean Cocteau, Jean Giraudoux and Henry de Montherlant.

Few productions made any reference to the war and none attacked the Germans. Examples of anti-Nazi remarks, even in cabarets, were rare. The best-remembered example was a joke by a comedian called Martini who would walk solemnly on stage giving a Nazi salute. As Germans prepared to respond, he kept his arm outstretched and added: 'Up to here. We're in the shit up to here.'

That audiences longed for moments of defiance was clear enough during performances of Henry de Montherlant's *La Reine morte*. At the time, the Paris-born novelist and playwright was Gallimard's most highly-paid author, but was an inside joke in the publishing house. Paulhan cited de Montherlant's literary output as an example to be followed by writers wanting to produce 'inept' works to undermine the credibility of collaboration.

Mauriac was to describe Montherlant as the 'prince of sham and bombast', contemptuously dismissing the austere, baggy-eyed Montherlant who was proud of being one of the rare French authors whose work was studied in German schools. Despite his obvious liking for the invader, Montherlant was applauded by audiences during performances of *La Reine morte*, a historical romance set in Spain, in which lines referring to the country's best men being in prison were spoken.

While the theatre boom never compared to the German-catering night club explosion – about 125 of the 200 central Paris cabarets were founded after the 1940 Armistice – it opened new horizons for Camus who was completing his melodramatic murder play, *Le Malentendu*. More important, it revived the possibility of staging a play built around the Roman Emperor, Caligula, originally written as part of a literary triptych with *L'Etranger* and the anti-existentialist essay, *Le Mythe de Sysyphe*. Under pressure from Malraux and Paulhan, Gallimard took the first two but *Caligula* had to be shelved.

Without the theatrical panel, the triptych was incomplete. Camus wanted the three to be seen together to illustrate his exploration of the Absurd, which he saw as the starting point for a search for a moral code. At the time, his allegory of the Occupation, *La Peste*, was under preparation. It may well have occurred to him that Paris, after three years of Nazi domination, was one of the greatest theatres of the Absurd. Camus's own life made him particularly suited to being one of its principal actors in the moments of its renaissance.

If the gods had wanted to test Jean-Paul Sartre and his analyses of the meaning of life, they would have invented Albert Camus. The Algerian writer had the looks, sociability and self-confidence that Sartre lacked while refusing to fit into the mould into which the philosopher tried to force him. Sartre's post-war years are littered with rows and misunderstandings inspired by a refusal to accept people as they were. His attitude has been compared to that of a butcher who is unable to recognise a cow until cut into many parts. Sartre tended to reconstruct the cuts to fit his own version of the complete model, a tendency which was to give a highly original view to his intellectual autopsies of Jews, blacks, homosexuals and, above all, the proletariat.

Camus was a member of the last category, born and raised in near misery by a working-class French family settled in Algeria, then part of metropolitan France. He so obstinately rejected the attitudes that the preordained Sartrian proletarian model was supposed to obey that when the two men fell out in 1952, Sartre wrote him off as a bourgeois, his worst insult.

Camus's life might have been a critical response to Sartre's in many subtle ways. Camus was a year old when his father was killed in the first battle of the Marne in 1914 while serving with an Algerian regiment of Zouaves. He was raised in circumstances emotionally, if not financially, similar to those of Sartre. The household in a poor whites' area of Algiers was run by his domineering grandmother who belted him and his older brother for the slightest disobedience while his mother could only plead that the boys should not be struck about the head.

Yet Camus revered his childhood. His mother, who was so upset by his father's death that she never spoke properly again, achieved a saint-like image for him. His childhood memories in the sun-filled streets were a safety net throughout his life.

Roger Grenier, a journalist at *Combat* after the liberation of

Paris when Camus made his reputation as editor, said he was not a simple man but 'nostalgic for simplicity'.

'As a child he knew a very physical life – beaches, sun, the sea – and he tried to translate all that. He was basically from Algiers and his roots were Algerian.'

This open-air life, much more than his family's illiteracy and the lack of books or cultural aids in the overcrowded family flat, separates Camus from Sartre as much as the Mediterranean is separated from the Seine. That they were ever seen, particularly from abroad, as representing a single view of life now seems incredible as their intellectual development was in total contrast.

Camus's life is marked by the impact of a series of brilliant or intuitive men who guided him away from taking up an agricultural labourer's job like his father and marked out the signposts towards the Nobel Prize in 1957. Only when his own vanity, inflated by unexpected success, set him above outside influence did his literary progression falter and he was beset by serious self-doubt.

Sartre's development, on the other hand, consisted in rejecting personal influences while seeking intellectual inspiration to fit his own preconceived ideas. His grip on internal certainties was to weaken when age and illness made him increasingly dependent on less than altruistic friends.

Certain aspects of Camus's life were constant, above all his illness that took all predictability out of his existence, destroying plans and pushing him towards depression. As a scholarship boy at an Algiers lycée – he was recommended by his primary school teacher to whom he dedicated his Nobel Prize – Camus appeared destined for the classic transition to the middle classes by becoming a high school teacher himself. But he twice failed his medical test because of incipient tuberculosis, an illness that also ended his footballing career as a goalkeeper for Racing Universitaire d'Alger.

His attitude towards women confirmed De Beauvoir's accusation that he was a Mediterranean 'macho', a judgment she made after he told her that her work, *Le Deuxième Sexe*, ridiculed the French male. He made it clear to her that he did not expect women to be intellectual. Gossips said he kept her at a distance because he was worried she would talk too much in bed. Outside marriage, the woman who suited his temperament best was the Spanish actress, Maria Casares, who played in his first production in Paris, *Le Malentendu*. As the daughter of a pre-Civil War Republican Prime Minister, Casares, like Camus, was a Mediterranean in her attitude to emotional relationships. Women were to play only a supportive role in his life. Patronage was a masculine affair, including his introduction into the Communist Party by one of his lycée teachers.

During his two pre-war years as a member of an Algiers' cell, the fusion between politics and literature was crystallised by another Left-wing professeur, Yves Bourgeois, four years older than Camus and a product of that distant and mythical institution, the Ecole Normale Supérieure.

Bourgeois's first-hand accounts of the rise of Fascism and Nazism provided a background to the election of Léon Blum's Popular Front in 1936, Camus's own voluntary involvement in teaching illiterate Arab children and his repugnance for colonialism. Among the first results of a commitment to Left-wing views was the establishment of Camus's Théâtre du Travail which opened with his own adaptation of Malraux's short novel, *Le Temps du mépris*.

Camus was then 23 and demonstrating another important and consistent factor of his life, a preference for collective effort that was fulfilled by the theatre and journalism. For Camus, collective effort was a passion. Le Théâtre du Travail's second presentation was an account of the revolt by Spanish miners in the Asturias in 1934. It was a joint effort involving several of the cast, particularly Bourgeois who wrote most of the dialogue. Camus acknowledged Bourgeois's direct, austere style as an influence on his own writing.

This ability to work with other people was another characteristic which differentiated him from Sartre. According to friends, the philosopher detested the give-and-take necessary in staging plays, a process which they felt was a 'torture' for him.

At the age of twenty-five, Camus still had no career prospects, earning a living through casual or temporary work either for the Algerian meteorological service or as literary adviser to an Algiers-based publisher. But in 1938, the man who was to have the most direct influence on the writer's adult development arrived in the North African city.

Pascal Pia was sent to Algiers to found the Left-wing *Alger Républicain* as opposition to the dominant *Echo d'Alger*. The Left's brief term of power in France under the Socialist, Léon Blum, had collapsed and the Right was taking its predictable revenge through its dominance of newspapers and broadcasting.

In 1938, Algeria, with a population made up of poor whites and even poorer Arabs, was a staging point for a rebellion against conservative values. It was not until twenty years later that the hopes were fulfilled when the struggle for Algerian independence provided the crucible for the fusion of disparate Left-wing factions that formed the basis for the present-day Socialist Party.

Pia, a huge man who readily worked twenty hours a day when running newspapers, was a friend since youth of André Malraux and had been closely connected with the Surrealists, leading to membership of the Communist Party. The journalist, Claude Bourdet, whose Combat movement Pia later joined, described him as a 'simple professional journalist'.

'He was also a funny guy with a great sense of humour who delighted in puns and practical jokes. After the war, he published a fake Rimbaud that took months to be discovered,' Bourdet said.

But there was ambiguity in Pia's character that lay behind his eventual quarrel with Camus after the Liberation of Paris when Pia was editor-in-chief of *Combat*, the organisation's newspaper, and Camus was editor.

'Pia was both arrogant and diffident', Bourdet said. 'He was content with a secondary role and never tried to outshine people but he wanted them to appreciate what he was doing all the same.'

As Pia arrived in Algiers from Paris with a list of possible journalists for his newspaper, supplied by the Communist Party, Camus's recruitment was no accident. He was already a productive writer, having published *L'Envers et l'endroit*, a collection of essays, while running a new theatre group, L'Equipe. He had also widened his horizons by visits to Europe and cut all links with his earlier ambitions by refusing a belatedly offered teaching post.

As sub-editor and reporter of a politically-committed paper too poor to pay his hotel expenses, Camus, who considered journalism a noble profession, was in his element. The newspaper was opposed to France's colonial policy. Camus carried out investigations into the exploitation of rural Arabs in articles that were devoid of flourishes of style but full of statistics on slave wages and food rations.

His health excluded him from the call-up and he continued to work for the *Alger Républicain* until the arrival of two French military censors, cavalry officers, at the beginning of the war. They interpreted their mission as forcing the newspaper to close. After more controversial articles, Camus was summarily expelled from Algeria, arriving jobless in mainland France.

Pia found him a job on *Paris-Soir* as a stone sub-editor but within weeks the newspaper staff left in the panic of the Fall of France, eventually settling in Lyons. At the time, the newspaper was France's top-selling daily, depending largely on a popular content which irritated Camus. The Germans founded their own *Paris-Soir* in the capital and the two rival editions circulated in the Occupied and Free Zones.

Camus completed the manuscript of *L'Etranger* two days before *Paris-Soir* left the capital and in Lyons married his second wife, Francine. Soon afterwards, Camus was sacked as part of an economy drive and the couple returned jobless to Algeria. For family reasons, they settled in the provincial town of Oran, a city Camus detested because it turned its back on the sea. Chance, though, had played another trick. The stupefying boredom of Oran was to inspire the framework for *La Peste*, published six years later, a book that was to reflect so much of Camus's wartime experience.

Camus's main earnings during this period came from giving language lessons. He wrote the original outline for *La Peste*, an allegory on the Occupation, while his wife was out of the flat teaching. He was always reluctant to be seen writing and tidied away the work before she came home. Later, in Paris, friends remarked that his study or office was always neat with as few papers visible as possible, as if his internal life had to be tucked away before he could assume his sociable and charming personality. Even as a full-time journalist at *Combat*, he kept his other preoccupations, such as theatre and the friends associated with them, in separate compartments.

In Oran, it was discovered that his tuberculosis had spread. In January 1942, special passes were obtained for him to be treated in mainland France. Relatives of Francine kept a small hotel in the tiny hamlet of Le Panelier in the Massif Central near the industrial town of Saint Etienne. By coincidence, the area was one of the most active Resistance hideouts, one reason for which some biographies wrongly insist that Camus entered the Combat movement in 1942.

Whatever his sentiments about the Occupation, Camus was too weak and depressed to think about much more than his regular hospital treatment at Saint Etienne, a dismal urban area that increased his melancholy. In October, the couple decided to return to Algeria and Francine left first to seek somewhere to live. But on November 7, 1942, the Allies invaded North Africa and the ferry service that Camus intended to take was cancelled as German troops took possession of all France without opposition from the Vichy Government.

One of the few good things to emerge from this terrible setback for Camus was the emotional content it provided for *La Peste*. He confided to friends that 'separation' would be a dominant theme of the book, as Oran was to be cut off from the world by bubonic plague.

'Exile weighs on me', he said, while confiding in his diary that he would also include a chapter on the effects of illness. In a brief outline, he noted: 'They learnt once more that physical sickness never came alone but was always accompanied by moral suffering (family, frustrated love) which gave it its depth.'

Wet, cold Auvergne added to the oppression of exile from the long, sunny days in Algiers, but he was to find many friends among the refugees and Resistants hiding out in the area. He also renewed contact with Pia, working for an underground movement in the Lyons area.

Pia, who was forming links with Combat, had done Camus another important favour before withdrawing from journalism, despatching the manuscript of *L'Etranger* to Malraux who enthusiastically recommended it to Paulhan. The 5,000-franc advance Camus received from Gallimard was both badly needed funds and an introduction to the publishing clan that was to influence his life almost as much as his connection with Pia.

In retrospect, Camus's period at Le Panelier resembles a process of weaning him away from the warmth and comfort of North Africa and transferring him to the more competitive climate of Paris's intellectual scene. Part of that process, again overseen by Pia, was a meeting with Louis Aragon and his Russian-born wife, Elsa Triolet; the couple who seemed pre-destined at that time to rule the Parisian literary roost after the war. Sartre and De Beauvoir were to usurp their place, but when Camus went to visit Aragon and Triolet in Lyons they seemed beyond challenge.

The most persistent common link between the pre-war literary scene, later wartime struggles and post-war controversies in Saint-Germain-des-Prés was the French Communist Party. All the central figures in the intellectual scene were either members, former members, fellow travellers or ardent enemies.

From 1927, when he joined, until his death in 1982, Aragon

Albert Camus, the original 'outsider', son of an Algerian farm labourer and
Nobel Prize-winner

was its most faithful member, swallowing policy change after
policy change without flinching, while observing that Party
members preferred 'faith to truth'. When asked what was a
good Communist, he said it was a militant who had worked

tirelessly for the cause all his life and was long since dead and buried.

Aragon took refuge in the south of France after Dunkirk, spending part of the time at Nice where he believed there was a plot to assassinate him. He moved to Lyons to seek protection of the highly-organised Resistance network and took refuge in the house of a publisher, René Tavernier, who also welcomed Elsa Triolet, a tiny, red-headed Jewess suspected of being a Russian spy.

There are only minor, irrelevant inconsistencies in Aragon's wartime behaviour. His reputation in the Communist Party, which provided most of the effective resistance to the Nazis, was second to none. Under the pen name of François la Colère, his poems provided inspiration for the underground movement while Elsa, whose political roots were anchored in the October Revolution, became the symbol of feminine defiance of Fascism.

She was feted in Aragon's poems in collections like *Les Yeux d'Elsa* and mastered French to become a major novelist. She was the only Jewess to have a book published and circulated openly in France during the war.

Her novel, *Le Cheval blanc*, one of the best-sellers of 1943 and a candidate for the Goncourt prize along with De Beauvoir's *L'Invitée*, was published by Robert Denoël who also published *How to recognise a Jew* and who accepted German participation in his firm. He knew Triolet's origins perfectly well as the Aragons stayed with him during secret visits to Paris as Monsieur et Madame Andrieux.

From his hideout in Lyons, Aragon influenced Communist literary policy more than he had as editor of the banned *Ce Soir*. Through contacts with Paulhan and another Communist poet, Paul Eluard, Aragon arbitrated in decisions on who was to be a member of the Comité National des Ecrivains which Camus was invited to join much later. One of the testing grounds for recruits was the review, *Confluences*, which Aragon controlled for his host, René Tavernier. Camus was invited by Aragon to reflect on 'Intelligence and the Scaffold' for an article on one of

Camus's favourite themes, abhorrence of capital punishment, for the July 1943 issue.

The Communist Party was spreading its net so wide at the time that it seemed to have dropped its old divisive doctrinaire attitudes. Among those whom Camus took to be welcomed by Aragon was a Dominican monk, Père Raymond-Leopold Bruckberger, a Resistance leader who strongly influenced Camus's ideas on religion.

Aragon, a slim, lively man who walked with a long, decisive stride, was by no means as self-assured as his poems and organisational ability made him appear. In many ways, he was the most bizarre of French intellectuals of this period with the exception of Drieu la Rochelle, a man closely linked with Aragon's failure to capitalise on his wartime celebrity.

Aragon was another sixteenth arrondissement bourgeois who suffered from the distress of a missing parent. As the illegitimate son of a Right-wing politician, he was given the surname, Aragon, in memory of his father's previous love affair with a Spanish aristocrat. The young Aragon was brought up in an all-female household where his domineering grandmother told him that his mother was his sister.

His adhesion to the Communist Party followed a classic route through Surrealism after First World War service as a medical auxiliary which brought him into contact with André Breton. In 1919, Aragon showed the first four chapters of his first novel, *Anicet*, to Breton who passèd them to Gide at Gallimard. His success meant that Aragon could abandon his medical studies and devote himself to writing.

Aragon's wartime medical service was a sort of Surrealist immersion. Breton insisted that his new friend share night duty with him watching over soldiers driven mad by the shelling. Breton later became such a strong influence that he could draw the most intimate confessions from Aragon, forcing him to admit at a public meeting that he had never had a complete erection. Aragon's emotional life was torn by a bisexual night-mare which included a harrowing affair with the British ship-

Louis Aragon, writer and committed Communist, and his Russian-born
wife Elsa Triolet. 'I was her dog' he said of their marriage

ping heiress, Nancy Cunard, and a physical fascination with
the unbalanced Drieu la Rochelle.

Aragon was still extremely vulnerable during the war. It was
said that Elsa Triolet treated him like a super-intelligent child
whom everyone wanted to hurt. She frequently threatened to
leave him, although they were only married in 1939, because of
his moods and impotence. Of his relationship with Elsa, he once
said: 'I loved a woman. I was her dog. It's my fashion.'

These pathetic details were long submerged by the impact of
his wartime work. He was admired in the Party for his strict

orthodox line as editor of *Ce Soir*, an attitude which led him to sacrifice close friends and colleagues like Paul Nizan who refused to accept the German-Soviet Pact. He was one of the rare intellectuals to be a genuine war hero as he was awarded the Médaille Militaire in 1940 as a medical auxiliary when he rescued wounded soldiers only yards from German tanks in the middle of a battle.

As irony plodded not far behind him all his life, Aragon, the most consistent intellectual disciple of Communism, had the arch-capitalist, Baron Guy de Rothschild, as commanding officer. It was the baron who ordered Aragon to give up his dangerous rescue work for fear he would be killed by German guns.

Aragon's poems are rare examples of pure literature contributing directly to Resistance morale. The fact that he was also publishing in his own name in the Non-Occupied zone and abroad increased the feeling among the Resistance that he was taunting the Nazis.

His most moving success was *La Ballade de celui qui chantait dans les Supplices*, which he wrote under the name of François la Colère to commemorate the execution of Gabriel Péri, a leader writer and foreign affairs commentator on the Party paper, *L'Humanité*. It was roneoed and handwritten thousands of times to become part of Resistance legend.

Et s'il était à refaire,
Je referais ce chemin,
Une voix monte des fers
Et parle de lendemains.

To the party rank and file, the poem shone with the simplicity of the proletariat, that mass of idealised humanity into which Aragon wanted to be absorbed as much as Sartre did. The working-man's voice that rose from the chains was so authentic that Aragon was often told that it could not have come from an intellectual.

That class transfer was only a minor consolation. The real,

rather than legendary, Aragon was a disappointment for French youth, even the Communists, after the war. He fought his post-war battles from alongside Saint-Germain-des-Prés but stronger personalities undermined his influence. Among them was Camus whose obstinate battle against Communism would contribute to ending Party dreams of Left-wing unity in which Aragon would have been the intellectual leader.

Before settling in Paris in November 1943, Camus spent some time in a Dominican monastery in Provence on the invitation of Père Bruckberger. The stay played an important part in Camus's subsequent hesitations over accepting Christianity.

Priorities in Paris were more immediate. Through the influence of friends, including Pia, he was offered a job as reader at Gallimard for 2,000 francs a month and moved into a hotel ten minutes from the office. Although still underweight and unhealthy looking, Camus was temporarily cured of tuberculosis and had to face up to playing some part in the Resistance.

Attitudes towards the Germans were considerably less complex than when Sartre returned from PoW camp more than two years before. By occupying the entire country, the Nazis had reunified France through a policy of universal oppression. The Vichy regime was a phantom administration with neither the will nor the power to inspire reaction on the French mainland.

Collaboration was no longer a matter of 'honour'. It meant cooperating with German brutality, including the handing over of all able-bodied men for compulsory work service in Germany. The demand was to swell the ranks of the Maquis as hundreds of thousands of young men went into hiding.

After joint protests by Jewish, Catholic and Protestant leaders, the national conscience had been awakened to the real purpose of the sinister round up of Jews. It was not known, however, until after the war that earlier indifference and Vichy callousness had condemned 80,000 French Jews to death.

But even those not concerned with the greater issues now wanted Germany ousted as rationing tightened, threatening widespread malnutrition. In Paris, the Germans turned on and off supplies at will. Their own troops' needs came first. What seemed once like an enormous bureaucratic aberration with eight different categories of rationing and wads of coupons for food, clothes and fuel, was a nightmare. In most working-class areas there was a fear that there would be nothing to eat at all.

Camus arrived as German reprisals and executions increased as the fear of defeat set in. Resistance was no longer a matter of personal dignity or a mystical union with an eternal France. It was a question of survival.

Even against this stark background, Paris's cultural life, supported by its large middle-class population, continued to prosper. For many, the war was only a nuisance, for others it was a chance to prosper. Fortunes were made out of entertainment, often to be spent at fine art auctions. Some of the most blatant collaborators, like the Champs Elysées cabaret-owner and popular singer, Suzy Solidor, died decades later still surrounded by enormous wealth made by accumulating paintings and antiques.

Bookshops were raided like corner grocery stores. Comparisons of under-the-counter prices for bestsellers like *Gone with the Wind*, show they were fetching seven or eight times their value, roughly the price of a black market kilo of ham.

To the public, which also financed the most intense era of French film production in its history, cultural figures were above reproach, however outrageously they behaved. Among the most extraordinary was Jean Cocteau, playwright, poet, cineast and artist who became the ubiquitous spirit of the war years, present at every important occasion, saying that great disasters thrilled him.

His behaviour was a subject of scandal among intellectual Resistants when Camus arrived in Paris. Among the more blatant of Cocteau's displays of contempt for Resistance orders to shun the Germans was his presence at the Institut Allemand-sponsored exhibition at the Orangerie of the giant statues of Arno Breker, Hitler's favourite sculptor. The exhibition, in

1942, was also attended by many other leading French cultural figures despite the presence of Nazis like Goering. Breker, in many ways as great a dandy as Cocteau, was a former resident of Montparnasse and was Hitler's guide during his rapid visit to Paris in June 1940. Breker and Cocteau were former lovers, but the French poet was now living with the handsome *jeune premier*, Jean Marais.

The Breker exhibition was to provide an insight into Cocteau's engaging silliness during France's greatest humiliation. While Paris argued about the rights and wrongs of honouring Breker's exhibition of enormous, naked men that seemed to be carved out of lard, Cocteau warned Marais: 'If the statues have an erection we won't be able to walk around'.

Marais, whose attitude was as flippant as his lover's, was banned from the stage by the Germans for wearing exhibitionist costumes in *Andromaque* but he was to buy his way back in French esteem by volunteering to join Leclerc's Second Armoured Division. When he returned to Paris, his place as the most striking of young French actors had been usurped by Gérard Philipe after playing Camus's *Caligula* in 1945.

Cocteau slid skilfully from one scene to the next, eventually turning up in Saint-Germain-des-Prés as part of the youth cult when nearing sixty. No one had the courage to condemn this artist of the 'shameful peace'. Simone de Beauvoir, usually so strict in her moral censure of others, described his behaviour during the war as 'poetic'.

'He said that the poet should remain distant from his century and indifferent to the madness of war and politics. "They're beastly to us", he said. "All of them, the Germans, the Americans, they're beastly to us."'

The French were far from beastly. They elected him to the Académie Française to sit beside thirty-nine other 'immortals' including the arch-Resistant Jean Paulhan.

In 1942, when illness and isolation were at their worst, Camus wrote in his diaries: 'The great problem to solve from a practical point of view – can one be happy and solitary?' Later, he wrote

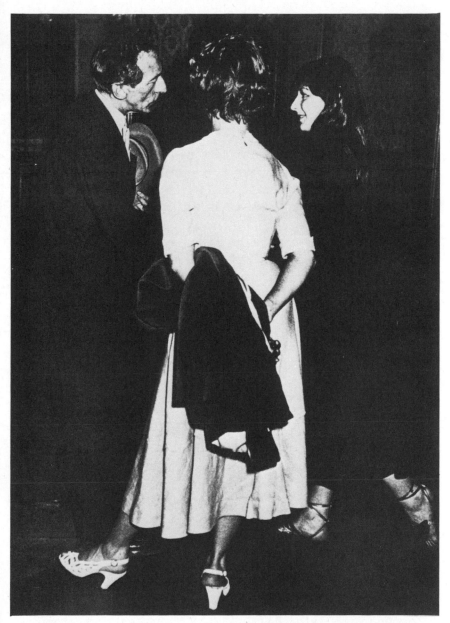

Jean Cocteau, whose Nazi sympathies were forgiven as 'poetic' with Anne-Marie Cazalis and Juliette Gréco

that he was more interested in being accepted than being the best.

During the months that followed his arrival in Paris in November 1943, his charm and talent enabled him to put aside these problems. He was happy, rarely alone and fully accepted by three different 'families'. Sartre and De Beauvoir made him the most important member of their group based on the Café de Flore. At Gallimard, he was to become an intimate companion of the brothers and sons in the publishing clan. Within weeks, he was invited to join the Combat resistance movement as a journalist, enlisting in a young, brilliant team that was to represent French moral renewal at the Liberation.

De Beauvoir described the group of friends, often former pupils, who gathered around Sartre as '*la famille*' which had close and distant relatives. When Camus joined, one of the favourite 'cousins' was the singer and actor, Marcel Mouloudji, who had drifted across from the '*bande à Prévert*' attracted by the young women De Beauvoir often introduced from her philosophy class. She encouraged him to write the story of his working-class childhood with a Moslem father and a Christian mother.

Mouloudji remembers the 'warmth and generosity' of Simone de Beauvoir as she spent hours correcting his grammar and style. Once in the grip of the didactic missionary, however, it was impossible to escape except by a process of 'excommunication'. Mouloudji won Gallimard's Pléiade prize for literature after Sartre's intervention in 1944 but lacked the commitment to carry on the crusade and fulfil Sartre's image of the young worker breaking from capitalist oppression.

Although Mouloudji remained a central figure in Saint-Germain-des-Prés he was gradually squeezed from the Sartre table where another promising recruit, the homosexual thief, Jean Genet, was being groomed. But Genet's spectacular progress from journalist to Saint-Germain's most controversial literary figure was still a long way ahead. Camus, on the other hand, already shone with the living proof that the working classes had the talent which the bourgeois denied and was to be shown off like a collector's piece.

The friendship between Sartre and Camus was sincere, but it still seems a relationship between a philosophy master and a brilliant pupil whose ideas needed straightening out. Many years later, Sartre said privately that he considered Camus a 'philosophical ass', even though Camus strongly resisted being labelled a philosopher. He was, though, deeply troubled by life and wanted moral certainties. In his diaries, Christianity fascinated him and he feared that if the world had no sense then totalitarians were right.

'I don't accept that they are right', Camus wrote. 'It is up to us to create God. He is not the creator. That is the whole history of Christianity. Because we have only one way to create God and that is to become him.'

This was written about the same time as Sartre was forming excuses for Marxist totalitarianism. The divergent paths that Camus and Sartre were to take were already well-illuminated at their first meeting as Camus had already described the existentialist 'German school of thought' as a 'modern tragedy'.

If the two men did not fall out almost straightaway, this was due to the open, tolerant atmosphere of the intellectual world at the end of 1943 until well into 1945. Anyone who sought post-war moral renewal was part of a great forum of hope. Even Gaullists and Communists were fighting side by side. Camus more than repaid Sartre's patronage by introducing the philosopher to the Combat movement, ensuring Sartre's all-important post-war Resistance credentials.

The date of Camus's own entry into the Resistance is still a subject to spark off petty arguments. His stature at the Liberation was so high that it became a political necessity to predate his association, sometimes by at least two years. The Combat movement itself puts the official beginnings at January 1944.

Claude Bourdet, a Parisian whose father was a well-established playwright, recruited Camus. The tall, handsome

Bourdet had been involved in espionage and sabotage since the Armistice in 1940 and recruited for Combat mainly from the middle-class Paris establishment. The Combat network maintained an independent image throughout the war, attracting intuitive, open-minded Resistants who spurned a common political or religious code.

'Unfortunately, the number of decent people in the Occupied Zone was very limited,' Bourdet said.

Camus's introduction to Combat came, inevitably, from Pia who was running Combat's monthly underground newspaper. Surprisingly, Paulhan, who saw Camus most days passing his office at Gallimard was not consulted although he was an active member of Combat. Bourdet knew Paulhan only as a rank and file member who delivered the *Combat* newspaper in Paris, unaware that he was recruiting writers for Editions de Minuit and *Lettres Françaises*, a new Resistance magazine.

Combat at first spurned intellectual resistance – 'We didn't realise how interesting literary resistance might be,' Bourdet said – but by late 1943 the war of ideas was more pressing. Camus was at first suggested as a colleague for a new literary magazine, *La Revue noire*.

The magazine was not to appear until after the Liberation after sabotaging itself. Camus arrived unexpectedly at the *Revue*'s secret workshop without an introduction. His shifty appearance panicked his fellow contributors who took him for a Gestapo agent and destroyed all the copy. When that misunderstanding was sorted out, production was halted by a case of adultery involving two leading contributors. The rivalry was immediately turned into a book and a play by the principals, leaving little time for the magazine.

Bourdet, who was later arrested and sent to a concentration camp, was not much impressed by the coolness of intellectuals when under pressure. The discovery by the Germans of a secret list of writers linked to the Comité National des Ecrivains caused a panic and he met François Mauriac hiding in the Métro carrying a bag full of pots and pans as he prepared to make a run for it. Similar panics were to send De Beauvoir, Sartre and

Camus, along with many friends from the Flore, into hiding in the country just before the Liberation. Most returned in time for the final insurrection.

When Camus joined *Combat*, he was introduced into one of the best-managed Resistance operations of the war. In 1942, when their paper was founded, about 10,000 copies were circulated. By May 1944, circulation had reached 250,000. Originally put together in Lyons when it was part of the Unoccupied Zone, *Combat*'s printing headquarters were transferred to Paris in August 1943 and placed under Pia's editorship. Fourteen flongs were pressed for distribution to provincial centres where local printers ran off copies to be circulated by hand. Hundreds of people were involved in distribution by the end of the war but the Germans never disrupted a source of information that rallied the French population at the lowest point of the Occupation.

Pia, who as 'Renoir' was known to the Nazis, was a hunted man. Although he had brief contacts with Camus in Paris, he was told to avoid the Saint-Germain-des-Prés area which was now known to be one of the main quartiers of organised Resistance.

'If the Germans had been clever, they would have arrested everyone in the boulevard Saint-Germain and sorted them out afterwards,' Bourdet said.

The first *Combat* edition in Paris was number 49, in October 1943, when the main burden of work was carried out by the secretary-general, Jacqueline Bernard, in a small workshop behind a concierge's lodge in a block of flats. Madame Bernard, a member of an Alsatian Jewish family with strong military links, puts the date of Camus's introduction to the newspaper as November 1943 when Pia brought him to the workshop and presented him as 'Beauchard'. Although this is disputed, it is difficult to see how Camus could have avoided casual links with the Resistance if he wanted to be 'accepted'. However, his first identifiable contribution was in March 1944 when he wrote an article calling for 'total resistance to total war'. Two months later, he wrote another article referring to mass executions by the Germans.

By then he was editor, as Pia had gone into hiding. His main work was lay-out and sub-editing for a single folio printed with the smallest body type. It did not interfere with his job at Gallimard where he was now part of the Readers' Committee alongside Paulhan and Sartre, among others. He was also preparing *Le Malentendu* and attending Sartre and De Beauvoir 'fiestas' – all-night parties that did not finish until the end of the curfew. 'Fiestas' assembled many of the personalities who would make Saint-Germain-des-Prés's post-war reputation and included some notable occasions. To pass one night in a friend's flat, Camus directed Picasso's *Le Desire attrapé par la Queue* in which Sartre played a role. Picasso, whose atelier was on the rue des Grands-Augustins, adjoining Saint-Germain, was present with his fellow painter, Georges Braque and the Comédie Française director, Jean-Louis Barrault.

Sartre, although a member of the Comité National des Ecrivains which met in a Latin Quarter flat with as many as twenty writers present, still felt excluded from active resistance. Camus invited him to join *Combat* after the philosopher said he was ready to do even menial reporting. Sartre now called himself by his underground name, 'Miro', while Camus, who was considered to be at considerable risk, was given false identity papers, calling himself Albert Mathé. But it was through his other 'family', the Gallimard's, rather than *Combat*, that he was introduced to André Malraux, now a colonel, who visited Paris secretly from his headquarters in the Dordogne.

By this time, Camus was living in a studio communicating with Gide's empty flat in the rue Vaneau, even nearer his office, and was recruiting professional journalists and typesetters for an expanded *Combat* after the Liberation. Resistance movements had decided that *Combat* would be one of three newspapers to take over the offices of *Paris-Soir* which was also the headquarters of *Pariser-Zeitung*. They were to be the core of the 'new Press' of a rehabilitated France.

This lofty assignment did not interfere with Camus's preparation for the first production of *Le Malentendu*. Sartre, meanwhile, had staged *Huis clos* at the Théâtre du Vieux Colombier. The play with its famous line: 'Hell is other people', is seen as the key production which concentrated public attention on Saint-Germain as an avant-garde cultural bastion.

Sartre's critical success with *Huis clos* was not matched by Camus and *Le Malentendu*, staged on the Right Bank at the Théâtre des Mathurins. The play, starring Maria Casares, opened after the Normandy invasion, causing uneasiness over its timing as well as its literary faults of construction and content.

The author's diaries show a curious tranquillity at what was generally seen as a failure which came close to affecting the value put on him by Left-wing resistance movements. The event, however, was a minor affair in a city where everyone was living in the future. Allied troops were coming closer and the Nazis were already packing their bags. A great festival of youth was about to begin in an explosion of joy at the Liberation.

3

Je suis comme je suis

In *Combat* dated August 24, 1944, Camus wrote: 'Paris fires off all its bullets into the August night. In this immense décor of stones and water, the barricades of freedom are set up again all around this river flowing heavy with history. Once again, justice has to be bought with the blood of men.'

The editorial was written in the offices formerly occupied by *Paris-Soir* and *Pariser Zeitung* in the rue Réaumur, not far from the Bourse in the second arrondissement. To get there from the Left Bank meant a long and dangerous walk dodging German snipers and trigger-happy members of the Forces Françaises de l'Intérieure, the FFI, as Paris was swept up in the exhilarating business of liberating itself. The Germans had left in such a hurry that they abandoned boxes of hand grenades in the offices that *Combat* took over. Camus helped organise their despatch to Resistance fighters ready to resist any German attempt to retake the rue Réaumur.

From a military point of view, the popular insurrection was little more than a spectacular firework show in which about 1,000 Parisians lost their lives. The Germans were ready to hand over the city peacefully as the French did in 1940. The advancing allies in 1944 saw no point in liberating Paris by force as the city had no strategic value. But Gaullists, Communists and other political interests needed prestige and they sought it by the most effective method: a battle. The Germans, who had refused Hitler's orders to burn the city to the ground, fought only for the right to leave in an orderly fashion. The Parisians, most of whom probably cared little for the political stakes, went into the streets not so much to free the capital as to liberate themselves from the shame of four years' Occupation.

In Saint-Germain-des-Prés, like elsewhere in the city, the popular mood resembled a collective commemoration of so many other uprisings since the Revolution. As in other rebellions, the intoxicating effect of overthrowing established authority was out of proportion to the numbers involved and the amount of violence.

For a week there was desultory streetfighting along and around the rue Dauphine under the guidance of half a dozen officially appointed FFI trying to organise or restrain anyone with a rifle. As nothing was recorded of the fighting, residents retain only an impressionistic picture of haphazard sniping at German patrols in narrow streets. In one incident, five inexperienced Resistants were submachine-gunned by a lone German infantryman. In another, a concierge stepped into a gunbattle to slap a badly-wounded German soldier. There were fleeting glimpses of armoured vehicles as the Germans sealed off the quartier. Little was known of what was happening elsewhere in Paris. The sporadic shooting stopped as suddenly as it had begun a week earlier and the Left Bank was flooded with GI's.

In one description, their arrival in Saint-Germain, is seen as 'Father Christmases on every corner', not merely handing out chocolate and chewing-gum, but hope. It was the beginning of a relationship with American ideals, literature, films and popular music that was to be an important element in the development of the area as a cultural centre. In the months to come, most Parisians would resent American presence after a double rejection of US influence by Gaullists and Communists. The youth cult in Saint-Germain made pro-Americanism part of their general revolt.

The Americans reciprocated but the cultural priority at the Liberation was to free Montparnasse. *Time* magazine's correspondents rushed straight to the pre-war literary cafés to report that the 'Dôme, Rotonde and Coupole were open for business as usual under striped awnings.'

'Americans who entered Paris last week were amazed', the magazine reported. 'They had expected to find Parisians starved, tattered, numb from oppression. They looked the same as they did before the Occupation. The women had smart clothes and cosmetics, the children were tubby and well-fed. The truth seemed that the Nazis entered Paris as a moonstruck lout courting a handsome woman. Paris had smiled grimly.'

The grim smile had been changed for euphoria. In Saint-Germain, there was a spontaneous wave of comradeship and forgiveness. When the official photograph of the quartier's 'guerillas' was taken, nearly two hundred people turned up instead of the twenty or so expected. No one was turned away.

The joy was not merely to celebrate the end of Paris's war. There was a feeling that the old divisions in France itself were over. Collaboration, corruption, political hatred, the petty interests of the bourgeoisie and the narrow-minded militancy of Communism were impossible to imagine in the great fiesta of the Liberation.

With the Collaborationist Press closed down, *Combat* and a handful of other newspapers emerging from the Resistance movement held the key to putting hopes into practice. Camus had returned from the countryside only days before the insurrection to take over as editor of *Combat*, published as a one-folio daily with Pia in overall command as editor-in-chief. Sartre was also in the city after returning from hiding and was assigned by *Combat* to report on the Liberation of the capital, producing a series of daily articles that finished with a downbeat warning on September 4. The 'week of glory is over', Sartre wrote. 'Tomorrow will be a very sad, deserted Sunday, a real let down after the

August 25th 1944. Parisians read the announcement in *France Libre* on the
morning of the Liberation

fiesta. And, come Monday, shops and offices will reopen. Paris will start working again.'

Optimism stayed resolutely in fashion, however. During the next few months, Camus and Sartre were swept along on a tide of good intentions. Camus's voice was heard through the editorials of *Combat*, sometimes elevating, sometimes goading, sometimes priggish. He reproached newspapers belonging to what he called the commercial 'rotten Press' for playing up the visit of Marlene Dietrich to a liberated Metz. He attacked the 'odious' purges of the Liberation when 10,000 people died in revenge killings, nearly all without trial. He solemnly wrote that 'justice for all' in a renascent France was 'in the submission of personality to the collective good'.

Camus was at the centre of most political and humane controversies, particularly those involving the punishment of Collaborators. He campaigned for the life of the author and poet, Robert Brasillach, editor of the Collaborationist newspaper, *Je Suis Partout*. Pro-Nazi newspapermen were among the scapegoats chosen by De Gaulle. Brasillach, at the age of thirty-six, paid for them all in front of a firing squad.

While *Combat* readers were fascinated by the new tone of newspapers that came out of the Resistance, the emergence of leaders just old enough to impress the young trendsetters of the post-war generation was even more significant. The comradeship between senior and junior staff at *Combat*, where all the money from the day's sales were put into a pot and then evenly shared out at night, formed bonds that have survived forty years.

Roger Grenier, recently out of lycée, was recruited by Camus on the staircase of the rue Réaumur building after defending the author in another newspaper against criticisms that he was an 'existentialist'. Those attacks came from the Right-wing of former underground movements but Camus was also criticised by the Communist Party which was gradually digging a ditch between itself and the younger forces of French social movements as its Press became increasingly doctrinaire.

Unfortunately, there was little substance to most post-war

political planning, except hope. The way *Combat* was run during the three years with Camus as editor provided a classic illustration. Although a sound, technical journalist, Camus refused to accept any commercial arguments, believing that the paper would thrive through idealism. As a result the newspaper's administration was 'amateur, even incompetent', according to Grenier. Pia, the editor-in-chief, on the other hand, was both practical and sceptical although Grenier saw him at the time as a 'sort of despairing nihilist'.

Pia told his staff that 'we will try to make a reasonable newspaper but because the world is absurd, we will fail'. Despite his misgivings, Pia often worked twenty hours a day in his slippers, a vacuum flask at his side, writing headlines, laying out pages and overseeing advertising.

Not suprisingly, young members of the staff felt closer to Camus, not only because of his reputation. 'He was not a person who liked to be devoured by his work', Grenier said. He rarely resisted invitations to a night's drinking, usually at the Méphisto cellar bar in Saint-Germain-des-Prés where Sartre and De Beauvoir spent most of their nights. He rarely discussed politics outside the office but, at work, it was Camus who set the tone for a paper in which he intended to 'substitute morality for politics'. Editorial conferences were a relaxed affair in which all the staff was allowed to state their views.

'I have never known so much freedom of expression in a newspaper,' Grenier said. The staff represented many political currents ranging from the centre Left to the edges of the extreme Right. Among contributors was the philosopher, Raymond Aron, who had returned from London without yet linking his future to De Gaulle, a decision that Malraux, who visited *Combat* in his colonel's uniform, had already taken.

When the editorial subject was fixed, Camus locked himself in his office to write but would often leave the leader for someone else to finish, either through laziness or a lack of inspiration. He was frequently away because of his tuberculosis, novel writing, staging plays and, particularly, his salaried job at Gallimard where he edited his own collection. Other journalists would take over editorial writing and deliberately imitate Camus's style even when they argued against Camus's own views.

'Camus did not want articles signed as he believed that all work should be collective,' Grenier said. 'It was a policy which gave rise to misunderstandings and eventually we had to sign editorials with initials.'

Behind that remark is a clue to the development of opposing camps of political opinion pulling for or against De Gaulle. They reflected a national debate which exposed the fragility of post-war unity.

During most of 1946, Camus was preoccupied with the completion of *La Peste* and his full-time job at Gallimard. He had to give up the editorship of *Combat*. The most influential leader writer was then Raymond Aron. Aron, a Paris-born Jew, whose secure childhood in Montparnasse with his two brothers, is an exception to the troubled background of many of his contemporaries, was a close friend of Sartre and Nizan at the Ecole Normale Supérieure. He was the author of several philosophical works and was interested only in an academic career until his meteorological unit was swept away in the retreat and he took refuge in England. He was given the editorship of the London-based *France Libre*, the starting point for a distinguished career in journalism over the next forty years as a columnist for *Combat*, *Le Figaro* and *L'Express*, until he died in 1983.

Aron was influenced into supporting De Gaulle after the war by André Malraux who was briefly Minister of Information for the general with Aron as his chief aide. As they had not met since before the war, Aron was surprised at Malraux's new found hatred for Communism although he did not explain even to his close friends the reason for his 'conversion'.

Partly because of Aron's influence and his connection with Malraux, *Combat* was seen as a mouthpiece for Gaullism or at least Gaullist ideas for a new Republic with an executive president. But this was not the only reason for its sales plunging from about 250,000 to hardly 100,000 by the beginning of 1947.

The readership wanted more entertainment rather than Resistance 'morality' but Camus was hurriedly brought back as editor under Pia in the hope of restoring prestige.

It was a serious error. According to Aron, Camus 'took initiatives and discussed the future of the newspaper as if he were the creator or editor-in-chief.' His arrogance deeply offended Pia. The damaging effect of disunity at the top was compounded by a national newspaper strike.

The haphazard financial structure born with the Resistance foundered, but Camus resisted an injection of capital from outside. Some of his colleagues felt he was deliberately sabotaging the newspaper which he considered as his own. He gave an impression of disillusionment in journalism as a whole.

His lack of enthusiasm turned a rescue attempt into a messy affair in which Resistance interests lost financial control. Months of bickering also shattered the long friendship between Camus and Pia which had begun before the war in Algiers and which sustained the Algerian writer during his exile at Le Panelier. Disillusioned and angry, Pia threw off his Left-wing sympathies and embraced Gaullism, later becoming a contributor to *Carrefour*, a magazine on the edges of the extreme Right. In 1957, he was among writers who attacked Camus when he received the Nobel Prize.

In his memoirs published in 1983, Aron, who left *Combat* to join *Figaro* as a columnist, said of Pia that his reaction was probably due to the fact that he could no longer bear the obscurity he had chosen.

'Perhaps he suffered from not fulfilling himself and turned the resentment he felt for other people against himself,' Aron said.

Camus lost another friend in the sad end to the original idealistic *Combat* which was taken over by commercial interests. His attitude during the last few weeks deeply offended Claude Bourdet, the man who had recruited Camus, and who unsuccessfully appealed to the writer for his support during the salvage operation. Bourdet, who later became a leading militant in the international anti-nuclear movement, was deeply involved in arranging the compromise that saved *Combat* from foundering altogether. But Camus made his disapproval of the deal clear in his last editorial for the newspaper when he left on June 3, 1947. Bourdet saw the article as a personal attack.

'Camus wrote such a nasty article about me, you would have thought I was his worst enemy,' Bourdet said.

Camus's main fault was a lack of loyalty to friends to whom *Combat*, even with commercial links, was a livelihood and a way of life. There were also elements of selfishness and vanity. By the time he quit *Combat*, Camus was on the verge of a new life. Just before his departure he handed around signed, advance copies of *La Peste* to members of the staff. He was already confident of an enormous success after publication of extracts in a review run by Paulhan. The allegory of the Occupation was perfectly timed. Within days, the first print order of 22,000 was exhausted. By autumn, 100,000 copies had been sold with Camus receiving 15 per cent of royalties on each volume with its cover price of 200 francs. Even though devaluation had reduced the franc to a third of its pre-war value, Camus was a rich man overnight and had joined Sartre at the peak of the French literary establishment.

He was also happy and settled in his private life after reuniting with Francine in 1945 and the birth of twins a year later. His first decision on publication of *La Peste* on June 10, 1947, was to return to Le Panelier with his family as if he wanted to remember the days of despair. His diary shows that he had at last come to terms with the Auvergne and, with it, France itself. Any ideas of resettling in Algeria were definitely dropped as he decided to dedicate himself to a literary life centred in Paris.

But it was also the summer when the Cold War set in, splitting French intellectuals and adding to divisions that had already developed over Gaullism. Camus, so clear and authoritative when writing, was embarking on a period of inner turbulence that would estrange him from the following around Sartre in Saint-Germain-des-Prés.

In terms of readership, the most influential journalist after the war was Louis Aragon, who dominated the Communist Party newspaper business as editor-in-chief of *Ce Soir*. He also ran the hardline monthly, *Europe*, from the rue Saint-André-des-Arts on the fringes of Saint-Germain-des-Prés and the most influential cultural weekly, *Lettres Françaises*, founded in the Resistance. The magazine was the official voice of the Comité National des Ecrivains of which Aragon was the dominant personality. Membership of the committee was considered the key to post-war acceptance even by right of centre intellectuals like Mauriac.

Aragon's audience, indirect or direct, was enormous as the circulation of Communist newspapers reached 10 million while the Party's vote at the first post-war General Elections represented 26 per cent of the electorate. When he joined the Party's Central Committee, he became not only the most eloquent spokesman of the Communist movement but the man most capable of imposing a doctrinaire line on its bourgeois intellectuals and fellow-travellers.

Backed by a Party that became increasingly pro-Moscow, Aragon used this power to considerable personal advantage. But he also accepted every humiliating twist and turn in Cold War policy by a movement that cynically exploited his prestige. His attitude towards the Communist Party often resembled his marriage to Elsa Triolet, a dogged, fanatical and often masochistic worship consummated in a literary abundance. The fear of rejection is evident in both relationships as Aragon continued a public struggle with his troubled personality through a deluge of poems and books.

While he eventually achieved the acceptance he yearned for, Aragon never inspired general admiration. With his wartime prestige, his huge captive audience and his hold over the literary establishment, he was better placed than either Camus or Sartre to become a post-war cult figure. At forty-eight, he still had a youthful, dynamic look but this belied a dry, irritable personality.

He lacked a fascination for young people as he was too closely identified with Communist morality. Except for a minority of adolescents fired by blind obedience to class war, Aragon represented rigorous discipline and moral sacrifice previously associated with the diabolical puritanism of Vichy.

In collaboration with the party leader, Maurice Thorez, who condemned the 'existentialist' movement that developed around Sartre as a manifestation of the 'rotting bourgeoisie', Aragon lost contact with the vital forces of youth, a process which was paralleled in the Catholic Church which often seemed an ally of the Party in a moral war against young people.

But if Aragon's literary stature had been maintained in the immediate post-war months, he might still have developed a following among the rootless middle classes that his own background represented. As it turned out, he was overshadowed by Sartre, Camus and even De Beauvoir, as a result of a major literary blunder.

Aragon spent much of the war writing what he thought would be his major novel, *Aurélien*. The 500-page book, written on what he described as '14 ridiculous school exercise books' was one of the greatest post-war flops. Only 1,500 were sold in France and the book was remaindered in the USA while both Sartre's and De Beauvoir's output, nurtured during the Occupation, were runaway successes. The hero of Aragon's novel was an amalgam of himself and Drieu la Rochelle. The two men had had a passionate relationship during the 1920s and the mutual fascination remained. But Drieu, fearing execution like Brasillach, had gone into hiding at the Liberation before committing suicide seven months later.

It was not so much the Collaborationist half of the hero that upset the Communist youth movement. General critical opinion considered the theme both outdated and 'bourgeois'. In Communist terms, Aragon was back to the point of departure as if he still bore his original class sin despite a long drawn-out conversion and baptism.

As a result, he was to try ever harder for political purity which would alienate him from much of the non-Communist intellectual establishment. But even his influence on hesitant fellow travellers was harmed by another incident not directly associated with his fidelity to Communist doctrine. Aragon was suspected by some of his enemies of being the man behind a black list of about fifty writers which the Comité National des Ecrivains wanted punished for Collaboration. The list was first circulated when Paris was freed but the backlash occurred only after Drieu la Rochelle committed suicide.

Word was put around that Aragon had personally drawn up the list which included Drieu. Although it was unlikely that Aragon was pressing for the execution of his friend, he was blamed. Paulhan said that no one took the list seriously except 'a man whom Aragon admired and who took it tragically'. As a result, Aragon was seen as the instigator of Drieu's suicide by sleeping pills and gas in 1945. Aragon was afterwards shunned by several friends from Surrealist days including André Breton.

Aragon's Russian-born wife, Elsa Triolet, with her October Revolution links, might have stopped the process of alienation, particularly with young Communists as she had immediate literary success after the war and had a wider audience than De Beauvoir. Triolet was the first post-Liberation Goncourt prizewinner with her novel, *Le Premier Accroc coute deux cents francs*, but no sympathetic current passed between her and Communist youth.

Dominique Desanti, a young Communist resistant during the war, first met the Aragons when Paris was freed and in 1983 published a biography of Triolet, *Les Clés d'Elsa*. When the Aragons came out of hiding, according to Desanti, 'the myth did not measure up to the real beings'.

Aragon, so lively in appearance, bored his young audience by talking about management problems in newspapers while Triolet spoke of her hopes of winning the Goncourt Prize which, in the universal thumbs down, was considered 'bourgeois'. During the war, Triolet was the romantic, almost legendary, inspiration of Aragon's poems on love and courage. But, in Desanti's words, the post-war Triolet 'discovered money and began dressing in Haute Couture'. A remark like that, circulating in Communist cells, must have been devastating for her image. Triolet's interest in high fashion, with Dior's New Look low hemline on the horizon, contrasted with widespread misery, particularly in the working-class areas of Paris.

Although haute couture was France's only significant export of the post-war period, good clothes were a dream for most of the population. Simone Signoret, pregnant by her married lover, Yves Allegret, a cineast, wore an overcoat cut from a tartan blanket at the time. When she went to the sixth arrondissement Mairie to ask for special clothing coupons for her unborn baby, she was given army surplus khaki wool.

Army leftovers, both Allied and Nazi, were something of a luxury in a country where five million people were homeless. By 1945, rationing in Paris was below subsistence level now that the orderly German supply systems had broken down. Fighting to liberate eastern France was still going on, distracting De Gaulle's provisional government from relief work. A crippling summer drought and an appalling winter were to cause more deprivation than the worst war years.

In the general post-war misery, increasingly compounded by political crisis, the younger generation had little to feel proud about. Most felt that their adolescence had been stolen during the war and they judged their elders severely. Middle-class parents, particularly, were tainted by Collaboration or at least passivity during the Occupation. The Church was closely linked with Pétain's dishonoured Vichy regime and was again propagating strict, old-fashioned morality. Teachers, particularly in lycées and universities, were associated with a profession that had been unusually selfish during the war, abandoning principles and Jewish friends to hang on to jobs. In looking for future inspiration, prospects were bleak. In 1945, politicians who had corrupted the Third Republic and voted Pétain full powers in 1940, were back in their seats at the National Assembly. Even De Gaulle was seen by many as an opportunist general, awakening Republican fears of the 'man on the white horse', the symbol of anti-democratic military leadership.

The young, especially the Parisian middle classes, needed

someone to lead them out of this maze of broken values. That was to be Sartre's role, not so much by establishing a new moral order but by making it permissible to make life your own work of art. He personified the rejection of the two great forces in post-war France, doctrinaire Communism and the Gaullist alliance with Catholicism, and was despised by both. But within months of the war ending, he already had a personal stature so great that political leaders feared he would inspire an intellectual *coup d'état*. He was to be the subject of attack from all the main streams of political opinion. Although photographs at the time tend to show him as a satisfied man, puffing on his pipe with an apparent air of self-fulfilment, he was to confide later that his years of glory were really 'years of hate'.

Not that he lacked admirers. Since his Liberation articles in *Combat* and a revival of *Huis Clos* at Saint-Germain's Vieux-Colombier Theatre in August 1944, Sartre had achieved celebrity on a scale unknown for an intellectual since the nineteenth-century writers like Dumas and Hugo. Françoise Giroud, a journalist who became France's first Women's Affairs Minister in 1974 as well as co-founding the magazine, *L'Express*, said he was 'better known than Greta Garbo'. His rise to fame was so fast that Paul Boubal, the proprietor of the Flore, had to install a special telephone line direct to the philosopher's table. Soon, so many admirers were turning up at the café to see him that he ceased working there and moved to a flat overlooking Saint-Germain square where he lived with his mother, now a widow. From the flat, Sartre was able to watch the scene below from what came to resemble a Papal balcony. Meanwhile, those who could no longer see him at the Flore queued up for audiences at Gallimard's offices just to shake his hand. The double-pronged attack by the Catholic newspapers like *La Croix* or Aragon's Communist Press stable only added to his notoriety. *La Croix*, representing a section of the Social Democratic Left and Gaullism, found itself in constant contradiction as it discussed Sartre. His atheistic philosophy was analysed by some of the Church's leading thinkers in high-flown intellectual argument and then dismissed as derisory in other articles because he passed his time in the cellar clubs of Saint-Germain-des-Prés with 'dissipated youth'.

'He was like one of those troublesome objects which make it impossible to close your suitcase', Giroud said.

Sartre's fame owed much to Camus who persuaded *Combat* to send him to America in January 1945 as the paper's correspondent for six months. At the time, the French government made the maximum amount of publicity out of overseas visits by French intellectuals, promoting them like export products. Sartre arrived like a prophet of the new France. His existentialist theories had an enormous impact on the American literary and university establishment. Accolades from the American intelligentsia flowed back to Paris like a seal of approval.

Anne-Marie Cazalis, poet and journalist, who helped launch Juliette Gréco's career in Saint-Germain, said that 'existentialism came back to us from the United States like the Marshall Plan'.

With the prestige of being one of the select few at *Combat*, Sartre capitalised on his growing fame in an extraordinary period of only two weeks in Autumn 1945. The first two volumes of *Les Chemins de la Liberté*, his novel based on his personal experiences in the years leading up to the Fall of France, were published and he founded the magazine, *Les Temps Modernes*, which was to become the main forum of progressive Left-wing views. Just as importantly, he emerged as a performer, putting to public use the 'powerful transference effect' that had hypnotised his adolescent pupils in his philosophy classes. His lecture, 'Existentialisme, est-il un humanisme?' was one of the great social events of the post-war years. His meetings were packed out. A spoof written by the novelist, Boris Vian, reported people tunnelling into the lecture hall or parachuting on to the roof. The small, squinting figure puffing on his pipe had an effect like a modern popstar with women fainting and men fighting in the hope of catching his words.

Sartre, who had dreamt of posthumous recognition, was clearly puzzled by the phenomenon and cared little for its material fall-out. Although he was reportedly earning as much as 20,000 francs a month from Gallimard alone, he still wore threadbare suits and worked at least six hours a day on his books and articles, the austere De Beauvoir writing at another desk in the flat. His social life, however, was continually demanding, often marked by all-night drinking sessions in Saint-Germain. To keep up the pace, he began to depend heavily on drugs but the terrifying consequences to his health and personality were some years away.

De Beauvoir had sufficient authority at the time to reduce Sartre's dependence on whisky and to see that his supply of tea was kept flowing, but she contributed much more to his fame than being a constant guardian. She had taken her own place on the existentialist scene with a collection of essays, *Pyrrhus et Cinéas*, in 1944, reinforcing the theory with her play *Les Bouches inutiles* and her novel, *Le Sang des Autres*, issued at the same time as Sartre's flurry of works in late 1945. For better or worse, the couple who refused anything resembling a conventional relationship were inextricably married by their ideas. While they resisted being called 'existentialist' because it was a Christian philosophy, they eventually had to capitulate and accept the label that was to become less a philosophical ideal than a general movement of political and social progress. As the popular Press seized on a number of controversial images, existentialism represented almost anything from the couple's '*union libre*' to the obscure Marxist clashes in *Les Temps Modernes*, an open tribune for the dissidents of Saint-Germain-des-Prés.

The electrifying effect on the young, educated middle classes of the couple's iconoclasm was described by Jean Cau, Sartre's secretary who won the Prix Goncourt for a novel in 1961. As Sartre emerged as an intellectual star, Cau was still at the Lycée Louis-le-Grand in the Quartier Latin. He wrote to Sartre who, in one of those spontaneous gestures for which the philosopher was well known, took Cau under his wing.

'In school, we grabbed Sartre's books,' Cau said, referring to the impact of *Les Chemins de la Liberté* and reawakened interest in *La Nausée*. Cau, who was studying philosophy, said that with his friends he was looking for a 'very sceptical new universe with a sort of commitment'.

'Sartre's was a new tone,' he said. 'It was very important for young people that a teacher, particularly a philosophy master, wrote like this. We had never known a professeur who used such hard language. The fact that a teacher, a great intellectual, could write *L'Etre et le Néant* was, for us, the equivalent of the Pope writing novels.

'It was the first time that a philosopher had written books in which you fucked and got drunk. We adopted his literature because it expressed the spirit of an age – an age of doubt, anxiety and self-questioning when all established values had taken a terrible blow.'

In 1948, Jean Cau co-authored an experimental film script with Anne-Marie Cazalis called *Ulysse ou les Mauvaises Rencontres* which was photographed in the streets of Saint-Germain-des-Prés. Shot in 16 mm by *Combat*'s film critic, Alexandre Astruc in a stream of consciousness style called '*camera stylo*', the production starred, among others, Simone Signoret, Juliette Gréco, Jean Cocteau, Jean Genet, Jean Marais and Boris Vian. Like most of the *camera-stylo* films – the first attempt to break from cinema tradition that was not to be achieved until the 1959 New Wave – *Ulysse* was never shown publicly. Astruc, who thirty years later produced a three-hour *camera stylo* interview with Sartre, hid *Ulysse* through embarrassment. Cau described the scenario as a 'completely burlesque script, a vague improvised story that ended in fiasco. It was a young people's joke.'

The cast list is part of Saint-Germain's history as it included two young people, Boris Vian and Juliette Gréco, who represented their whole generation. Vian's reckless life style and early death resemble one of his own helter-skelter novels that were not appreciated until two decades later. His scattered genius had to be reassembled to recreate the quartier's most appealing personality who fascinates contemporary adolescents. Gréco, who became one of France's best-known singers in the Fifties, was an orphan of circumstance, a Sartrian godchild and an image of the indestructible life-force of French youth as it emerged from its wartime chrysalis. Anne-Marie Cazalis, who sponsored her career as an intimate friend, felt that as Gréco was 'both penniless and beautiful, she was the symbol of post-war youth'. Gréco's adolescence coincided with her own discovery of Saint-Germain. Even if she had not become famous, her story is one of the most enlightening episodes of the period.

In both conversation and in her written memoirs, Gréco tends to idealise situations and people as if reality is too much to accept. 'The meeting of so many great and varying talents in this quartier can only be due to some great astrological coincidence', she once said. The truth, in her case, is more brutal.

She came to the area for the first time in the winter of 1943 direct from Fresnes prison where she had been held by the Gestapo along with her sister, Charlotte. Her mother, a Resistance worker had been arrested earlier in their home town of Bergerac in the south-west while Gréco and her sister were seized soon after arriving in Paris where they hoped to contact friends. Their father, a Corsican police commissaire who was forty years older than their mother, had long since walked out of their life. As Gréco was only sixteen and unaware of her mother's Resistance activities she was released from prison while her mother and sister were deported to Germany.

Alone in a strange city, Gréco sought out a former Bergerac lycée teacher, Hélène Duc, who kept a boarding house in the rue Servandoni in the Quartier Latin. Many of the other residents were connected with the stage, including the then unknown Gérard Philipe. Gréco dreamt of being a classical actress, taking free courses under a well-known teacher, Solange Sicard, who also coached Signoret, and participated in one of the great theatre productions of wartime France, the Comédie Française's staging of Paul Claudel's, *Le Soulier de Satin* in 1944.

Gréco's contribution to the *Soulier*, the most expensive production of the war, was as a background wave in a sea chorus recruited from the youngsters at Solange Sicard's acting school.

She is remembered only as being somewhat fleshy for such an ethereal role.

Her weight – she was known as La Ronde Toutoune – may also explain why, despite a deep, powerful voice, she did not fulfil her ambition to emulate Sarah Bernhardt as a classical actress. But over the next four or five years she underwent a physical transformation that brought her closer to Cazalis's description of 'beautiful'. It would open the way not just to a singing career but fame as an international cinema star.

There seemed little likelihood of that in 1945. Gréco was prepared to return to Bergerac with her mother but when she went to greet her and her sister on their release from concentration camp Madame Gréco announced that she was going to Indo-China as a naval officer. The two girls were left to make the best of their lives in the boarding-house in the rue Servandoni. While Gréco was bitter about this act of abandonment it was the passage to adulthood and the entry into the more serious world of Saint-Germain. She had already discovered the atmosphere of cafés like the Flore and was at the right age to be dazzled by the reputations of men and women at the centre of local gossip and national respect.

The village-like atmosphere of Saint-Germain quickly established a network of friendships among young people whose main fascination was cinema. Cafés like the Bar Vert in the rue Jacob became discussion centres for groups who would spend much of the day at free showings in the Cinémathèque where constantly changing groups of friends around Gréco included future directors Roger Vadim and Alain Resnais.

The easy contact between established personalities and young hopefuls made the most extravagant ambitions seem realisable. Living mainly off money orders sent from their mother, the two Gréco girls became regulars at the downstairs bar at the Pont-Royal, a luxury hotel only a few paces from Gallimard's office which became the local for an entire generation of writers and publishers.

The French contingent was reinforced by outsiders like

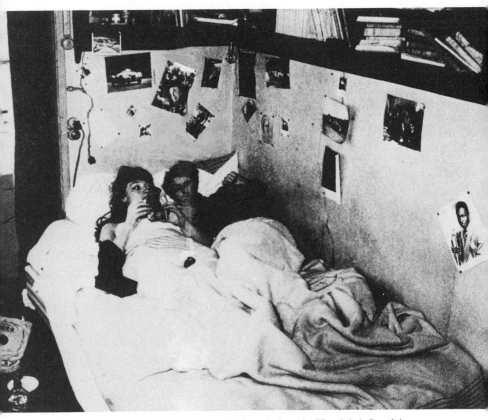

Juliette Gréco and friend, fashion model Annabel, at the Hotel de la Louisiane.
Photos of Miles Davis are on the walls

Arthur Koestler who was assimilated into Sartre's group despite mutual antipathy and political animosity. But the man
who introduced Gréco into the philosophers' enchanted circle
was Maurice Merleau-Ponty, editor of Sartre's *Les Temps
Modernes* and one of the clearest exponents of existentialism
and its relation to Marxism. The same age as De Beauvoir,
Merleau-Ponty was the most attractive of the intellectuals
circulating around Sartre and, according to Gréco, used his
'brilliant intelligence as a powerful aid to amorous adventures'.
   Gréco was, to all intents and purposes, an intellectual

'groupie' who was so fascinated by the broadmindedness and generosity of Sartre's friends that she even took over Sartre's hotel room in the Hotel de la Louisiane where the hook on which he hung his bicycle was still implanted in the ceiling. Sartre, who preferred the company of women, admitted her to his entourage. While he complained that she was something of a clinging ivy, he treated her like a persistent, amusing child and was ready to discuss all her moods. Several years later, he was to be instrumental in starting her singing career.

Sartre had many women friends but never betrayed any urgent pressure to prove himself physically with the women he fascinated. He flirted intellectually saying 'I will make conversation to you' as other men would say 'I will make love to you'. He created an atmosphere of trust that consoled Gréco for her absent father. But her 'cult of admiration' concentrated on Simone de Beauvoir whose strictness and self-discipline recall aspects of Gréco's mother.

Gréco still speaks of De Beauvoir in the terms of a high-school girl with a crush on a teacher, calling her a woman of 'troubling beauty with a Madonna's face, a beautiful and intelligent genius'. It was a fascination that was far from rare among adolescent girls who came into contact with de Beauvoir.

Absolutely sure of herself among a crowd of self-doubting young people, De Beauvoir had an incalculable effect on the moral values of adolescent middle-class French girls whose upbringing amounted to little more than a series of prohibitions. The effect of this strong-minded independent woman with her own moral code was evident long before she published *Le Deuxième Sexe* in 1949. In 1943, she lost her high-school post because the Vichy authorities felt she was a bad influence on her Catholic pupils. For much of the Saint-Germain generation, the publication of *Le Deuxième Sexe* was only a restatement of standards they had been encouraged to live by for years.

While De Beauvoir's theme was a general call to women to liberate themselves from oppressive traditions, the strongest impression in the public mind at the time was that she was preaching a sexual revolt based on her own way of life. Mauriac, after reading the book, was to write to a friend at Gallimard's to say that he now 'knew everything about your patronne's vagina'. De Beauvoir's own relationship with Sartre reinforced the limited view that she was a prophetess of decadent sexual morality that was to become one of the main reproaches levelled against the Saint-Germain youth cult.

A transference from an intellectual identification with sexual freedom to a physically active one became fixed in the public mind with the opening of the cellar club, Le Tabou, in the rue Dauphine in April 1947. From outside the quartier, particularly in the better off arrondissements where clean-cut Bobby-soxers were the only youth movement, Saint-Germain was to take on an image of a sexual Free Zone. For the young, crossing to the Left Bank was often an act of revolt, a choice between parents and Sartre, between discipline and 'existentialism'.

Middle-aged Frenchmen and women who lived through this period as teenagers still become angry at accusations of orgies and drug parties in the name of a loose interpretation of Sartre's philosophy. They point out that drugs and alcohol were too expensive while ignorance of contraception limited sexual daring. What excesses occurred, they claim, were only shocking in relation to a particularly repressive moral climate.

At the time, Parliament spent more hours debating the closure of brothels than in trying to solve the most stringent food rationing of the decade. The main obsession of most of the population was remembering the dead. The opening of Le Tabou was seen by many as an insult to a nation in mourning but the choice of Saint-Germain for a gathering place for youth in revolt would probably have happened even without its unique atmosphere.

During the war, the quartier was one of the centres of the Zazou movement, a strongly Anglophile phenomenon that developed into a loosely organised protest against Vichy severity. The main inspiration was American big band jazz, offensive to both Vichy and the Nazis more because it was black than because it was American. 'Le Swing' became a secret activity with dances held in cellar bars. The police had no difficulty in persecuting Zazous as they were easily recognisable. The boys gummed down their excessively long hair with salad oil and wore long jackets and tight trousers. The girls dressed badly in cheap skin coats, rolled neck pullovers, skirts held together by safety pins and laddered stockings. For both sexes, an ugly, unpolished pair of shoes was essential while the universal recognition sign was a rolled-up umbrella which was never opened even when it rained.

Elegance was hardly a hallmark for 'existentialists' either, mainly because clothes rationing was stricter than ever. Fashion depended entirely on imagination and available material but the aim was to shock outsiders and be immediately recognisable. Gréco and Anne-Marie Cazalis became fashion leaders, going through a variety of cheap materials including surplus field-grey and parachute silk before settling on tartan trousers which were considered particularly provocative. Basketball boots – 'les baskets' – took over from the Zazous' dirty shoes as the universal footwear for boys and girls.

While Gréco was to become the better known of the partnership, Cazalis was the main inspiration of the popular image of Saint-Germain through her journalistic talents and her promotion of Le Tabou of which she and Gréco were founders.

A slim, red-haired girl, Cazalis spent the war in the south of France being buffeted like an unwanted animal from one part of her family to another. She developed a shrewd, independent personality that was able to absorb the shocks in life with something approaching indifference. It was more as an observer of a curious event than as someone in great danger that she described one of the symbolic events of the Liberation. She watched De Gaulle's triumphant return to Paris in August 1944 from a balcony in the Louvre. A boy beside her was shot by a sniper's bullet and she watched him die.

This acquaintance with random violence was to be common to many of the personalities of Saint-Germain, not least Boris Vian whose father was murdered in the kitchen of their suburban house just after the Liberation.

In Cazalis's case it toughened her approach to life although her first ambition was to be a poet. In 1946 she won a prize presented to her by France's most revered contemporary poet, Paul Valéry, but she preferred a tough, Hollywood style of journalism as a career.

Her success as a journalist came from exploiting the mystique around Sartre and De Beauvoir. She went to Saint-Germain from the suburbs where she was staying with friends to seek out the couple who welcomed the forceful, entertaining young woman into their group. Soon afterwards, while sitting with the couple in the Bal Nègre, a Montparnasse club, they introduced her to Gréco. By that time, Sartre's old room, where Gréco stayed, had been equipped with a bath which turned the hotel into a free and easy meeting point for young people with an artistic life-style but little opportunity to wash.

Cazalis was absorbed into the group as Gréco's most influential friend and was to become the unofficial manager and public relations specialist of the 'existentialist' movement.

Looking back on those years, Cazalis has a curious puritanical attitude, complaining that the exploitation of Saint-Germain by popular French newspapers deliberately exaggerated the area's importance to 'extend the Occupation era and enrich themselves'. In fact, she herself awakened the interest of two mass circulation papers, *Samedi-Soir* and *Paris Dimanche* when the cellar club, Le Tabou, opened in April 1947 under her supervision with Gréco by her side.

With the Tabou's opening, the term 'existentialists' for the movement – an expression which Cazalis is credited with inventing – was to spread, sparking off a series of articles, not least in *Life* magazine. The United States interest is still considered the supreme accolade, catching the tone that young people themselves wanted to project by their lifestyle. The magazine published a series of photographs of the 'bohemians of Paris' in Saint-Germain whom it saw as the successors of Manet, Van Gogh and Picasso who 'struggled up from the same Bohemian environment'.

Life's black and white photographs of groups of young people 'discussing philosophy' in the smoke-filled cellar of Le Tabou to the background of jazz and poetry readings or sitting on pavements waiting for the dawn were a simplistic summary of a whole post-war generation as it struggled out of adolescent contradictions. The title of a Jacques Prévert poem, 'Je suis comme je suis', was to become its slogan. For a brief, ephemeral period, all the innocent ambitions of the young seemed to be concentrated in the Tabou's musty cellar with its dance floor covering barely ten square metres.

Saint-Germain had other clubs before the Tabou, notably the Méphisto, the Bar Vert and the Lorientais, a jazz club which opened from 5 pm to 7 pm before turning into a Chinese restaurant. It was in these clubs that friendships formed that had nowhere to blossom after closing time. The Tabou, which in those days had the uninspiring outside aspect of a rundown village café, was open all night to serve newspaper deliverymen. When Cazalis and Gréco discovered its downstairs cellar, already equipped as a club, the problem of an all-night meeting point was solved.

At its inauguration, it was little different from the nearby Méphisto with music on a gramophone interspersed with poetry readings. All the music was American, including popular songs and jazz for dancing the Jitterburg. But the Tabou quickly gained a reputation for being much livelier than the Méphisto. While it was possible to talk normally at the Méphisto, philosophical discussions at the Tabou were impossible. Even so, Sartre, De Beauvoir and Camus, who now exploited a resemblance to Humphrey Bogart and dressed like a private detective, were among the first comers. Jean Cocteau who was one of the flamboyant regulars in the Saint-Germain scene also visited the club to dance with Gréco and Cazalis. When Orson Welles turned up, Americans realised that the centre of Paris progressive culture had switched from Montparnasse.

The club might have remained a fantasy world for young bohemians as in the image created by *Life* magazine if the newspaper, *Samedi-Soir*, on Cazalis's initiative, had not seized on it within a fortnight of the opening. The closed village atmosphere of Saint-Germain, to which few outsiders were admitted on equal terms, became, overnight, a national attraction for anyone interested in a marginal life-style. Commercial interests rapidly followed.

According to *Samedi-Soir*, Saint-Germain was overflowing with poor existentialists between the ages of sixteen and twenty-two who were, for the most part, 'cursed by their fathers'. They lived in hotels until presented with the bill and then walked out. Throughout the day, they gathered in the Bar Vert whose lavatory became a wall newspaper for existentialist thought such as: 'DON'T KILL TIME, KILL YOURSELF'; 'ASK FOR AN ARSENIC-MINT TO SATISFY YOUR THIRST FOR ETERNITY', or: 'I HAVE SUCH A RESENTMENT FOR MAN THAT I WOULD LIKE TO BE REBORN IN A TRAIN CRASH'.

After midnight, according to the newspaper, existentialists took refuge in the Tabou 'the true sanctuary of a new generation'. The journalist could detect nothing worse there than flat broke young people staring into glasses of tepid water or dancing the Jitterbug 'like hard-labour convicts'. His main concern was how they survived without any money apart from 'selling a few old books, taking a job as an extra in a Sartre play or running up debts'.

The description of how they dressed – the men with shirts open to their navels and the girls refusing makeup – was the nearest the newspaper got to suggesting that the young people were degenerate, but within weeks the Tabou came to be seen as a den of vice.

The club's attraction had been increased when Boris Vian and his two brothers arrived to form a jazz band and by August the noisy comings and goings sparked off a civil war in the rue Dauphine. The road was still inhabited mainly by workers who needed their night's sleep. They tried to stop the Tabou by threats of violence or direct action such as emptying chamber-pots on the heads of young people. The publicity attracted more sightseers who queued up to enter the club where Gréco and Cazalis viewed applicants from behind a grille in the door to the cellar, admitting only their friends or the most bizarre newcomers.

Advertisements appeared from residents recalling that the rue Dauphine had distinguished itself during the Liberation of Paris and intended to set up a militia to liberate the Tabou. As a result, descriptions of the activities of the young dancers became increasingly incredible as journalists competed for sensation. The *pisse-copies*, as Boris Vian called them, excited the condemnation of editorials. *France-Soir*, the successor of *Paris-Soir*, called the existentialist dancers 'delinquents, drug traffickers and tarts who should go and philosophise elsewhere'. Attacks on existentialism in the Communist and Catholic Press mingled with philosophical and political criticisms of Sartre and De Beauvoir. The confusion between popular and intellectual Saint-Germain 'existentialism' was firmly fixed.

Sartre made feeble attempts to reject 'parentage' of the existentialist movement saying that 90 per cent of the young people who went to Saint-Germain had never read his books. Paulhan was not far from the truth when he said that *L'Etre et le Néant* was bought mainly 'to weigh the jam'. But identification with the youth cult's excesses was added to by spoofs including one which showed Sartre as hesitating between two decadent nightclubs – L'Etre and Le Néant.

In fact he was hurt by allegations he was corrupting young people and defended what was essentially a craze for dancing the Jitterbug in a sympathetic atmosphere. 'I find the dance which animates these young people has nothing cynical or sensual about it', he said. 'It is an innocent, gay and healthy exercise which does them the greatest good physically and after which they are much too tired to have any dirty thoughts.'

Even with this defence and Cazalis's insistence that the Tabou, where bread turned mouldy after half an hour because of the damp, was 'all Coca-Cola and the Andrews Sisters', the club was closed down in August 1947, four months after opening.

It reopened in autumn in much stricter conditions. After the windows were smashed by irate local residents, the rue

An evening at Le Tabou. Raymond Queneau and Boris Vian are in the centre.
Alain Vian is on the right

Dauphine learned to live with its notoriety. The Tabou, though, was firmly stuck in the public mind as an image of a new, controversial way of life to be found on the Left Bank. The publicity unfortunately destroyed Saint-Germain's innocence in two ways. The delinquent element was attracted in growing numbers until the newspaper articles on Saint-Germain's decadence became more and more justified by the early Fifties. It also brought in commercial interests who saw Saint-Germain's daring image as essential to launching progressive ideas. Although this was to take the area out of the hands of its amateur village promoters, it was to have the creative side-effect of launching playwrights like Beckett, Ionesco and Genet or attracting talent like Brel and Brassens who would change the direction of French popular song.

The Tabou was quickly absorbed into this commercial circuit as other cellar clubs opened to exploit its success. For dedicated 'existentialists' it was to become just another assembly point among many. By mid-1948, to be *'dans le vent'* – a phrase equivalent to 'with it' which Cazalis invented – the centre of attraction was the bigger Club Saint-Germain-des-Prés. The quartier's Pied Piper, Boris Vian, had taken up residence there, followed by the Cazalis-Gréco entourage.

4

L'Arrache-coeur

By mid-1947, France faced a moral, social, economic and political crisis as damaging as the worst moments of the war. Until 1945, there had been the excuse that outside forces brought about France's humiliation. In 1947, the truth had to be faced that the nation was destroying itself.

The burst of national unity and good intentions at the Liberation withered to nothing. Resistance movements exhausted themselves in internal quarrels and by the end of 1946 their influence had already gone. De Gaulle resigned in disgust as national leader in January 1946, beginning a long 'crossing of the desert', as Malraux called it, that would last until the *coup d'état* of 1958. The Communist Party, which commanded more than a quarter of the electorate and controlled key industries through the trade unions, was thrown out of government in May 1947 as the Cold War intensified. It would be thirty-four years before they were to share power again.

The two best organised underground movements were now in much the same position as they were before the Liberation. Only this time they were rivals, both determined to undermine the Fourth Republic which had reassembled the elements of weak pre-war and bigoted Vichy leadership. Gaullists saw the only solution as a new Republic with a moderate dictator while the Communists again flirted with Stalinist revolutionary ideas. The only common factor between Gaullists and Communists, apart from their contempt for Parliamentary rule, was hatred for the Americans. The intellectual establishment split as it scurried to support one side or the other. Those, like Sartre, who believed in an alternative solution sought marginal ground that created ever more misunderstandings.

The restoration of weak leadership inherited from the Third Republic and Vichy had been subtle, beginning with the purge of Left-wing Resistance elements in the army as soon as the war ended. The economic damage caused by the war allowed private capitalism to dictate economic priorities even though De Gaulle carried out a wave of nationalisations. In the public service, *fonctionnaires* who had been condemned by the Resistance were comfortably reinstalled at their desks, advising members of the National Assembly and Senators whose war record was often disgraceful. In officialdom, Collaborationists who had been punished were considered unlucky rather than shameful.

With the Resistance Press, like *Combat*, undermined by strikes and internal quarrels, the commercial Press increased the national divide by preparing the population for an imminent war against Bolshevism. But in the public mind, still impressed by Gaullist and Communist arguments, most resentment was saved up for the Americans. The Marshall Plan was made out to be an attempt to turn France into a colony while American soldiers were made to feel part of an occupying army.

Reports in US newspapers at the time reflect a feeling by the Americans that they were treated with more contempt than the Germans. Paris was no longer the extravagant rest centre remembered by the Wehrmacht. Puritanism and post-war purges had closed most of the night clubs and introduced prudishness in the big cabarets. *Life* magazine quoted unhappy, bewildered GI's asking: 'Where are the naked girls?' Images of plump, well-dressed Parisians seen in August 1944 were replaced by reports of a grim, hostile, hungry population.

For the working-class Parisian, life really was much worse than under the Nazis as the working week had increased from forty to forty-five hours since the Liberation, while purchasing power had dropped by a third. The daily battle to find something to eat was harder than the blackest days of the war, with bread rationing down to two-thirds of its 1942 level. Communist strikes paralysed one industry after another.

The daily anxiety over finding food, clothes, fuel or transport was compounded by the instability of Fourth Republic governments whose main recipes were devaluations of the franc and increasing doses of austerity. At the same time, they reinforced the pattern of chaos and division by events full of menace for the future such as the despatch of an expeditionary force to the colonies in Indo-China and the refusal to consider independence for territories like Morocco and Madagascar.

It was the young who most felt the disappointment of these post-war years. Their adolescence had been put between parentheses during the war. Now their elders had let them down again as self-interest gained the upper hand over idealism. Many more wasted years were in prospect, but Boris Vian's voice rallied a whole generation to get on with the business of living. His life-style was not only an antidote for general depression, but a counter argument to Sartre's vision of political commitment as a remedy for the world's ills. Vian's recipe was direct and simple.

'Stop feeling responsible for the world,' one of his characters says in *L'Automne à Pékin*. 'You are partly responsible for yourself and that's enough.'

In photographs taken in Saint-Germain-des-Prés after the war, Vian rarely smiles. Much taller than most of the area's personalities, he stares at the camera as if trying to hypnotise. There is a look of an automaton in his stiff stance, his pale skin and beak-like nose. Sometimes, he looks appallingly tired as if the early death for which he knew he was destined was keeping him waiting.

When it eventually caught up with him in 1959, when he was only thirty-nine, the circumstances were so bizarre that Vian's place as the spirit of a whole generation was assured. He died of a heart attack after sneaking into a film première of *J'irai cracher sur vos tombes*, the book that launched him in the post-war cultural scene. The book both made him and ruined him while the shock at the poor film adaptation killed him.

'One day, Vian will become Vian,' wrote his mentor and friend, the poet and author Raymond Queneau who regretted that Vian's talent, verging on genius, was not fully appreciated in his lifetime. In Saint-Germain, he often seemed purposeless, flitting from one obséssion to another, as if life were some reckless experiment in which everything had to be experienced superficially. It was only after his death that his treasures were reassembled to find that in his fifteen-year productive time span, he was the most versatile and most enlightening of all the leading figures of Saint-Germain.

He outwrote everyone, producing seven novels, seven plays, three operas or musicals, twenty-eight film scripts, four hundred popular songs and hundreds of articles on jazz, now bound in volumes as thick as anything Sartre produced. In addition, he turned out a wide-ranging series of translations from Strindberg to the American general, Omar Bradley. Everything was written out in long hand, often in sessions of eighteen hours, so painful that he had to construct a special elbow support to defeat writer's cramp.

Even so, many of his friends still see him as a dilettante, a profligate whom they remember flitting from one social occasion to the next, organising interminable *surprise parties* between jazz sessions and trips to the summer resort that owes its creation to Saint-Germain's holiday expatriates – Saint Tropez. The idea that Vian worked hard for his living, sits oddly with this amusing, friendly personality who seemed always available for any enjoyable waste of time.

Vian's certainty that his weak heart would cut his life short at any moment brought him into physical relation with one of the key elements of Saint Germain's youth culture; the belief that living, or at least pleasure, was going to be destroyed suddenly by a new wave of misery or another war. Even Sartre told De Beauvoir that they would soon be swept away by an atomic bomb. This gloomy preoccupation, so often summed up in the quartier's graffiti, became part of an elaborate game to justify an attitude of let the dead bury the dead. Nothing caught this tone better than the title of Vian's novel, *J'irai cracher sur vos tombes*, published in 1946 as war memorials throughout the country were engraved with the names of the Second World War dead. Vian's life style, though, was not so much spitting on other people's graves as on his own.

Despite being the spirit of Saint-Germain and a friend of all its leading figures, Vian does not fit easily into any preconceptions. He did not even live there. When he came to Paris during the war he lived in his parents-in-law's flat in the rue du Faubourg Poissonnière on the Right Bank. Later, he renovated a flat over the Moulin Rouge in Montmartre next to Jacques Prévert's. He was neither a lost provincial 'orphan' attracted to the open hearth at the Flore nor an intellectual afraid of losing touch with the Left Bank's vital forces like the Sorbonne, the Beaux Arts or the Ecole Normale Supérieure.

Unlike many of Saint-Germain's trendsetters, he had a trouble-free childhood, apart from rheumatic fever, in a united family. He was shaken when his father was murdered in the family house at Ville d'Avray, a Paris outer suburb, in 1944, but by then he was old enough, twenty-four, to take the shock. He had a network of family friends as well as two brothers and a sister to whom he was very close. By 1944, he had also been married for three years to Michelle Léglise and had a salaried job in what was probably the best ordered office in Paris, the headquarters of the French standards bureau, the Afnor, an official body drawing up norms for industrial products.

Ville d'Avray, where he spent the first twenty years of his life, has the look of solid, predictable contentment with its large family houses and its rich or famous residents. The Vians had inherited money from a grandfather's fortune in bronze-casting

and maintained an air of respectability even when this trickled
through their fingers before and during the war. To make ends
meet, the big family house, next door to that of Jean Rostand, a
biologist and member of the Académie Française, was let before
the war to the Menuhins.

The Vians moved into a gatekeeper's lodge, while the main
house, 'Les Fauvettes', became a rendezvous for some of the
world's most famous musicians including Sir Edward Elgar.
The Vians and the Menuhins played together like one family
and there is a photograph of the seven children standing in
descending order on the lawn at Ville d'Avray, Yehudi, the
eldest, with his hands on the shoulders of the biggest Vian boy,
Lelio while Boris's younger brother, Alain, holds the shoulders
of Hephzibah. But while Yehudi and Hephzibah went home to
play their classical music the three Vian brothers were already
fascinated by jazz.

Later, Boris's father built an 80-square metre dance-hall
which could accommodate 400 dancers in the garden at Ville
d'Avray. The jazz band formed by the three Vian brothers, with
Boris on the trumpet, played twice a week to 'surprise parties'
for the local middle-class children. The chaste occasions, overseen by the local lycée masters, which even the headmaster's
daughter attended, created an extended family atmosphere that
was recognisable later in Saint-Germain-des-Prés. In the lycée
days, Vian's speciality was the Foxtrot. After the war, when
Vian's parties moved from flat to flat for as long as week, the
music was Be-bop.

'I really loved my father,' Vian wrote. Loyal to his father's
traditional ideas on education, Vian agreed to study engineering
rather than pursue his youthful literary fantasies inspired by the
clown of the Belle Epoque, Alfred Jarry. Vian's war years were
spent partly at the engineering school, l'Ecole Centrale, whose
former pupils included Louis Blériot and Gustave Eiffel. One of
the results was his first published work, a manual on physical
chemistry in relation to metal products.

L'Ecole Centrale increased Vian's neutralism in politics
which was to differentiate him from most of the other leading

The Menuhins and Vians were once next-door-neighbours. Left to right:
Yehudi Menuhin, Lelio Vian, Boris Vian, Alain Vian, Hephzibah Menuhin,
Yaltah Menuhin, Ninon Vian. Photo taken by Boris Vian's father, Paul, at the
Villa 'Les Fauvettes'

literary figures in Saint-Germain. Vian placed his friends politically by whether they chose Saint Cyr, the officer training
college, or the Ecole Normale Supérieure to complete their
education. Saint Cyr was Right wing, the Ecole Normale Left
wing and, according to Vian, L'Ecole Centrale 'stood in the
middle counting the blows'.

Even though he had a high level of mechanical skill, which he
showed in his obsession for vintage cars, and was a fine carpenter, Vian was ill at ease as an engineer. After his father's
unexplained murder, he felt released from filial obligations. By

1946, he was pursuing a full-time literary career, having given up his job at the standards' bureau. His father's death broke another solid link as the house at Ville d'Avray had to be hurriedly sold.

By then, Vian's cultural influences were clear. The first was Alfred Jarry whose *Ubu Roi* is Europe's greatest anarchistic classic. Vian's particular fascination was for Jarry's *Dr Faustroll*. Vian's determination to update Jarry brought him within the orbit of Raymond Queneau, secretary-general at Gallimard, whose humour and style were in part a reaction to the pomposity of much of the publisher's stable.

He was also fascinated by Jacques Prévert whose constant good humour and brilliant mixture of talents made him a predestined neighbour for Vian. Queneau, Vian and Prévert were eventually to combine their talents as members of the Collège de 'Pataphysique, an institution dedicated to Jarry's Science of Imaginary Solutions.

Jarry was the inspiration of Vian's first two novels, *Troubles dans les Andains* and *Vercoquin et le plancton* which Queneau published in his own collection at Gallimard although Paulhan always claimed that he was the first to have read and supported what can be called a nonsense novel. Queneau, a friendly, well-rounded family man, twenty years older than Vian, was a perfect surrogate father as well as being, in Vian's words, 'the only French writer who has a unique language, style and ideas'.

Queneau's humorous novels, such as *Zazie dans le Métro*, his poetry and his skilful use of language in Saint-Germain intimate revues like *Exercices de style*, brought him a steady, modest success during the Saint-Germain period although his presence had been noticeable there since winning the first Prix des Deux Magots for a novel *Le Chiendent* in 1933. In the literary world, he is remembered, first of all, for his natural kindness which Vian described as 'a providence for young authors'.

Apart from his brother, Alain, who was especially close to Boris during the Saint-Germain years, two other men were strongly influential in Vian's literary and personal development. Inevitably, one was Jean-Paul Sartre. The other was

Jacques Loustalot, five years younger than Vian, who was to contribute to Saint-Germain's legends by his eccentricity and extraordinary death in 1948 and who is identifiable as the ubiquitous Major in many of Vian's works.

Vian's relationship with Sartre could be seen as an epic struggle between political commitment and hedonistic detachment. In the middle was Vian's wife since 1941, Michelle, who preferred Sartre's message, leaving Vian at the end of the decade 'not so much for Sartre but for Sartre's group', according to Vian's friend and biographer, Jacques Duchâteau. From then on, Michelle was regularly in Sartre's company as he gradually assumed a more active participation in proletarian street politics.

The fascination with Sartre's overpowering influence on French youth was the subject of Vian's best novel, *L'Ecume des Jours*, where a philosopher called Jean-Sol Partre is murdered – his heart is torn out while writing in a café – by the lover of a man who spends all his money on buying useless Partrian relics. The internal family struggle on commitment and detachment in the Vian household was already well-developed by then with Michelle and Boris on the fringes of Sartre's group while playing different roles.

Vian contributed to *Les Temps Modernes* only to make fun of the seriousness of Sartre, De Beauvoir and Merleau-Ponty, mixing up their names in articles about Meloir de Beauvartre or Pontartre de Merlebeauvy whom he judged 'too weak' and capable only of producing 'stupid articles'. But his attitude was based on personal experience as, with Michelle, he was often at the centre of major political disputes. It was at the Vians' flat that Camus had his first row with Sartre when they fell out over a book by Merleau-Ponty, *Humanisme et Terreur*. This was in 1946 when Camus, in Sartre's description, was in a violent mood, taunted by the 'cold, pale Merleau-Ponty'.

Sartre intervened to give a third point of view in the hope of reconciling the two men, but neither of them would speak to him again for six months. Witnessing events like these contributed to Vian's contempt for political intellectualism but his only attempt at a coherent counter-argument, *Traité du civisme*, that he worked on during the Fifties, is incomplete.

By then, Michelle had left him for Sartre's camp which was becoming increasingly committed to the Communist revolutionary line while Vian was absorbed into what was seen as the reply of the uncommitted – 'Pataphysique.

Sartre plays a less revealing part in Vian's literary life than Jacques Loustalot, the glass-eyed eccentric friend of his school days. Loustalot, the mayor's son from a small Atlantic coast holiday village, became the absurd representation of doomed and nonchalant youth whose manic-depressive fantasies are the key to Vian's appeal to adolescents.

Vian met Loustalot at about the same time as he met Michelle Léglise. The Vians and the Léglises took refuge in Capbreton near Bordeaux in 1940 where the Ville d'Avray party scene restarted. Loustalot became part of the family until his death eight years later when Saint-Germain's youth cult was at its peak.

Loustalot's nickname, The Major, arose from early meetings with Michelle when he told her: 'The well contented major returning from India, is me.' At the time, he was only fifteen, five years younger than Boris, but they appeared the same age. Loustalot claimed that his glass eye was the result of an attempted suicide at the age of ten and suicide would again be discussed when he died at the age of twenty-three in Saint-Germain.

Michelle was fascinated by the extreme naturalness of The Major's absurd gallantry, such as lighting her cigarette with an expensive lighter and throwing it away in the sea with a flourish. The glass eye which The Major was constantly removing became part of Saint-Germain's legends. When Juliette Gréco refused to let anyone into the Tabou unless they could prove they were 'interesting', Loustalot swallowed the eye.

Despite the difference in age, The Major and Boris Vian were inseparable. Vian projects his friend in his novels like an inner self expressing Vian's own extravagant ambitions.

In 1948, when one of Vian's week-long parties was in full swing, The Major walked out of a sixth-floor window in Saint-Germain and killed himself. There was no proof that it was suicide as Loustalot often used to threaten to walk out of windows when a girl refused to dance with him. But only six months before, Boris Vian had written The Major's epitaph in a short story for *Samedi-Soir* called *Surprise party chez Léobille.*

'As for the Major, his body twisted quickly in the air and, thanks to a few judicious turns, became straight. He had the misfortune to fall into a red and black taxi with an open roof which carried him far away before he could realise it.'

With the commercialism of the Tabou and the death of The Major coming so close together, Vian might well have lost interest in the area that had served to prolong his adolescence but distracted him from earning his living. He was kept there by his love of jazz, the dominant cultural influence in his life and his introduction to the area in the first place.

Vian's life is so diverse, offering a key to so many aspects of post-war France, that it inevitably becomes disjointed, rather like many of his own novels which seem to owe their construction to the peculiar methods of work he learnt at the standards' bureau. Most have to be dismantled and reassembled to be properly understood. The interworking relationship of each part is not always obvious. Music was the only consistent expression in Vian's life and jazz was its dominant theme. As a good trumpeter, who particularly admired the U.S. jazzman, Bix Beiderbecke, Vian first came to Saint-Germain in 1944 as a musician at the short-lived Club de Nouvelle Orléans. His trumpet was again present at the Lorientais and the Tabou and he was the moving spirit behind the Jazz Club de Saint-Germain, founded when the atmosphere at the Tabou changed. The club, a few yards from the Flore, became the European capital of jazz with Vian known both as a performer and a critic for specialist newspapers and *Combat*. But although jazz was the main reason why Vian stayed loyal to the area, it was only background music to a frenetic life.

If Vian had not been so sure that he would die young, the dispersion of his genius into too many areas would seem like fecklessness. But as he was fully aware that he was condemned by his weak heart and chest, the rush to fulfil his eccentric gifts is like the action of a man afraid to lose even an hour of his time. Even while he had a salaried job, he would work, play jazz or amuse himself throughout the night, refusing rest and going straight to his office without a break. Unfortunately, his rush spoiled many of his works as far as style was concerned, frustrating his secondary ambition to achieve financial independence. In 1945 and 1946, he wrote five novels, *L'Ecume des Jours* among them. But this, his most popular work, was not recognised until years after his death when it rapidly sold more than a million copies and became an inspiration for the 1968 student movement.

The only book for which he would receive national recognition in his lifetime was produced in less than a fortnight in 1946 while on holiday at the seaside. It was written to earn some quick ready money but made Vian a small fortune. Unfortunately it also cast a shadow over the rest of his life as it was the centre of France's most important literary scandal which dragged on for so long that it undermined both Vian's health and talent.

To add to the irony, the book was not even released under Vian's own name. *J'irai cracher sur vos tombes* was published in 1946 by the new Editions du Scorpion under the name of Vernon Sullivan, a nom-de-plume made up of the names of two jazzmen. The book has little literary merit but captures some essential elements of the Saint-Germain period including a popular fascination for American-style thrillers, an identification with the Black struggle in the United States and the horror moralists saw in the tiny Left Bank Quartier.

When Vian hurriedly wrote the book he was hoping to cash in on the success of the newly-formed Série Noire, translated American thrillers, published by Maurice Duhamel, which is still a popular French institution. Série Noire rivals like Scorpion were faced with a shortage of American originals and

Vian, as Vernon Sullivan, was asked for a pastiche of two of his favourite writers, James Cain and Horace MacCoy.

Vernon Sullivan was supposedly a coloured American working for the US forces near Paris, which justified the claim that the book had been 'translated from the American'. The story concerned a southern American Black whose skin was pale enough to allow him to cross the colour line. But when his younger and blacker brother is lynched for going out with a white girl, the hero seduces and murders two daughters of a white racist before being killed himself.

The book passed almost unnoticed at its publication, the only notable review claiming that it was such a poor novel that it was rejected by American publishers. After some months in circulation, the provocative title caught the attention of a puritanical Gaullist-linked group called the Cartel d'Action morale et sociale who were involved with other protests such as the attempt to stop the circulation of the untranslated versions of *Tropic of Cancer* and *Tropic of Capricorn* by Henry Miller. The organisation demanded that the book should be banned under laws to protect the family while condemning the theme as pandering to an unhealthy fascination with American decadence.

The accusation caused sales to soar. Just as interest waned, a commercial traveller murdered his mistress in a seedy hotel, leaving open Vian's book at the page where the hero strangles a woman. The Cartel's campaign intensified and by 1950 about 600,000 copies of the book were sold with the 'original' American version, translated by Vian, also in circulation. Eventually in 1953, seven years after the book was released, Vian was fined 100,000 francs, given a fifteen day jail sentence and ordered to destroy the remaining copies. He was saved from prison by a general amnesty that included wartime Collaborators and child molesters.

Vian made more than four million francs out of the book, compared to the salary he received at the standards' bureau of 20,000 francs a year. He was able to live without a salaried job for more than eight years even though all his other work, including other Vernon Sullivan 'translations', earned barely a pittance. But friends say that Vian did not rejoice in the irony. He suffered considerable anxiety. The constant interrogation by examining magistrates, attendance at trials and appeals, and the accusation that he was a 'pornographer' sapped his ability to concentrate on worthwhile literary work.

It was the title, more than the content, that raised the anger of puritans as there was nothing to justify a pornography charge except that, at this time, Proust was considered even more provocative while Lawrence was too dangerous to be translated. While the controversy was at its height, Vian wrote a stage version but street posters were not allowed to carry the title and referred only to 'the play by Boris Vian'.

Vian's persecution was by far the most scandalous attack by moralists during this period but it was by no means the only one. A publisher took a tremendous risk in producing anything adventurous. Jean-Jacques Pauvert whose first release as a publisher was a reflection by Sartre on Camus's *L'Etranger* at the Liberation, fought a constant war with the Government's Censorship Committee and groups like the Cartel as he interspersed Cocteau, Malraux and Marcel Aymé with titles by Sade and Genet. The battle with censorship went on late into the Fifties with the publication of *Bonjour Tristesse* by Françoise Sagan in 1954 to a national outcry for a new ban.

'You must remember what France was like during those years', Pauvert said. 'It was an old, backward country where the trains had hardly begun to run again and where luxury was practically non-existent. It was governed either by gloomy Socialists or austere pro-Gaullists. Frankly, it was a sinister age with a moral climate similar to that MacMahon introduced after the Commune in 1870. We really touched the lowest point.'

Pauvert said that the atmosphere in bookshops was 'pre-1914'. Once he asked for a copy of De Laclos's 1782 classic, *Les Liaisons Dangereuses* and was told by the shocked woman assistant: 'We don't sell that sort of literature here.' By 1958, attitudes had changed so much that one of the original youth cult figures of Saint-Germain, Roger Vadim, turned the book into a film starring another long-established resident, Gérard Philipe.

Saint-Germain's fascination with Black America was on two levels, again represented by the attitudes of Vian and Sartre. For Vian, Black America was the inventiveness of its jazzmen and he fulfilled an adolescent dream when the Club Saint-Germain developed under his guidance as the principal European stopover for the United States' best popular musicians. Among them were Duke Ellington, Charlie Parker, Miles Davis, Errol Garner and Count Basie. The Club Saint-Germain became the headquarters of modern jazz while the rival Vieux Colombier, underneath the theatre where Sartre's *Huis Clos* was performed, remained the reserve of New Orleans' traditional jazz under the direction of Claude Luter, one of Vian's closest friends. Among Luter's resident players was the Black American clarinetist Sydney Bechet who settled in Paris.

Jazz was as much a way of life as entertainment. It was still frowned on by much of the middle class which associated it with drugs and sexual decadence. The memory of the ban on jazz by the Vichy government was fresh, so that it became part of the youth rebellion. To be accepted by young people, it was necessary to 'talk jazz'. Simone de Beauvoir recognised the need and left it to Vian to make a record collection for her and Sartre.

Sartre's interest in Black America was, however, purely intellectual. While in the United States in 1945, he met Richard Wright, author of *Black Boy*, and a protégé of the Paris-based Gertrude Stein. Wright, who died in 1960, came to live in France on Sartre's insistence and was overwhelmed by the reception which began with meeting Gallimard's stars, including Gide, at a cocktail party. At first, he felt he was treated more as a golden captive rather than a Left-wing pioneer whose political convictions were much more mature than Sartre's. A Communist since the Thirties, he dedicated a poem to Aragon in 1936.

He was ill-at-ease with Sartre's intellectual approach to politics and returned to the United States. But there, the burden of being a Black Communist, even in New York, was too much to accept and he returned to France with his family to settle in the rue Monsieur-le-Prince near the Odéon, just off the boulevard Saint-Germain. Although Sartre made him famous in France, serialising *Black Boy* in *Les Temps Modernes* and turning it into a bestseller, Wright preferred his own 'court' of exiled American Blacks who followed him. They included James Baldwin, William Gardner Smith and Chester Himes who at first treated France only as a refuge from racism and McCarthyism. They were fully aware that the French attitude to Black persecution in the United States was in contrast to the average Frenchman's contempt for North African Arabs. But the welcome they received in Paris, where cafés like the Tournon and the Monaco next to Wright's flat became meeting points for exiled Blacks, increased their determination to take leading roles in Black American movements at home.

Vian himself placed the peak period of Saint-Germain in 1949. It was a hinge year in which the innocence of Le Tabou was still fresh at the moment when the area was invaded by commercial backers ready to take high risks promoting new clubs like La Rose Rouge, L'Echelle de Jacob, Le Vieux Colombier or L'Ecluse where a whole new generation of inventive talent would be launched.

Vian's own life was also undergoing profound changes as he approached thirty. The break-up with Michelle, spread over many months, also marked the rupture with the carefree days dating back to Ville d'Avray. The Major's death began the process which continued with the developing relationship with Ursula Kubler, a ballet dancer Vian met at one of Gallimard's receptions and whom he married in 1954.

They moved into an attic room in Clichy before Vian renovated the nearby flat over the Moulin Rouge which brought him next to Jacques Prévert.

There were a series of other minor or major events that changed Vian's life during 1949 and 1950. The Club Saint-Germain, with its parade of American jazzmen, had fulfilled a childhood dream but the young, penniless audience of the Tabou days was replaced by an increasingly chic middle-class. Cazalis and Gréco had followed him to the Club but both agreed that the essential atmosphere of Le Tabou was never recreated. At about the same time, Vian was warned by doctors that his lifestyle was too hard and he abandoned playing the trumpet.

A more subtle setback was the increasing justification of a scandalous side to Saint-Germain which mingled with accusations of pornography in Vian's long-running legal case. Newspaper reports of drug addiction, sexual excess and even violent crime were sometimes uncomfortably close to the truth as Saint-Germain's tourist population increased.

Vian kept his own cuttings on the increasingly outraged reaction of the Right-wing and Communist Press. He alleged that most newspaper reports were the fantasies of *pisse-copies* under pressure from news editors. Some of the reports, such as an accusation that Simone de Beauvoir used such foul language that she offended a group of lorry drivers were obviously made up in newsrooms. Some, like a quote from the Russian *Literatournaia Gazeta*, aimed indirectly at Sartre, were hysterical propaganda.

Saint-Germain, according to the *Gazeta*, was the refuge of impoverished youth who lived in filth.

'It is the youth of darkest corners of Paris, a curious mildew of hate, jealousy, stupidity and the most vulgar sexuality. This is the real face of the existentialists, this is their life.'

Saint-Germain was also becoming the centre of exhibitionism and publicity seeking. As journalists were among the highest proportion of 'regulars' in cellar bars, it was easy to start a rumour that some famous star was about to make a visit. Cameramen were rushed to the spot just as some starlet stripped, adding to the legend of endless debauchery.

Other journalists did the area just as much a disservice by overstating the area's innocence. In Vian's collection of cuttings, there are quotes from *Samedi-Soir* describing the quartier as 'the most chaste in Paris'. The entry of the Cellar Rats, a young group of dancers specialising in formation Be-bop dancing, was praised as 'a wave of purity'. Other newspapers, not least *Combat*, were so determined to project an air of middle-class respectability around Saint-Germain that Vian was afraid that it would be destroyed less by condemnation than by ridicule.

Vian, though, remained in the public image as a pornographer, condemned not least by the Communist Party. When he pioneered the Theatre of the Absurd in 1950 with his play, *L'Equarrisage pour tous*, a provocative send-up of the Normandy Invasion, Elsa Triolet took to the front line of Communist puritanism. *L'Equarrisage*, she said, compounded her 'solid antipathy for Vian's shameful spittle'. His image was hardly improved when Jean Cocteau, whom the Communists hated even more, took his defence, comparing the play to Apollinaire's *Les mamelles de Tirésias* and his own *Mariés de la tour Eiffel*.

There are many signs that Vian was becoming increasingly detached from Saint-Germain during this period and rethinking his entire life. One of his escape routes was an increasing fascination with vintage cars or his open-topped white Austin-Healey sports car. His favourite vehicle was a 1911 Brazier with a pierced back seat for relief en route, a practice which Vian carried out when passing policemen. The cars helped to increase his distance from the political-intellectuals of Saint-Germain as his friends say that Vian, an exceptionally skilled mechanic, preferred to spend his time with working-class, marginal trade unionists who helped him restore his cars in primitive workshops in the outer Paris suburbs.

But the most important reason for a change in Vian's priorities was simple necessity. In 1950, the tax authorities caught up with him after examining the accounts of Les Editions Scorpion which showed he had earned 4.5 million francs. To meet the taxmen's sudden demands, he was obliged to concentrate more on quick translations and during this period worked eighteen hours a day on a French version of Omar Bradley's *Soldier's Story*.

A desperate rush for freelance earnings that was to include

broadcasting and oilpainting was to have a tragic effect on his novels. He rushed into a contract with a small shaky publishing house, Editions Toutain, for his novel, *L'Herbe rouge*, but nearly every copy was pulped when the firm collapsed. A time-consuming project to produce a 300-page *Manuel de Saint-Germain-des-Prés* did not appear until 1974. Meanwhile, in 1950, Gallimard refused his last novel *L'Arrache-Coeur*, that was not to appear until after his death. At thirty, Vian's first literary preoccupation, novel writing, was given up in despair. The second phase of his career as scriptwriter, song writer and creator of revue was barely started.

As Vian's first marriage dissolved against a background of personality conflict and political priorities, his divorce was something of a symbol for what was happening in the Saint-Germain scene in general, where the atmosphere moved relentlessly towards the general destruction of intellectual unity and a rupture between intellectual leaders and the youth cult.

With the declaration of the Korean war in 1950 and the increasing disarray and instability in the French political scene, the domestic and international Cold War was now at freezing point. The battle lines had been clearly drawn between Aragon's Communists and Malraux's Gaullists. Most of the leading intellectuals had taken sides behind these two great movements, but the two most influential men on the cultural scene, Camus and Sartre, remained undecided, one on the right and the other on the left of the ever-widening political gulf.

Their eventual decisions of political allegiance which led to their public row in 1952 coincided exactly with the final dispersal of the French Left. It took nearly thirty years before the Left recovered from the trauma and became strong enough to take over government.

5

La Troisième Force

Between November 1947 and June 1951, when national politics were dominated by a Third Force coalition opposed to Communism and Gaullism, France had eight governments, two of which lasted only two days. Superficially, the Third Force was a Centre-Left alliance dedicated to preserving parliamentary democracy from the extremes of Left and Right. Within weeks, it became little more than a series of self-interested compromises that dismayed the electorate and opened the way in 1952 to a return of the conservative Right, dominated by former Vichy elements.

De Gaulle described members of the Third Force as 'little parties cooking their own soup by the corner of the fire', a repugnant image to leading intellectuals obsessed by the grandeur of political ideals. No one of the cultural stature of Malraux or Aragon, the prophets of Gaullism and Communism, rallied to the Third Force. Some opinion leaders, like Sartre, went in search of an alternative solution, founding the Marxist-inspired Rassemblement Démocratique Révolutionnaire which saw itself as potentially as powerful as Bolshevism.

The parliamentary Third Force had neither the freshness of Gaullism nor the strength of Communism and it quickly adopted a backward-looking image. In the Fourth Republic, Parliament sat as an electoral college to choose the national President. In 1946 it elected Vincent Auriol, a Socialist deputy since 1914 and Minister of Finance in Léon Blum's Popular Front in 1936. The Third Force was dominated by pre-war Socialist and Radical members of the National Assembly while opportunist men of the Right joined its ranks only to undermine the Government's credibility. The result was creeping administrative paralysis while policy differences between the various factions became difficult to distinguish. Only the Communists, isolated on the Left, maintained an easily recognisable parliamentary identity in ideological terms.

Dominance of the Third Force by men of the past hid the essential fact that it contained the foundation members of the Socialist government that would ally with the Communists to govern France from 1981. In 1947, the most important element was the Section Française de l'Internationale Ouvrière, the SFIO, with its traditional, moderate working-class support from the North. The SFIO inherited the name by which the Socialist movement had been known since 1905 and which it kept when the Communists split from the movement in 1921 because it was not sufficiently radical.

Most of the little parties and independent members of the National Assembly who professed left-of-centre politics were eventually to bring their minor flocks to Socialism when the present-day Socialist Party was created in 1971. With them came recruits from the rump of the once great pre-war Radical Party whose last moments of triumph were under the 1954 government of Pierre Mendès France.

The man who united these elements in 1971, recreating much of the discredited Third Force, was François Mitterrand who became President of the Republic in 1981. Mitterrand's triumph obscured the historical fact that he, as much as anyone, contributed to the Left's disarray in the post-war years. He was the object of contempt for progressive intellectual forces, although his original ambition had been to emulate Left Bank radicalism.

François Mauriac was to say of the Fourth Republic politicians: 'Contemplate them, my heart. They are really horrible.'

Mitterrand cannot be excluded from that general judgement. He was a Minister eleven times during the eleven years of the Republic, having been elected a member of the National Assembly on a Right-wing platform for a party claiming to be on the Left-wing. The colours of the governments he served during those years changed with the seasons. As a young Left Bank student before the war, he yearned to be a major cultural figure. Immediately after the war, as a newspaper editor, he was noted for his vigorous, clear editorials supporting freedom of opinion.

Yet he was to become the most repressive Minister of Information of the post-war years, alienating much of the intellectual Left and earning the nickname 'Goering' from the Communists as he imposed rigorous censorship on the broadcasting system.

He would almost certainly have been plunged into obscurity when the Fourth Republic collapsed in 1958 if he had not, in the meantime, come under the influence of Pierre Mendès France in 1954. Mendès France was to become the symbol of French anti-colonialism, creating the common ground that was to unite the Left during the Algerian war and prepare the way for Mitterrand's 1981 victory. There was a certain justice in Mitterrand's gathering the fruits. His political twists and turns in the Forties and Fifties reflect an entire generation's search for its point of balance against a background of moral betrayal.

Mitterrand's political development was inspired by his period as a student on the Left Bank and his close wartime relations with some of Saint-Germain-des-Prés' leading political and literary figures, notably the writer Marguerite Duras. The boulevard Saint-Germain was the central point of his student life. He went to Law School in the Quartier Latin, controlled by extreme-Right student parties, and to the Institute of Political Science on the fringes of Saint-Germain-des-Prés where the Left held sway. The physical clashes between these two groups were constant reminders of pre-war political tensions. Mitterrand also attended meetings at the area's main conference hall, La Mutualité, centre of big Left-wing rallies dominated by Gide and Malraux. At the same time, he was fascinated by Drieu la Rochelle, but refused approaches to join the pro-Nazi Action Française. Mitterrand was caught up by the literary-political osmosis and dreamt of a writer's career, submitting short stories to Left Bank magazines.

His hesitation in choosing sides was due to his provincial background. Mitterrand was from a Catholic middle-class family from the south-west. His father was a stationmaster at a time when the job had social rank equivalent to a local bank manager. The family atmosphere was dominated by a rigid allegiance to the Catholic Church and a puritan attitude to the corrupting influence of capitalism. The young Mitterrand was educated privately by priests and for his Left Bank studies he boarded at a Marist fathers' pension behind Saint Sulpice church. This was to cut him off from complicity with the mainly atheistic Paris middle-class student whose political allegiances had been formed from lycée days.

Mitterrand was something of a renegade to his caste which was to provide so many recruits for Pétainism, because he detested militarism and refused officer-training when he was called up at the age of twenty-three in 1939. Wounded as an infantry sergeant at Verdun in 1940, he was to succeed in one of the most reckless PoW escapes of the war, leaping over the camp wire under fire from German guards. He outpaced his pursuers by only a few yards before finding a prearranged Resistance hideout.

Not long before that escape, Mitterrand was jilted by his fiancée. On his return to the Left Bank, Marguerite Duras was struck by his carelessness for his own safety, an attitude which some friends traced to his reaction to his broken love affair. His apparent determination to tempt fate, such as smoking English cigarettes during secret missions in occupied Paris, became part of a daring approach as one of the most successful intelligence agents of the war. Under the name of Captain Morland, Mitterrand created his own network among prisoners-of-war, using the Left Bank as a base and Duras as his contact with the Gestapo.

Mitterrand drew heavily on the aid of Communist intellectuals. Duras' flat in the rue Saint-Benoît in Saint-Germain was a key meeting point for Communists, a role that it was to play increasingly after the war. The tiny, ebullient Duras, who was Mitterrand's age, took on the dangerous task of misleading the Nazi police on the whereabouts of Captain Morland. She held meetings with a Gestapo agent in the Flore to pass on false information.

Duras' friends saved Mitterrand's life when his Left Bank hideout was discovered in June 1944 and several members of his network were captured. Mitterrand escaped with the aid of leading intellectual Resistants, including Albert Camus.

By then, antipathy between De Gaulle and Mitterrand had been established during a meeting in Algiers in 1943 when the general humiliated the young Resistant, who responded by refusing to accept Gaullist orders to fuse his network with another close to De Gaulle. The clash not only inspired a lifetime's enmity for De Gaulle and his constitutional projects, but complicated Mitterrand's political ambitions as he was considered a Communist 'mole'.

The Liberation of Paris came with Mitterrand aged only twenty-eight but equipped with enormous resources for a political career. Apart from being one of the best-known figures among the 1.8 million French soldiers in captivity who formed his intelligence network, Mitterrand's Resistance reputation had been moulded alongside popular heroes like Claude Bourdet for whom he had a strong sympathy. Mitterrand was not only unmarked by any association with pre-war political movements, but was considered part of the mainstream of a new, rejuvenated Left. His image as a Left-wing sympathiser had been reinforced by his marriage to Danielle Gouze, then only nineteen, whom he first met in a restaurant in the boulevard Saint-Germain in 1944. Mademoiselle Gouze, sister of Christine Gouze-Rénal, one of France's best-known film producers, was just out of lycée and a courier for the Resistance. Her family had strong links with the SFIO. In addition to these credentials, Mitterrand was editor of the returned prisoners' newspaper, *Libres*, where he expressed opinions that exactly reflected popular Left-wing calls for a government of national unity.

Mitterrand's ambitions were at first cut short by De Gaulle who, because of their mutual antipathy, refused to confirm Mitterrand as Delegate for Returned Prisoners in the first provisional government after Paris was freed. As a result, he began a search for new political impetus, at one point joining Bourdet to discuss the possibility of a new Socialist force which, Bourdet said, was intended to 'sacrifice short-term solutions for a new long-term plan'.

'François Mitterrand felt it was too long for him to wait,' Bourdet said. The future president was in a hurry and his impatience would destroy his credibility with the intellectual Left.

Mitterrand marked his distance from the idealistic Left when he rejected Bourdet's long-term hopes of creating a new form of socialism. He put himself beyond the pale when he sought election as a candidate for the UDSR, the Union Démocratique et Socialiste de la Résistance, a movement that was originally torn between the Socialist SFIO and the centrist Radical Party. This party, to which Bourdet also belonged at its beginnings, had so many opportunist currents that one of Mitterrand's biographers, Franz-Olivier Giesbert, wrote that 'despite being rich in inventions, French politics has rarely given birth to such bric-à-brac'.

The party, with its variable location on the parliamentary compass was to serve Mitterrand as camouflage for his search, as Giesbert put it, 'for fame, respectability and social success'. Socialism was dumped by Mitterrand in November 1946 when he campaigned at the age of thirty-one for a parliamentary seat in the central French department of the Nièvre. His platform was flagrantly Right wing, opposed to Socialist principles such as nationalisation and to any hopes of general Left-wing unity by being powerfully anti-Communist.

Mitterrand has made it clear in conversation that he chose the multi-faction UDSR because he was too unsure of himself to make headway in Socialist movements like the SFIO. But the idea of obtaining political experience inside a tiny group was contrary to his ringing editorials in *Libres* when he condemned the 'weakness and division of democracies' for their contribution to the rise of Fascism.

'Fascism's luck inside France,' he wrote in 1945, 'was in the incoherence and shabbiness of our democracy'.

Mitterrand's post-war choices were to contribute to an even shabbier and more incoherent political scene, making it appear that the new ranks of professional parliamentarians were as self-interested as the old. While it would be unfair to say that he discredited the Fourth Republic, he was to become a symbol of its weaknesses. His readiness to take high office despite obvious unpleasant compromises disqualified him from claiming that he was merely overwhelmed by the period's mediocrity. He went a long way to creating the atmosphere when the UDSR became part of the Rassemblement des Gauches Républicaines, an electoral camouflage for a group well right of centre. The Rassemblement's chairman was a politician whom Mitterrand once relished attacking in his editorials, the man of Munich, Edouard Daladier.

The confusion that Mitterrand created in the minds of the small circle of opinion-makers on the Left Bank was considerably less important than that stirred up by André Malraux. Nothing he had written or said during the war hinted that Malraux would emerge as a Gaullist crusader and an implacable enemy of his pre-war friends, the Communists.

As Gide was too old to take more than a peripheral interest in post-war politics, Malraux, who was forty-four when peace was signed, was the most influential Left-wing cultural figure of the immediate post-war months. He believed he could attract much of the Left to the ranks of Gaullism and set about the task with mystical fanaticism.

To make his new allegiances clear, he used the stage at La Mutualité, the Left Bank's conference hall, in January 1945, when 2,000 delegates of a short-lived Mouvement de Libération National met to discuss fusion with the Communist Party. The movement represented nearly every facet of the Resistance outside the Party. Malraux's speech during the three-day discussions was decisive in the progress of French post-war politics.

Dressed in his colonel's uniform with calf-high riding boots, Malraux attacked the Communist Party head on, refusing any form of alliance and warning that the Party would use its highly-organised structure and discipline to take over total control of any coalition. Malraux's was the voice of experience and authority on Communist matters and it stopped any idealistic notions of an across-the-board Left-wing movement. Mitterrand was in the audience. The anti-Communist diatribe fitted in exactly with the young Resistant's view of the Party despite, or rather because of, his relations with Marguerite Duras's Communist circle. Like Malraux he considered the Party as being too strong to be a loyal partner.

At that moment, Mitterrand's career could well have followed Malraux's. They were both still attracted by the Left without any definite point of attachment and both were fundamentally anti-Communist. Both had commendable Resistance backgrounds and the young Mitterrand needed someone of influence to help his political career. However, considerably more divided the men than united them. Above all, there was a major problem of character.

Mitterrand was ill at ease with men of dominant reputation. Malraux intimidated him. The young politician admitted to friends that he joined the heteroclite, mediocre gathering in the UDSR rather than a big party because he was afraid of being swamped by the prestige of established political leaders. Despite his legal training, which he later put to use as an advocate

at the Paris Bar, Mitterrand was quickly rendered inarticulate
at party meetings and had to arrive at his ends by political
cunning. One of the reasons he took so long to impose himself as
national leader was that he surrounded himself with advisers
of poor quality. One of Mitterrand's Resistance companions,
Pierre Bugeaud, a Communist, said that the future president
'tended to give responsibility to people in relation to their
fidelity to him, rather than because of their own talents, and he
was even ready to put up with mediocre advisers as long as they
were faithful to him'.

Malraux would have looked with contempt on such a pact
with the weak. For him, politics was a virile confrontation and
he wanted to be surrounded by the strong. His own personal
confidence expanded in front of an audience and he was never
more sure of himself than when facing men of character.
Even Gide said that 'in front of Malraux you don't feel very
intelligent'.

The great gulf between Mitterrand and Malraux, however,
was in their relation to De Gaulle. The first meeting which the
former infantry sergeant had with the haughty general in 1943
still stuck in Mitterrand's throat. He was further humiliated
when De Gaulle threw him out of the post-war provisional
government. From then, Mitterrand's whole career was to be
dedicated to wrecking the general's ambitions.

In contrast, Malraux placed his entire hopes in De Gaulle,
revering him and trying to manipulate him at the same time.
Having abandoned fiction for cultural analysis, Malraux surrounded the general with an invented mysticism that he trans-
mitted to the mass electorate. The mission paralleled Malraux's
personal ambition to become a benign cultural commissar, a
role he was to play as De Gaulle's Cultural Affairs Minister from
1959. Before that, his political relationship with De Gaulle
appeared like a theatrical operation, as if Malraux were an
artistic director pulling together a production for a player with
enormous talent.

'I have known a relatively high number of statesmen but
none, by far, have his grandeur', Malraux told Claude Mauriac,

the journalist son of François Mauriac. Gaullism was not so much a political theory like Marxism or Fascism, Malraux said, 'but a movement of public salvation'.

Once, when De Gaulle asked Malraux how he intended to explain Gaullism, the writer said he would 'talk of chivalry'. The general's campaign filled the place held by Malraux's days as a pilot in Republican Spain, particularly as it appeared to have developed into an apparently hopeless cause by 1947. Both De Gaulle and Malraux played on the public's nerves by exaggerating the threat from Communism. The general warned that the Red Armies were only the equivalent of 'two laps of the Tour de France' away from Paris, while Malraux told journalists that he knew of plans for Soviet invasion via Italy and parachute drops on the Paris suburbs.

Malraux's attitude was often ridiculous and highly emotional and his former friends on the intellectual Left usually replied by mockery, stressing his feverish chain-smoking and facial tics as if warning the public that Malraux had gone round the bend. Malraux's 'chivalry' however was that of a roving knight, as nothing predestined him to being a faithful member of the intellectual Left.

His childhood in the Paris suburbs where his father, an occasional inventor, committed suicide at the age of 30 did not prepare him for the company of men like Sartre and Aragon. As someone who was self-taught, who did not even have a baccalauréat, he had thrust himself into national esteem by the force of his personality.

During the Spanish Civil War, he was the first to discover the fragility of the European Left in the face of Fascism, and, by the time he met Sartre in the South of France in 1941, he was convinced that political commitment was a waste of time without something resembling a benign Fascist structure that would stand up to the 'hegemony of the strong' on both Left and Right. More than for anyone else on the French intellectual scene, the war was to compound a sense of personal loss and defeat which would underline the need for an alternative solution to sterile extremes.

His two brothers, Claude and Roland, who in many ways were as colourful and as courageous as André, were both killed during the war, breaking the most stable emotional links in Malraux's life. Claude was executed by the Nazis. Roland, another Resistant, was killed by Allied bombs in the Baltic in 1945 while captive in a Nazi ship full of hostages. The war also destroyed the only peaceful idyll of Malraux's life of military and political adventure when Josette Clotis was killed accidentally in November 1944.

Clotis, a minor novelist who tended to ridicule Malraux's obsession for world problems, provided Malraux with a brief glimpse of domestic routine during the period in the South of France when his two sons, Gautier and Vincent were born. Her disinterest in militant Left-wing preoccupations was a total contrast to the commitment of his first wife, Clara Malraux, who remained faithful to Marxism. Josette Clotis's apoliticism undoubtedly contributed to a reassessment of priorities in Malraux's mind.

He was absent with his fighting unit in eastern France when Josette slipped while trying to catch a moving train and fell under the wheels.

Having committed himself to Gaullism, Malraux attacked unorthodox Marxists with as much virulence as he did mainstream Communists. He was particularly scathing about Sartre's commitment to an idealistic proletariat saying that 'literature is full of good souls who believe that the proletariat is made up of noble savages'. He was openly irritated by Camus's vacillation as he dithered over breaking away from the 'clique from the Flore'.

Malraux was confident that most of the Left would rally to De Gaulle and was among those who persuaded the general to resign in January 1946, convinced that he would be back in power within six months with an overwhelming majority. When this tactic failed, Malraux accepted the role of Propaganda Delegate in De Gaulle's newly-founded Rassemblement du Peuple français, set up in 1947. His title was particularly offensive to the anti-Fascist movement that had already decided that De Gaulle was Europe's new Hitler.

The Rassemblement's support was made up of 80 per cent of former Vichy supporters, but Malraux was not over-concerned. His main initiative in trying to maintain Left-wing links was to ask François Mauriac to remain loyal to the general. Mauriac relished the irony of finding himself considered 'to the left of Malraux'.

But Malraux had other literary recruits, including Pascal Pia, the publisher Gaston Gallimard, and Raymond Aron. Of these, Aron's adhesion was the most symbolic as he had been among the trio of pre-war friends at the Ecole Normale Supérieure which included Paul Nizan and Jean-Paul Sartre. Aron, as an academic and leader writer for *Figaro*, set about destroying illusions in 'unity of the Left', the slogan of Saint-Germain intellectuals.

He argued that there was no such thing as Left-wing unity, as the French were interested in neither Labourite solutions nor a classless Scandinavian society. He saw the post-war debate as a continuation of the rivalry within the French Revolution of 1789, saying that the only contemporary Left-wing experience that fascinated the post-war Left was the violent Russian Revolution.

Up until 1947, Malraux made several attempts in private meetings to convince men like Sartre and Camus to join him, but after that he was rapidly isolated from the mainstream of discussion around Saint-Germain. He was to watch the ebb and flow in the area from his favourite bistro in the rue du Dragon, just over the road from the Café de Flore. It was an ideal situation to judge the high and low moments of intellectual Marxism as the rue du Dragon linked the rue Saint-Benoît and the rue de Rennes.

Marguerite Duras' flat in the rue Saint-Benoît was the main informal Marxist discussion point, prolonging meetings at the official Communist cell at 44 rue de Rennes. One of the topics discussed contemptuously at both places was Malraux's Gaullist crusade and among those who hurried between the two nerve centres of Marxism was Malraux's former wife, Clara.

Malraux was not the only pre-war personality to sow confusion in the intellectual Left. For different reasons, André Gide also played a part. In 1947, the year of so many turning points as the domestic and international Cold War set in, Gide was awarded the Nobel Prize for literature just ten years after another French writer, Roger Martin du Gard, and ten years before the honour fell to Albert Camus. The prize consecrated Gide's lofty status at the age of seventy-seven when he was barely in control of his faculties. This in no way stopped conflicting interests from trying to exploit his reputation and he became an embarrassment to the Left as he signed petitions he did not understand and contradicted himself in interviews. Attempts to persuade him to stay out of the political scene only made matters worse as Gide could bear no criticism and was determined to live up to his role as the doyen of literary political pundits.

When he died in January 1951, there was a feeling of relief on the Left. The nastiness of the Communist Party, which never forgave his Thirties' repudiation of the USSR, was not entirely misplaced when *L'Humanité* wrote that 'a corpse had just died'. Gide, the paper added, had been 'living dangerously in three thicknesses of flannel', a reference to his huddling around a stove in the tiny Left Bank room where he would sign almost anything that was put in his hand and then forget that he had done so.

Until De Gaulle's *coup d'état* in 1958, Malraux appeared to have once again chosen a lost cause. His confident predictions of a rapid return of Gaullist power withered despite the mediocrity of Parliamentary parties who established rule by immobility. Parliament's philosophy was coined by one of the Fourth Republic's least-remembered Prime Ministers, Henri Queille, a country doctor and member of most governments. He was to advise members of the National Assembly to 'delay solutions until they have lost their importance'.

De Gaulle's hesitation in face of pressure to use unconstitutional means to regain power and the immobility of the Third Force provided an ideal climate for the Communist Party to launch a massive offensive. Its disciplined hold on the working classes, who felt they were being prepared for a popular revolution, was paralleled by a brilliantly successful propaganda campaign to rally French intellectuals. Nearly every leading member of the intelligentsia who played even a marginal political role after the war was tempted at some time to adhere to the Party. Some were repelled immediately, some hung on as fellow travellers and many threw themselves into a crusade of blind obedience.

The extraordinary fascination that the Communist Party had for French intellectuals during the Cold War was inspired by a medieval fervour similar to that which Malraux wanted to introduce in Gaullism. Sartre said that intellectual party members 'took themselves for an order of chivalry, calling themselves the lasting heroes of our time'. It was an order with religious overtones, with Moscow being compared to Jerusalem and bourgeois militants publicly confessing their long conversion from decadent middle-class ideals to the purified state of an honorary member of the proletariat.

The vows of the chivalrous order were rigidly set when Moscow set up the Kominform in 1947 to create a single orthodox line. Andrei Jdanov, a member of the Soviet Political Bureau who was a general at the Battle of Leningrad, was appointed as defender of orthodoxy which became known as Jdanovism. In France, a Commission of Intellectuals was created in the Party, and this in turn set up a Cercle des Critiques whose leaders included Louis Aragon, his fellow Resistant poet, Paul Eluard and Marguerite Duras. Although the Cercle was the centre of passionate discussions in private, members were obliged to show unity outside meetings and support violent attacks on non-Communist writers, particularly Paulhan and Sartre.

Using its tremendous organisational ability and its Press outlets, the Party distorted the importance of artists. For Communist faithfuls of the day, the greatest novelist was André

Stil whom the Party compared to Stendhal and who won the Lenin prize. The most praised painter was André Forgeron whose realism obeyed the dictates of Jdanovism. Both owed their success to the unrelenting patronage of Aragon. Stil became the most translated French author of his day.

The Party gave generous aid to any writer prepared to be seen as supporting Communist principles. Many intellectuals played along for material reasons while others were rewarded for a genuine belief in Party priorities. Dominique Desanti, for instance, who had been so disappointed by Aragon as a young Resistant after the war, typified the simplistic belief in Communism's purifying process by writing a novel called *A bras le corps* in which a rich girl from Paris's sixteenth arrondissement falls in love with a worker and sees the error of her birth. The story was barely a novel as it typified many bourgeois conversions.

To be published in literary magazines, authors accepted straightforward rewriting by senior party officials who would not even bother to consult the authors until routine references to Stalinist orthodoxy had been written into the text. The Party was even stricter when it concerned behaviour of the working class.

Simone Signoret had introduced a new star to the Left Bank by marrying Yves Montand, whose Communist family had fled Italy before the war. Montand, a former Marseilles docker, was launched as a singer by Edith Piaf and was to become one of the Party's most precious assets during the Cold War although he never took out membership. With Signoret, he was at the forefront of all the Party's main protests during the period, rallying many of its supporters from the entertainment world. During the Cold War, Montand accepted Communist pressures to censor his repertoire which was considered 'erotic' and offensive to Jdanovism.

Puritanism was part of the Communist doctrine, a factor which complicated the already bizarre relationship the Party had with Sartre and De Beauvoir. For most of the public, Sartre and his companion were resolute fellow travellers, pointing the way to orthodox Communism. Inside the Party they were prime targets for abuse. Roger Garaudy, a political bureau member who later dumped Communism and converted to Islam, was in charge of intellectual purity for a time and led the attack on existentialism calling it a 'philosophy for dropouts which destroys manliness'. De Beauvoir's *Le Deuxième Sexe* was the subject of a general mobilisation of hate, being described as 'lowering instinct to the level of animals' and 'encouraging perverse sexual desire'.

Having accepted the German-Soviet treaty of 1939 without complaint, Louis Aragon found no difficulty in identifying with the Party's hardline in the Cold War. The policies he supported were as varied as condemnation of American cinema and all forms of psychoanalysis, while he secretly covered up knowledge of Stalinist crimes that reached the Party a decade before Kruschev's staggering revelations in 1956.

As a literary man and journalist, he helped rewrite Communist Resistance legends while preparing long and adulatory propaganda works like the six-volume book, *Les Communistes*, or writing fawning poetic appreciations of the Party leader, Maurice Thorez. For outsiders, it was impossible to say whether Aragon was manipulating or being manipulated, as he appeared to be his own master in cultural contacts and distributed favours generously. His parallel life as the most influential contemporary poet was important in developing new forms of popular song to replace the shallow romanticism of the Thirties and Forties. In his role as a pure poet he was 'charming, elegant, handsome and aristocratic' according to Catherine Sauvage, a singer whose pioneer career in Saint-Germain clubs was based on the first adaptations of Aragon's poems in song. Léo Ferré, another Saint-Germain discovery, whose successes were also inspired by songs using Aragon's poems, was struck by Aragon's charm but disturbed by his tendency to 'talk only about himself'.

However, inside the Party, Aragon's behaviour was unpredictable and his apparently easy-going aristocratic nature

Catherine Sauvage, a singer, whose pioneer career was based on adaptations of Aragon's poems, with Léo Ferré

would often be replaced by childish rages in which he wept or begged to have his way. He was often called to order with stunning severity, the best-remembered occasion being when Stalin died and he published a Picasso drawing of the dead dictator as a virile, handsome man instead of the avuncular patriarch of the current Party line.

His acceptance of the Party's iron discipline, particularly after he learnt of Stalinist crimes, seemed to contain elements of the fascination of power which his friend, Drieu la Rochelle, felt for Nazism. It was a relationship which recalled his marriage with Elsa Triolet, the woman he 'loved like a dog' and who increasingly dominated him. Triolet was the main organiser of book shows, conferences and exhibitions throughout the country, that developed an ever-increasing Communist hold on literary output. She was also a more popular writer whose work had an immediate propaganda effect on a large public.

In an exceptionally productive post-war period, her most important work was *Le Cheval roux* which, although not published until after Stalin's death, showed how totally she was involved with Party structure without being a member of the Party. The two-volume novel, which concludes with Elsa shouting 'Adieu, Louis' as the American Air Force plane she is travelling in crashes, was an anti-nuclear work, which fitted in with her prominent role in the Mouvement de la Paix. The movement, a Communist organisation, included Frédéric and Irène Joliot-Curie, who won the Nobel Prize for discovering nuclear fission. Frédéric Joliot-Curie was the technical adviser for the novel.

Between them, Aragon and Triolet built up a climate of guilt around writers who increasingly felt that in not adhering to the Communist Party, or at least following its line, they were betraying the proletariat. Eventually, even Sartre would succumb to this formidable moral pressure, putting his magazine, *Les Temps modernes*, at the service of Communist orthodoxy and censoring his own works to obtain Aragon's imprimatur. His public association, however, was not visible until the Party's power was shattered by the 1952 general elections and it became more than ever the focus of persecution by the resurgent Right.

By then, Sartre needed the comfort of the Party almost as much as Aragon did, as he had lost most of his intellectual friends because of his quarrelsome nature and his often offensive political and social theories.

6

L'Homme révolté

The row that caused a split between Sartre and Camus in 1952, burying any hopes of intellectual political coherence in Saint-Germain, was not the result of a sudden flare-up. A complex web of theoretical clashes divided literary opinion-makers during the seven post-war years against a background of a constantly shifting debate on Marxism. Differences of temperament, however, were as important as the theories themselves. Many arguments came to a fiery conclusion while enmity lingered for decades. In the case of Sartre and Camus, already separated by their bourgeois and working-class backgrounds, personality was also decisive. Sartre's often impatient intellectual over-confidence was always on a collision course with Camus's often irritating moral hesitation. The main reason they did not fall out earlier was because they were not so close during this period as propagandists for and against Communism were to make out when the row was exploited for its Cold War value.

One of the reproaches Sartre used to make of his school friend, Raymond Aron, was that he was afraid to '*déconner*' – to stick his neck out. That was never Sartre's failing, but for

Eugène Ionesco, Romanian playwright and one of Sartre's strongest critics

every one who felt that the philosopher showed political courage through his progressive ideas, another saw his behaviour as opportunism. One of his strongest critics was Eugène Ionesco who set out through his plays to counteract what he considered the vacuity of Sartre's fluid Left-wing debate, which led to Sartre's belated rejection of Marxism not long before he died.

Ionesco felt that Sartre was 'supposed to be the conscience of our time, when he was in fact its inconsequence'.

'He was not an opportunist materially, but he was an ideological opportunist who followed the dominant ideology', Ionesco said. 'After Heidegger, who was close to the Nazis, he wrote "Existentialisme est-il un humanisme?" because it was a fashionable argument.'

Sartre wrote to please at a time when unorthodox Marxism and progressive social theories were the daily bread of his

Left-wing entourage. The hurry to seek applause, particularly from De Beauvoir betrays immaturity. Sartre himself said that until he was thirty-five, when war broke out, he was still a child. The ten years that followed the conflict often look like adolescent experimentation. Nothing brings this out better than his own *Lettres au Castor*, published three years after his death, in which he describes in detail immature relationships with women for the approval of Castor, De Beauvoir's pet name.

His attitude to money at the time recalls his schooldays at La Rochelle when he stole cash from his mother's handbag to buy cakes to win over his tormentors. Robert Gallimard, his publishing contact in the family firm, remembers that Sartre was always in debt to the firm although he lived simply. This was because he took his royalties in wads of notes so that he could distribute money generously to his friends or give big tips. Some of the loyalty he acquired was bought. He was known as 'an easy touch'.

Sartre's inability to sustain conversation with men, whom he found 'boring', was partly responsible for his failure to come to an understanding with his associates in the Rassemblement Démocratique Revolutionnaire, the political party he helped found and which he abandoned after two years.

The party's 'new Bolshevism' which intellectuals believed would provide an alternative to the discredited Socialist-led Third Force and authoritarian Communism foundered largely because of the atmosphere created by Sartre. Raymond Aron said Sartre was unable to resist castigating associates who did not share his view that political and moral choices were indivisible.

Sartre's own moral choices were often ingeniously personal although argued with intellectual authority. As side issues to the main political argument for or against identification with the Communist Party, Sartre carried out his own sociological enquiries involving Jews, Blacks and homosexuals as part of his campaign to break down outdated rigid ideas. Each enquiry was intended to increase acceptance of these marginal groups. Each did them a disservice.

His 'Réflexions sur l'antisémitisme' rejected the idea that Jews were a race apart and implied that they were an Aryan invention. The attempt to banalise the Jewish identity only angered the Consistory which interpreted the essay as both absurd and anti-semitic. Later, an anti-racist pamphlet, 'Orphée Noir' said that white skin was obscene and that whites should have a layer of black skin under the first layer. The black Communist writer, Richard Wright, considered the statement 'reverse racism'. He broke off his association with *Les Temps Modernes* and joined the Congrés pour la Liberté de la Culture, an anti-racist organisation which Sartre condemned as a collection of *'pâles demoiselles'*.

Sartre's most insensitive tract was his effusive argument for homosexuality, *Saint Genet, Comédien et Martyr*. It was not so much that the public was totally unprepared for a revolutionary moral idea that made the work offensive. Sartre took no account of the feelings of Jean Genet, a friend from the wartime days of the Flore. The highly emotional playwright felt that his personality had been usurped and he had been turned into an abstract, intellectual product.

Genet had never been able to assume his complex character with the flamboyance of his protector, Jean Cocteau, and wanted to throw all his writings on the fire. It took Genet several years to recover from Sartre's analysis and start writing again. Sartre, however, rated *Saint Genet* along with *Les Mots* and the 1951 play, *Le Diable et le Bon Dieu*, as his most successful work.

Ideological clashes with Malraux, Aron and Merleau-Ponty had already ended contacts with them well before Sartre fell out with Camus while the philosopher was barely on speaking terms with most of the literary stars at Gallimard after letting contemptuous opinions on their work circulate through conversation. A break with Malraux had been inevitable as, even before the war, Sartre had described the writer as 'a cunt' in a letter to De Beauvoir. Their meeting during the war widened the rift and Malraux took the first opportunity to show his own contempt for Sartre when the philosopher took part in a broadcast in

which De Gaulle was compared to Hitler. Malraux told Gaston
Gallimard that *Les Temps Modernes* had to be expelled from its
offices in the Gallimard building and the magazine was hurriedly transferred to a neighbouring publisher, Julliard.

Malraux was as much to blame as Sartre for this estrange-
ment, as many writers were resentful of the way Malraux threw
his weight about. Boris Vian went as far as accusing him of
'blackmailing' Gallimard by threatening to withdraw his books
from the firm. He alleged that Malraux's excessive demands
reduced the amount of money available to encourage new
authors. Sartre, on the other hand, approached the publishing
temple with humility, according to Robert Gallimard, sitting
patiently in the imposing foyer like an unpublished author,
never demanding a revision of his contracts and signing agree-
ments without discussing terms.

The friendship with Aron was another victim of the De
Gaulle–Hitler broadcast as Sartre felt that Aron had taken
Malraux's side. He refused to make up, even though Aron went
round to his flat and apologised. Merleau-Ponty was dumped
after the younger philosopher rejected an existentialist flirtation
with the French Communist Party when the Korean war broke
out. But personality differences were already evident in the
twice-monthly meetings to prepare *Les Temps Modernes* where
editorial policy was chaotic, because of the conflicting views of
contributors and Sartre's inability to chair meetings with
authority. Merleau-Ponty was one of the victims of Sartre's
compulsion for gossip, much of which was to find its way into
De Beauvoir's *Mémoires*. Merleau-Ponty was made out to be
unstable according to stories spread by Sartre, who made much
of Merleau-Ponty's heavy drinking and womanising. At parties, according to Sartre in a letter to De Beauvoir, Merleau-
Ponty would get so drunk that he would ask all the women
present to sleep with him and slap those who refused.

Each quarrel was to create its own pool of controversy as
Sartre was, in turn, attacked by the central figure involved, or
by his train of acolytes. But François Mauriac openly said that
Sartre enjoyed the role of a Saint Sebastian, receiving arrows

from all directions. Mauriac, who himself had a quarrel with Sartre dating back before the war, said the philosopher was a 'masochist' who deliberately invited attacks from 'his brothers'. Camus, in contrast, was a moving target ideologically and was further protected by a practised charm.

After the success of *La Peste*, Camus's life was marked by professional and personal disappointments. A stage adaptation of *La Peste* called *L'Etat de Siège* was a commercial and critical failure. He was to retrieve some of his reputation as a dramatist with *Les Justes* in 1949, but by then his tuberculosis was again evident. With voyages abroad, his illness and other demands on his time, his home life was spasmodic and he was conscious that it brought him less satisfaction than it should have done. His diary and published work were full of enigmatic or open references to self-doubt and the need for some stable, predictable values, either political or religious.

His contacts with Saint-Germain were irregular after his departure from *Combat*, but he was still enthralled by Sartre's theories, particularly over the justification of violent revolution. If Camus had broken away from this fascination earlier, he might have shed one of the distractions that affected his literary creativity which he felt was drying up. Instead, much of his work during this period was an ambiguous indirect discussion with Sartre that increased mutual identification in the public mind long after the two men had lost sympathy for each other's views.

Sartre was always more nimble when covering the treacherous ground over which Camus was tempted to follow. He used a debating technique that he often boasted about. When he was pushed into a corner, Sartre would relaunch the discussion in a completely new direction so that he always appeared right. Camus plodded on behind fascinated by Sartre's erudition and forgetting to analyse problems from his own point of view as a man from a working-class background.

In 1947, Camus remarked that 'nearly all French writers who today claim to speak in the name of the proletariat were born to well off or rich parents. This is not a fault as there is chance in birth and I find it neither good nor bad. I limit myself to alerting the sociologist of an anomaly or a subject of study.'

Sartre, like much of his generation, carried his birth like original sin and must have envied Camus. But the Algerian writer, who before the war had so consciously identified with the problems of the poor, adopted the abstract tone of the bourgeois intellectuals who he knew were unqualified to speak on behalf of the proletariat. Recently, almost miraculously, separated from his own poverty, he seemed to be unaware that France was struggling with mass deprivation in the post-war years, as well as exploiting millions in the colonies. Instead, he was drawn into a sterile debate with Sartre over the justification of revolutionary terror. Both put off a clear commitment for as long as possible, as the answer would amount to a rejection or acceptance of Communism. Neither wanted to abandon a moral no-man's land.

Sartre enjoyed delaying the decision as he preferred to raise questions rather than provide answers. For Camus, it was part of a long struggle to sort out his personal conscience. One of the most enlightening pieces of reporting on their way of thinking is contained in Camus's *Carnets* when he describes a meeting set up by Malraux in 1946 in an attempt to find common ground with Camus, Sartre and the Hungarian-born author, Arthur Koestler, whose *Darkness at Noon* had been a runaway success in France. Koestler alerted French intellectuals to Stalinist crimes and had a strong influence on Camus. Malraux was confident at that time that Camus would join the Gaullists.

At their meeting Koestler increased pressure for a clear rejection of Communism and Stalin's regime, saying: 'This conspiracy of silence is our condemnation in the eyes of those who follow.' Sartre's answer to this appeal was recorded as: 'Yes, etc etc', while Camus was more worried that: 'We are all responsible for an absence of values.'

That meeting took place before the Cold War set in but already Camus was sketching out the theme of *L'Homme révolté*, the basically anti-Stalin work that would cause a split with

Sartre. Until the book was published, the argument between them seemed to be on the degree of acceptable State violence rather than whether it was justified at all. As Sartre had a wider and more immediate audience than Camus, the two men were drawn together by Sartre's 'Yes etc etc', which was interpreted as an intellectual justification for Soviet mass murder by many observers. The impression was reinforced by Sartre's hysterical anti-Americanism.

Sartre's often naïve extremism during this period is now forgotten and has to be read in the context of a time when fanatical views were common and usually formed on the basis of distorted propaganda. Raymond Aron said that Americans held the same place in Sartre's 'demonology' as Jews in Hitlerism. Sartre compared the Americans to Nazis and called on Europeans to break all links with the United States to avoid 'catching rabies'. In contrast, the Soviet Union appeared as a sort of paradise, justly achieved through rightful purges. An article in *Les Temps Modernes* in January 1950 reported that 'in no country in the world is the dignity of work more respected than in the Soviet Union. Forced labour does not exist because the exploitation of man by man no longer exists. The diverse measures applied in American prisons contrast singularly with the equitable dispositions of collective work in the Soviet Union.'

The 'existentialists' of the cellar clubs of Saint-Germain had become less susceptible to Sartre's influence when this sort of nonsense was written, and continued to idealise the United States. The influx of young Americans seeking cultural fortune, like Marlon Brando and the writer, James Baldwin, showed that the fascination was mutual. Sartre's anti-Americanism contributed to his decline as a popular influence on the young but the general debate on the merits and demerits of super-powers was largely surpassed when the Sartre-Camus differences broke into the open with the publication of *L'Homme révolté* in 1951. The two supposed opinion leaders chose their sides much later than the general public.

The political essay was one of the most difficult works Camus undertook and he needed eighteen months of intense mental effort to draw up what amounts to a public confession of a long internal struggle. He explored source material going back to the Greek legend of Prometheus to break out of the intellectual fabric woven round Sartre's theories. While the work often read like a laboured attempt by a self-conscious pupil to answer an overbearing master, the message was clear enough, *L'Homme révolté* was anti-Communist and anti-Sartre.

The book appeared in November but it was not until mid-1952 that Sartre decided to review it in *Les Temps Modernes*. He shied away from criticising it himself because of embarrassment with the key passage which pointed out the 'ultimate contradiction of the greatest Revolution in history . . . which claimed to be just against the background of a uninterrupted cortège of injustice and violence'. In Camus's view, the contradiction was the way the Soviet Revolution incorporated 'a guilty people' in an unrelenting search for 'an impossible innocence under the bitter regard of its Grand Inquisitors'. In one sweeping sentence, Camus condemned the entire Russian proletariat, its universal brotherhood and all those, like Sartre, associated with justifying Soviet oppression and terror.

In rejecting or approving such an attack, a critic would be obliged to choose sides in the domestic and international Cold War. Sartre put the moment off by asking for a volunteer among the magazine's contributors and the task was undertaken by Francis Jeanson, whose overeagerness to flatter Sartre was well known. Simone de Beauvoir said later that Jeanson, who made a living out of interpreting Sartre's life and works, 'turned the hot iron in the wound' more brusquely than Sartre would have liked. Jeanson treated Camus contemptuously saying he had the 'moralising and ineffective attitude of a do-gooder'.

Stung to the quick, Camus sent a reply to Sartre at *Les Temps Modernes* addressing it to 'Monsieur le directeur' and saying he was tired of 'receiving lessons from critics who had never placed their armchairs in the direction of history'. The affair became public when *Combat* published large extracts of the letter to the surprise of much of the public who presumed that Camus and Sartre lived in relative ideological harmony.

The row was not only announced in huge headlines in the national Press but was exploited abroad, particularly in the United States, as proof that Camus, considered a paragon of moral values, had at last admitted his conversion to Western ideals and turned his back on Communism.

Putting aside the outdated argument on the justification of mass terror in the service of Revolution, the underlying reasons for the rupture were personality differences. By 1952, Camus was a more irritable and vain man than the young Resistant fascinated by the Parisian intellectual scene. He had a right to feel that he was Sartre's literary equal, but Sartre's opinion that he was a 'philosophical ass' must have reached him indirectly. Camus himself has implied that his natural charm had become more practised, an actor's method of getting his way. In addition, the writing of *L'Homme révolté* had been a dour experience, increasing the tiredness he felt from his illness and the doubts he had over his intellectual powers. The book needed meticulous research which he interpreted with constant glances over his shoulder for approval from the Paris élite. The review in *Les Temps Modernes*, which he saw as being ghosted by Sartre, hurt his pride as it appeared to be a rebuke as much for his scholarship as his political choices.

Because he was wounded intellectually and probably regretted that he had wasted time that could have been used for more useful literary work, Camus would have found it difficult to accept reconciliation with Sartre in any circumstances. The idea was put beyond question by the ironic savagery of Sartre's published reply to Camus's letter addressed to 'Monsieur le directeur'.

In conversation, Sartre said that there were always good reasons for the rows he had with his literary contemporaries but 'in the end it was always me who took the decision to end all contacts'. His reply to Camus is basically insulting, written in bursts of cold and hot anger, in which he calls Camus 'perfectly unbearable' and implies both physical cowardice and class treachery. It is a sad letter particularly as Sartre felt it was one of his better flights of literature and incorporated it in *Situations*, a seven-volume work of some of his journalistic output.

He was under abnormal physical and mental pressure at the time, constantly trying to catch up with his own reputation. The demands on his time were enormous, particularly as he felt that he was going through what he described as a 'bourgeois' idea of progress, moving to some peak of self-perfection. Constantly surrounded by his group of flatterers, his literary and practical worries were paralleled by an intense social life in which heavy drinking was a constant factor. To meet the demands on him, he became increasingly dependent on drugs. The double effect of overwork and abuse of drugs was particularly noticeable between 1952 and 1958 when Simone de Beauvoir noted that he 'stuffed himself, one after another, with belladonal, optalidon and corydrane', a cocktail of stimulants and tranquillisers.

By the time he fell out with Camus, he was already suffering from the irrationality created by his way of life and was on the verge of a series of physical crises. The damage had accumulated over several years. All-night parties in the wartime and post-war years, some of which had dramatic consequences, are often described in De Beauvoir's memoirs.

After one of these parties in 1946, when Koestler threw a glass at Sartre and then punched Camus, the Algerian writer asked Sartre: 'Can we go on drinking like this and work as well?' The answer was evident as neither Camus nor Sartre ever recreated the abundant literary output of the wartime years. Both overestimated their physical capacities.

The row with Koestler was the result of an increasingly exhausting mixture of intense intellectual life, complicated by heavy drinking and womanising. The political arguments over the validity of revolutionary Communism were particularly tense between Koestler and Sartre who both felt they held the ultimate truth. But rational discussion was rarely possible during nights of heavy drinking where virility often seemed as much at stake as political commitment. Koestler suffered from an often morbid Don Juanism, Camus developed a melancholy compulsion to seek new women companions while Sartre was obsessed by his image of a cool, baiseur-intellectuel in which he said he was 'less a lover than a masturbator of women'.

Politics, alcohol and sex were all near the surface on the night of the row in which Koestler accused Sartre of trying to sleep with his wife, Mame. Camus, who held his drink badly, tried to make peace but after Koestler's reaction went home severely depressed. Not long after that, Koestler broke away from both Sartre and Camus, later confiding that 'he was sick to the teeth of the frogs'.

Sartre came to the logical terminus of his pro-Marxist analyses by deciding that a rejection of Communism was a betrayal of the proletariat and became the French Party's most useful fellow traveller of the Fifties. His personal political campaigns flickered on in an intermittent guerilla war that troubled the harmony occasionally, but Aragon now had an invaluable propaganda ally.

Camus, meanwhile, continued in the ambiguous path that would irritate, at different times, Malraux, Koestler and Sartre who thought, on occasions, that they had won him over to their causes. With *L'Homme révolté* in 1951 he created enough doubt to make himself exploitable as an ally of the conservative Right, even making it seem that he was on the verge of conversion to Christianity, until he began a new struggle with his conscience with *La Chute* in 1956.

The tragedy for the France of the Fifties was that the two men whom public opinion had elevated to the position of the nation's most respected moral guides quit the centre stage without providing a set of values as a domestic alternative to the chaos created by traditional political forces. As they went their separate ways, the parliamentary Left also collapsed.

The only sure judgment that can be made of the intellectual-political Left-wing debate of the post-war years is that it was self-destructive. Torn by its own contradictions, the parliamentary Left, particularly the SFIO, brought down most of the eight governments in the four years to 1951. The obsession with castrating Communists and Gaullists resulted in a disastrous gerrymander in that year's general elections. Despite winning five million votes, Communists ended up with only 11 seats in the National Assembly compared to 183 before. De Gaulle's party won only 117 seats. Although parties allied to Gaullism won more than half the votes, their members were from the conservative Right. The Socialist-dominated Third Force now had nothing on its wings to protect it from the resurgent Vichy Right. After two years of crisis, Parliament elected René Coty President of the Republic, while Joseph Laniel became Prime Minister. For the first time since 1877, ultra-conservatives held both offices in a democratic system.

Vichy's revenge on the Resistance leaders was total. It would take a colonial war in Algeria, in which a million people died before the demoralised intellectual and political Left would again find a common rallying point.

7

Le Deuxième Sexe

While Saint-Germain was arguing over political and philosophical issues that would soon be overtaken, Simone de
Beauvoir published *Le Deuxième Sexe*, the most important
sociological essay of the period. The book, released in 1949,
relaunched international debate on women's liberation and
underlined the pioneering role played by the women of Saint-
Germain-des-Prés in preparing the moral climate of the second
half of the twentieth century.

After the publication of *Le Deuxième Sexe*, the worldwide
reputations of the quartier's residents like Juliette Gréco,
Marguerite Duras or De Beauvoir herself and those directly
influenced by the area's liberalism, such as Françoise Sagan or
Brigitte Bardot, gave the impression that they were the natural
products of a tolerant Left Bank society which encouraged
well-educated women to express themselves fearlessly. In fact,
their own personalities were the dominant force in a revolt
against middle-class prejudice and they often had to accept
ridicule from their male contemporaries to carry it through.

Independently-minded women attracted by the Left Bank's

intellectual atmosphere sought their freedom by many different routes, sometimes causing scandal, but they were united by a fundamental reassessment of relationships with men and male-imposed values. An unorthodox lifestyle was, however, rarely a spontaneous choice as parental irresponsibility, divorce, an unhappy love affair, selfish ambition or emotional instability were more likely to act as catalysers than a careful analysis of traditional sexual role-playing.

It was because De Beauvoir's message was clinically precise, reflecting a logical choice to reject received ideas, that *Le Deuxième Sexe* would make many women hesitate before assuming time-allotted roles as mother and housekeeper. She put her case not as someone taking advantage of an ever-expanding social and moral debate, but as a reflection on a lifetime's principles at the age of 41. Nothing she had seen, read or heard had changed her mind over the fundamental argument that marriage and motherhood were not merely questionable states, but wholly undesirable. A woman, she said, needed a career and freedom to choose her lifestyle if she was ever to be content with herself. In other words, she was man's equal.

De Beauvoir had lived by those standards since rejecting her convention-ridden middle-class family in Montparnasse more than twenty years before, and was so confident that she was right that she lived out her convictions in the area where she was born among the people with whom she grew up. Over the years, she had proved to an ever-growing circle of admirers that a celibate woman could cope emotionally with life without the constant presence of a man. Sartre's love letters and her own books were to show that it was she who dictated the terms of their long companionship in which she was the more stable partner. Now, as far as her career counted, *Le Deuxième Sexe* elevated her to a status equal to the world's most influential writers and philosophers and she had sacrificed none of her personal liberty to achieve it.

De Beauvoir was too sure of herself to be called courageous for writing a book which shocked even her close male contemporaries in Saint-Germain and made her wonder if she had gone

Simone de Beauvoir, life-long friend of Sartre, taken in the late 1940s

far enough in condemning male intolerance. But for a French-woman to buy the book and read it openly in the France of the late Forties was an act of rebellion.

De Beauvoir's indictment of marriage was even more relevant in 1949 as married Frenchwomen lived under male tutelage. A woman was obliged to give up all financial and legal rights on marriage under laws which treated her like a juvenile or a mental defective. Even with the introduction of female suffrage in 1945, women were excluded from any part in national reconstruction despite the fact that many played a crucial, voluntary role in the Resistance. A general atmosphere of intolerance persuaded women like the author, Marguerite Yourcenar, who became the first woman member of the Académie Française in 1980, to settle in the United States and take out

American citizenship. Even women who were playing influential roles in France were not given credit until many years later. Although Marguerite Duras was often said to have been the arbitrator of the Marxist debate in Saint-Germain, she remembered that in the immediate post-war years she was allowed only a limited part in discussion even in her own flat. She spent most of her time cooking or looking after the baby while listening to exchanges among men, which, she said, contributed to her development as a writer. Another author, Nathalie Sarraute, whose books added so much prestige to the Nouveau Roman movement of the Fifties recalled that a woman could not even publish a book unless her husband signed the contract.

Women's rights were not a popular issue. Even Sartre, who supported underprivileged groups reflexively, ignored the question. There was nothing to suggest in his two volumes of love letters to De Beauvoir, published in 1983, that he felt that women had a major contribution to make to the post-war debate, except by listening to men. His appreciations of De Beauvoir herself were often patronising. He admired her, he said, because she had 'the beauty of a woman and the mind of a man'.

However, De Beauvoir felt that her opinion was treated with respect until the publication of *Le Deuxième Sexe*. She then discovered that while the men of Saint-Germain could consider revolutionary changes to political and philosophical systems, they could not accept the idea that women were free to make up their own minds. Several years later, De Beauvoir admitted she was still shaken by the way the book was received.

'I was astonished at people's reactions', she said. 'Camus was furious. He reacted with typical Mediterranean machismo, saying I had ridiculed the French male. Professors hurled the book across the room. Maurice (Merleau-Ponty) wrote staggeringly rude things about me.' De Beauvoir added that she was also 'sniggered at in restaurants' because it was considered scandalous to have written about female sexuality.

'Men kept drawing attention to the vulgarity of the book, essentially because they were furious at what the book was suggesting: equality between the sexes. In the life I was leading then, there wasn't much difference between men and women. It was not until *Le Deuxième Sexe* was published that I noticed that some of my friendships were very deceptive.'

This reaction from men she had known for years and whom she had met socially and professionally since her schooldays hurt far more than the vicious attacks led by the Communist Party and the Catholic Church, but De Beauvoir's revenge over narrow-minded intellectuals was crushing. *Le Deuxième Sexe* sold 22,000 copies in its first week of publication and became an international bestseller throughout the world. More than a million copies were sold in the United States alone. De Beauvoir established her independence from Sartre and was to reinforce the message even more dramatically in her autobiography, *Mémoires d'une fille bien rangée*. The two books were treated like the Old and New Testament of women's liberation, but by the time the autobiography was released in 1958 other women were also spreading the message by other means. The most effective was popular song.

The success of Le Tabou had encouraged the opening of more cellar bars and clubs in Saint-Germain where cultivated audiences applauded experimental works by singer-composers, usually accompanied by only a guitar or a piano. Outside the Left Bank, the entertainment world had taken up its conventional pre-war style in which popular singing was based on stylised ballads for men and songs of emotional suffering for women, both with lavish orchestral backing and expensive costumes. Maurice Chevalier and the Corsican tenor, Tino Rossi, the two dominant male vocalists of the pre-war years, had shaken off thinly-based accusations of Collaboration and were again crooning to millions in sugary radio shows that offset mass misery in a torn country. Chevalier, who was one of the first to be denounced in a Resistance black list in 1942, had been given clearance by Louis Aragon, but some female singers were less lucky.

The public took a much more serious view of Collaboration

by women, particularly if there was a sexual implication. One of the most successful pre-war romantic singers, Suzy Solidor, was hounded out of Paris as her club on the Champs Elysées had been the most popular rendezvous for German officers. Mistinguett never recovered from allegations that she dined with German officers at Maxim's. In contrast, Edith Piaf, whose career had blossomed in 1939 when she starred in Jean Cocteau's play, *Le bel indifférent*, now became a national idol, using a style directly inspired by Solidor. Piaf's tragic love affairs, notably with the world middleweight champion, Marcel Cerdan, who died in a plane crash, increased her popularity. Piaf's patronage was important in launching two new stars: the singer, Charles Aznavour, who would later become a favourite actor of the cinema's New Wave, and Yves Montand. Although attached to the Left Bank by his politics and his relationship with Simone Signoret, Montand, like Aznavour, had a mass heart-throb appeal which had nothing to do with Saint-Germain-des-Prés' image.

There seemed to be no short cut to fame as new singers lacked the aid of an enterprising recording industry which, like the big music-halls, depended on established stars. The disc industry had been one of the hardest hit by purges at the Liberation when all artistic staff who worked during the war were dismissed. Politically-acceptable replacements lacked experience and flair. The biggest pre-war record producer, Polydor, which launched Piaf, had been confiscated during the war when its Jewish owners fled to the USA. The firm was little more than a name in 1945 but was to recover because of a remarkable partnership with the new wave of singers in Saint-Germain, eventually relegating men like Maurice Chevalier to a sort of folk museum. The Polydor company introduced to mass audiences talents like Georges Brassens and Jacques Brel, but it is doubtful whether these two men would have ever been accepted without the impact of two women innovators, Juliette Gréco and Catherine Sauvage.

Yves Montand, singer, the Communist party's best advertisement,
shown here on the cover of 'Autumn Leaves'

Juliette Gréco had already earned the title 'muse of Saint-
Germain' before she began her singing career in 1949, two years
after the success of Le Tabou. Within months she came to
represent the physical manifestation of De Beauvoir's call for
female independence in *Le Deuxième Sexe* with its statement
that freedom of sexual choice was a crucial part of women's
liberation. When she began singing, Gréco was, from a pro-

fessional viewpoint, no more than an out-of-work actress who had played two small stage roles. But she was one of the most photographed and talked about people in the quartier.

Even though she was slimmer and more attractive than the bouncy teenager who had become known with the success of Le Tabou, there seemed little likelihood that she would capitalise on her reputation. Since leaving Le Tabou in 1947 with her friend, Anne-Marie Cazalis, she had helped Boris Vian run the Club Saint-Germain but, like the novelist, was unhappy at the jazz cellar's increasingly chic clientèle and wanted to experiment elsewhere.

Le Tabou's former backers decided to reopen Le Boeuf sur le Toit, a Right Bank cabaret founded by Jean Cocteau and closed by the Germans in 1943. What Gréco was expected to do there except attract photographers and sift potential customers was not clear until she and Cazalis had dinner with Jean-Paul Sartre in a restaurant on the Place du Tertre in Montmartre. While walking down the steps from Le Sacré Coeur to Pigalle, Sartre took up a suggestion that she should sing and offered to choose the lyrics.

Sartre played the piano in his flat, overlooking the Place Saint-Germain, for half an hour each day – the instrument took up much of the room in Jean Cau's secretarial office – and it was after his morning practice the following day that the philosopher went through lyrics with Gréco. He had spent much of the night choosing them. One, 'Les blancs manteaux', about a guillotining in a street in the Marais district of Paris, had been written for *Huis clos* and then dropped. It was still part of Gréco's repertoire more than thirty years later.

As she did not like Sartre's original musical accompaniment, the writer arranged for her to visit Joseph Kosma in the nearby rue de l'Université. Kosma lived in a barely-furnished attic room, despite the fact that he was one of the most popular composers in France whose successes included 'Les Feuilles mortes' (Autumn Leaves) with words by Jacques Prévert. Kosma, who worked with Kurt Weill before the war, also set to music a poem by Raymond Queneau which later became

Gréco's first record, 'Si tu t'imagines', a bitter-sweet reflection on the fleeting pleasures of youth.

She sang three songs at Le Boeuf sur le Toit when it opened in 1949. The cabaret was crowded, the audience sitting on the floor because there were few chairs. But the Right Bank was foreign country to Gréco and she left after only ten days. In September 1949, after a singing holiday at a jazz festival in the West Indies, Gréco returned to perform at La Rose Rouge, a former basement restaurant in the rue de Rennes that was to become Saint-Germain's most successful cabaret.

There is no simple explanation for Gréco's success story. Other women singers at the time were given as much publicity without leaving a deep mark on popular imagery. As radio stations depended on an uncontroversial diet of Chevalier music-hall style songs based on java, tango and rumba rhythms, Gréco's appeal was spread mostly by recommendation. She was, at first, only a supporting artiste at La Rose Rouge where the stars were the singing comedy team, Les Frères Jacques and the mime, Marcel Marceau. She was reluctant to cut records and most of the crowds who went to see her at La Rose Rouge heard Gréco's voice for the first time. Her reputation, however, had already been established as an independent, experienced young woman, free to choose the sexual adventures she wanted and refusing any judgment on her behaviour.

Gréco herself said that her image had already been established during the success of Le Tabou, two years before her singing début.

'At the time, a girl of eighteen was still a child,' she said. 'People imagined that I used to make love to Sartre on marble tables in bistros even though marble is very cold.'

At La Rose Rouge she changed her style, abandoning her image as a carelessly-dressed teenager, and wearing a simple black dress, a Balmain model picked up in the sales which she altered by cutting off the gold satin train. It became part of her stage personality as she broke through the innuendo and censored lyrics of music-hall songs by introducing words like 'sex', 'making love' and 'naked' into popular song.

Sexual freedom was explicit in her choice of lyrics, particularly in 'Je suis comme je suis', whose theme by Jacques Prévert set to music by Kosma was seen as pornographic by the older generation. It was not her fault, she sang, if her lover was not the same one every time.

> *'J'aime celui qui m'aime,*
> *Est-ce ma faute à moi*
> *Si ce n'est pas le même*
> *Que j'aime chaque fois.'*

Her deep voice, her training as an actress and her tendency to cling to the microphone 'like a shipwrecked man clinging to a lifebelt', as one critic put it, all contributed to a mixture of innocence and experience. The black dress, she said, was 'like a blackboard on which the audience gave full rein to its imagination', and much of what she sang was a true reflection of herself.

'I was not exactly innocent of the image that other people had of me', she said. 'I was an object of scandal but only because I was normal. I experienced women's liberation in a completely natural way, a long time before people talked about it. It was not just the liberation of women. It was liberation pure and simple – an explosion of freedom, joy, laughter and companionship.'

Gréco also explained the difference between her and Piaf, one of the few singers she admired.

'Our language was not the same as I didn't inspire pity,' she said. 'I didn't cultivate pity either. My body was both surprising and disturbing and did not provoke any tenderness in the audience. People believed I was incapable of suffering in my love affairs like Piaf did.'

Gossip writers contributed to Gréco's popularity, particularly as she was associated with other young stars like Marlon Brando who came to Paris for acting experience. Gréco said that Brando used to take her home from La Rose Rouge on his motorcycle, but even without this friendship she was quickly known in Hollywood. La Rose Rouge, which the actress Anouk

Aimée ran with her Greek husband, Nico Papadakis, was reputed as a talent pool and attracted Hollywood scouts following up recommendations from established stars like Charlie Chaplin, Myrna Loy and Rex Harrison whom Gréco remembered meeting there.

The cafés of Saint-Germain-des-Prés were where Orson Welles spotted Eartha Kitt, then an out-of-work dancer scraping a living by singing at the Right Bank lesbian night club, Carroll's. Welles gave Kitt the role of Helen of Troy in his production of *Dr Faustus* and dubbed her 'the most exciting woman in the world'. Within years she was starring in Broadway musicals.

By 1951 Gréco had already been given a show at one of Paris's biggest traditional music-halls, the Bobino in Montparnasse, an event which signalled the beginning of the transition of Saint-Germain values to national popularity.

The most important ingredient of Left Bank popular song was the quality of the lyrics. Gréco's were written by the best known literary figures of her generation including François Mauriac, who won the Nobel literature prize in 1952. Mauriac said he wrote Gréco a song because he was jealous of Sartre's contribution. But it was Louis Aragon, one of the strongest critics of Existentialism that had given birth to the cellar bar youth cult, who was to have the most impact, raising lyric-writing to new artistic levels.

Aragon's influence owed much to Cathcrine Sauvage who was almost the same age as Gréco but was much closer to the intuitive political anarchy of Saint-Germain youth. Her record producer at Polydor, Jacques Canetti, who played a key role in making the area's performers into national stars, said that Sauvage 'looked like a revolutionary from a mile off' when she came from the provinces at the age of eighteen to study theatre under the Comédie Française director, Jean-Louis Barrault. Her anarchist lyrics were among the first real pacifist protest songs, but her use of Aragon's poems had nothing to do with her Left-wing views and the fact that he was a Communist. To

Sauvage, Aragon was a pure poet who had written some of the best love poems of the twentieth century.

'His poems were not politically committed,' she said. 'In this respect he had less influence on the public than Sartre. For us, he was a classical poet. Most of the poems I sang were written before or during the war and we appreciated them for their aesthetic and not their political quality.'

Aragon was flattered even though the main audiences for his work were the supposedly corrupt youth which the Communist Party condemned. Sauvage said she saw only the best side of his personality and he was genuinely appreciative of her interest. In 1952, he took a bundle of records of his poems, set to music by George Brassens and sung by Sauvage, to Moscow and distributed them to the Soviet Union's political bureau.

Poetry reading and poetry singing were an important part of Saint-Germain cellar life when Sauvage arrived in the area in 1947 and audiences knew that they were expected to listen attentively. Performers usually got little more as a reward than applause and free drinks but few could accept the different commercial atmosphere of the Right Bank.

Left Bank performers were invited to cabarets across the river as objects of scandal. For Sauvage, the good pay given by Right Bank clubs never compensated for the audience's lack of attention. They were usually composed of 'call girls, bosses with secretaries and tourists', Sauvage said. Waiters carried on serving during acts and the audience chattered. In one club, Sauvage sarcastically claimed that the piano accompanying her was preventing her from hearing the audience's conversations. Brassens, who appeared with her, walked out saying that the customers were only a 'bunch of cunts'. But this type of aggression was what the audience hoped to see.

After a hand-to-mouth existence in Saint-Germain during her first two years there, Sauvage was signed up for three months at Le Boeuf sur le Toit when it reopened in 1949 but, like Gréco, quickly returned to Saint-Germain. Pay was so bad that she had to appear at as many as seven different clubs and restaurants in one night to earn enough to live. More than

Gréco, Sauvage typified the wandering minstrels of the area and she appeared in clubs which nationally-known singers now quote like battle honours – Le Quod Libet, Le Caveau de la Huchette, l'Harlequin, l'Ecluse, l'Echelle de Jacob and La Rose rouge.

The atmosphere in Saint-Germain broke down the barriers between artists and public whom she considered 'my pals'.

'We knew the public and there were no compartments which exist now,' she said. 'We were only teenagers but we had lived through the war and seen deportation and death. I was aggressive and we sang songs that expressed a thirst for justice and peace. We brandished the banner of poetry. We were not jealous of each other as we were all opposed to the same stupidity and hypocrisy.'

Sauvage, like all of Saint-Germain's artistic pioneers, rejects stories of orgies among young people because 'we were too busy talking the night away and remaking the world'. Women's clothes, particularly baggy trousers, shocked the '*bonne bourgeoisie*', she says, but 'by comparison with today's standards we were choristers'. She feels that much of the puritan backlash was simply because parents felt it was shocking that young people sang of adult emotions.

'It was unbearable for the older generation, used to pre-war singers who were mature women.'

Sauvage worked closely with Léo Ferré who had a similar interest in protest songs and in Louis Aragon's poems. Many critics believe that Ferré made the biggest contribution to popular song in the post-war years but his popularity has always been affected by his caustic character. Although he used the 'language of the street' from the time he arrived in Saint-Germain just after the Liberation and took up the cause of the poor, he only began to be listened to widely when France was emerging from economic depression in the late Fifties. He was the first post-war European 'protest singer' to use his own lyrics, and it is hard to dispute Catherine Sauvage's claim that the singer-poets of Saint-Germain 'sang protest songs fifteen years before the US anti-war songs were all the rage'.

A prickly character who, when young, resembled a beady-eyed, down-at-heel secondary school teacher, Ferré had an uncompromisingly personal and bitingly anarchist style. He caused a scandal by attacking Pope Pius XII's failure during the war to condemn persecution of the Jews in a song called 'Monsieur tout blanc' and became the voice of pacifism during the Indo-China war with his anti-militaristic 'Regardez les défilés'. His anti-militarism became dangerous during the Algerian war when he was threatened with death by the extreme right OAS secret army which detested his pacifist lyrics.

Ferré was a misfit in Saint-Germain and speaks about it with hatred. His background was more than usually unconventional as he was born in Monaco, the son of the staff manager at the casino. Despite his anarchy, his singing career was encouraged by Prince Rainier who went incognito to his shows in Saint-Germain. A self-taught pianist, Ferré first came to the Left Bank before the war and lived in the rue Saint-Benoît while studying at the Institute of Political Science at the same time as François Mitterrand. During the war he worked on a farm but on returning to Monaco was introduced to Edith Piaf who said he had a future as a singer.

He eked out a living in Saint-Germain's cellar bars as a singer poet but, to him, the area had none of the Left Bank romance so often evoked by veterans of Le Tabou's brief period of innocence. The commercialism at the turn of the decade disgusted him. Singers were exploited and his main preoccupation was wondering whether he would have enough money to buy a packet of cigarettes or pay for his cheap hotel room.

'The quartier was a commercial enterprise run by people who made money out of bistros and Sartre's reputation', he said. 'It was a kingdom of hotel owners and alcohol merchants. I never mixed with other singers and I didn't want to know them. They were all queuing up in front of the future, a fragile future, being dragged along in Sartre's wake.

'It was surprising that Sartre let himself get involved. He was one of the great intellectuals of the century, even if part of his work is unreadable. I am sure he did not understand what he had written himself when he read it back. *L'Etre et le Néant* is ridiculous and he hated poetry.'

Ferré, whose white hair gave him a benign appearance from middle age, was much admired by other singers including Gréco who said his songs were 'masterpieces'. But Ferré harboured a strong resentment for 'the muse of Saint-Germain-des-Prés'.

When Gréco was running Le Tabou in 1947, Ferré asked if he could present his songs and was told to come for an audition at Gréco's hotel. She was ill and he had to sing three unaccompanied songs standing at the foot of her bed. She told him to report to Le Tabou at 10 pm but, after waiting for half an hour without seeing Gréco, Ferré left. Since then, Ferré has made no secret of his feelings for Gréco and her work. He described her first song, 'Les Blancs Manteaux', written by Sartre, as 'bloody stupid'.

'Gréco built up her popularity and her singing career by mixing with the right people,' he said. 'She used people like candles, lighting them and putting them out.'

Ferré's grudges are legion. There are many singers he dislikes, such as Yves Montand, because they turned down his songs. He also hates the Communist Party which he joined 'for five minutes' in 1947, tearing up his newly signed membership card at his first cell meeting because he could not stand the rigid discipline of the debate.

Many leading artists, including Edith Piaf and Gréco, included Ferré songs in their repertoires. He was also accepted as a poet in his own right by leading cultural figures like André Breton and Louis Aragon at a time when the two men were no longer speaking to each other.

Although Catherine Sauvage and Leo Ferré can make strong claims to inventing contemporary protest songs, they were not directly involved in the first national controversy over pacifism that would foreshadow the tensions of the Algerian War. The row claimed two victims, the veteran habitué of the Café de Flore, the singer-actor, Marcel Mouloudji and the novelist, Boris Vian. The controversy developed over a pacifist appeal called 'Le Déserteur' which Vian wrote and which Mouloudji sang and recorded in 1953. Vian was to stir up a new wave of national hostility against himself that enforced another change of direction for his varied talent. Mouloudji suffered worse as the song wrecked his career.

'Le Déserteur', in which a conscript asks the President to be excused national service, was released in the poisoned atmosphere of growing concern over French participation in the Indo-China war. In a trial run that would unite much of the Left during the Algerian conflict, protest concentrated on the arrest of a young sailor, Henri Martin, a Resistance hero and member of the Communist Party who volunteered for naval service in 1945 to fight Japan but felt he had been pressed into defending colonial policies in Indo-China where he kept a diary of French war crimes. Accused of sabotaging a ship in 1949 after he was refused permission to leave the navy, his trial and appeal stretched over the next four years, providing a rallying cry for the scattered Left, until he was quietly pardoned when the row became obscured by the Algerian War.

The Martin affair was the first national issue which bound Jean-Paul Sartre closely to the Communist Party, as he supported the Party's case with tracts of his own. Later, general concern over Indo-China policy as it lurched towards the disaster at Dien Bien Phu in 1954 attracted much of the Left and Centre around a coherent protest, that would eventually involve politicians like Pierre Mendès France and François Mitterrand. Inevitably, the politically uncommitted like Boris Vian, whose anti-military views reflected a strong personal disgust for violence in any form, were also identified with the cause, even against their will.

Vian's song, 'Le Déserteur', one of the few he performed on stage himself, was a logical development of his good nature rather than a political statement. It nonetheless added another ingredient for the general amalgam of hate which former Vichy supporters, now in government, reserved for Vian's Saint-Germain. The Right already saw the area as a centre of pornography, destructive atheism, subversive Marxism, drug abuse and sexual perversion. Now it came to be seen as a hotbed of treachery against democratically-chosen conservative government. This was by no means the limit of twisted logic as the song's interpreter, Marcel Moulodji, found out. The Right also resurrected another of its essential elements, racism.

Mouloudji was something of a monument in Saint-Germain even though he was only thirty-two at the time of 'Le Déserteur'. He had been linked to Jacques Prévert's group at the Flore since he first appeared on stage as a boy soprano at the age of twelve. He was as adaptable as Boris Vian. Gréco once remarked that his talent was 'astonishing' and that he could write, paint, act and sing equally well while modestly hiding behind a disarming smile. He was at the peak of his career when Vian asked him to record 'Le Déserteur'. He had appeared in thirty films and won Gallimard's Pléiade literary prize for a novel. He appeared frequently on stage but felt more attracted by writing and painting.

His decision to continue his singing career with Vian's songs was intended to finance these two interests, but his choice of lyricist was doubly provocative. The novelist's reputation as a pornographer was so fixed in the public mind that many established singers refused to use his songs. In defying already unsympathetic attitudes, Mouloudji forgot to take into account the impact of his own parentage. His mother was a Breton charlady and he was born and brought up in France. But what counted for the Right was the fact that his father was an immigrant Algerian manual worker.

While 'Le Déserteur' might not have caused a stir if it had been sung only in the clubs of Saint-Germain, Mouloudji first performed it on stage in Pigalle and was booed. Two months later, his recording of the song was ordered to be withdrawn from the shops and it was banned on the radio, now controlled by the Right in the traditions set by François Mitterrand.

Mouloudji was boycotted as an entertainer. For the first time, the lyrics of Saint-Germain had passed the dividing line between provocation and subversion.

Mouloudji's career went rapidly into obscurity when the Algerian war developed. He was an innocent victim as he was even more apolitical than Vian, and did not consider the song as a protest but a statement of a commonly held philosophy among his friends. He maintained his pleasant, easy charm after the setback, although he had good reason to feel a grudge against some of those friends who shied away from making an issue out of the controversy with its overtones of racial discrimination.

'The affair rebounded on me because my name is Algerian although I am French,' he said. 'It was unfashionable to protest at the time and, as I was not a member of a political party, I got no support.' In the wake of 'Le Déserteur', Mouloudji had to issue a replacement song for the record company. The title was 'On m'a dit' and Mouloudji included the line: 'They told me to shut up'. Sadly even the politically committed opinion-makers of Saint-Germain also chose silence.

While Vian, an object of so much contempt himself, could do little to help Mouloudji, he did everything possible to save 'Le Déserteur'. Eventually, the song became part of France's folk treasury, but it also contributed to accelerating Vian's failing health and obliged him to take a salaried job again. After Mouloudji's setback, Vian decided to start a cabaret career of his own, as he missed contact with the public since abandoning the trumpet on doctor's orders. He was taken on at Les Trois Baudets, a theatre-cabaret a few yards from his home above the Moulin Rouge. Its owner, Jacques Canetti, who had for several years been reconstructing the Polydor record company and arranging tours for Saint-Germain singers, included Vian in a supporting bill for a second-act comedy based on *Les Carnets du Major Thompson* by Pierre Daninos.

Canetti was determined that Vian should join him as assistant in the record industry but Vian wanted to be an artiste. It was often said at the time that Canetti, a hard, dry businessman, let Vian have his own way to prove to him that he was incompetent as a stage performer. Vian was so bad that it was never clear whether his wooden appearances, in which he appeared paralysed by stage fright, were at the root of the audiences' hostile reaction or whether they were just continuing the fight against Vian's key number, 'Le Déserteur'. Vian, thin, white faced and obviously ill, troubled even sympathetic crowds. His only record, which he made for Canetti, was a flop and his only tour, again sponsored by the record producer, took a terrible toll of his health. Along with other Canetti stars, Vian travelled throughout France in 1954, when his singing of 'Le Déserteur' caused constant trouble among audiences. He was often nearly exhausted when he started his act, as he drove his white Austin-Healey throughout the tour to venues hundreds of miles apart, and then joined other artistes in a constant round of parties and receptions.

For part of the tour, he was pursued by hostile groups of soldiers who heckled his performance and he was also shaken by public rows in which he was threatened with violence. When he returned to Paris, his chest troubles worsened and he accepted a job as artistic director with Canetti whose Polydor label had been absorbed by Philips. As a result of the merger with the powerful Dutch-managed group, many of Saint-Germain's performers who believed that their careers were restricted to a specialised audience became internationally known stars.

Over the next five years, Vian played a central role in recommending songs and singers, but it was not until well after the writer's death that the general public accepted Canetti's belief that Vian wrote the best songs of his generation. During his lifetime, Vian's songs hovered over the entertainment industry like albatrosses. Brigitte Bardot tried unfruitfully to launch her own singing career on an album of Vian songs. The subsequent failure obliged her to concentrate on a film career.

Vian's decision to work full-time with Canetti was a signal that Saint-Germain's innovators were now controlled by commercial interests. But without the presence of dynamic financial backers, the area's influence would have been stifled by its own introversion. Even thirty years later, popular singers were to take Saint-Germain as a reference for quality while Vian's own repertoire of 400 songs was still being drawn on for 'new' lyrics and music. This could never have happened without the most imaginative impresario of the period, Vian's new boss, Jacques Canetti.

Canetti, Bulgarian born but naturalised French, is the brother of the 1981 Nobel literature prizewinner, Elias Canetti, who took out British nationality. Joseph Canetti is known as the 'Napoleon of the chansonnette' by French singers who both despised and relied on his gifts as a sharp businessman and a superb opportunist talent scout. His commercial realism seems in retrospect more like an unselfish suicidal risk as he opened the way for new singers who would eventually join a popular Panthéon that included Georges Brassens and Jacques Brel.

A former radio journalist, Canetti spent the war years in Algeria before returning to take over the shattered Jewish-owned Polydor record label after the Liberation. The company had no money and Canetti had only a part-time job. The firm could not afford to finance Piaf, its biggest pre-war discovery, and she signed for the rival producer, Pathé-Marconi.

'It was a real catastrophe for us,' Canetti said. 'Our catalogue was so old-fashioned it was unsellable. We had no American repertoire left and no Jazz.'

His solution was to build up his own stable of artistes by creating Les Trois Baudets, a Montmartre cabaret which mixed new acts and new plays.

'I was mad,' he said. 'I had no idea of the difficulties lying ahead but I was impatient to get back to work after the war years. It seems enormously thoughtless to record the unknown singers that I did.'

Canetti's talent hunting ground was Saint-Germain with Les Trois Baudets serving as a half-way house that enticed performers to try their luck in the outside world. Risk was limited as Canetti could not afford the lavish orchestras of the traditional music-halls and audiences began to expect to see an untried singer accompanied by only a guitar or piano. The first part of

The 'Rats de Cave' dancing be-bop. Note the uniform of plaid shirts and basket-ball boots

the bill at Les Trois Baudets was used as a testing ground in front of audiences that were far less indulgent than those of Saint-Germain. A singer would either crack or break through. Occasionally, when Canetti was sure he had found talent which needed time to adapt he would persist with his hunch against hostile audience reaction for months.

When La Rose rouge moved to the former underground restaurant in the rue de Rennes, under the offices of the French state electricity company, Canetti spent much of his time there despite the fact that tobacco smoke affected his own chest problems, an illness which was said to have increased his sympathy for Boris Vian. Even without the smoke it was often difficult to breathe as there were no safety restrictions and customers would fill every inch of the floor space and the stairs.

The stage was only twelve feet across, considered big by Saint-Germain standards, but was still so restricted that a pianist had to sit underneath. Performers changed in the corridors. The make-up 'studio' was an interior telephone-box. In these conditions, only the best could survive and a talent scout could make his judgments sitting, like the audience, within touching distance of a performer.

As the state-owned radio still subsisted on a diet of music-hall songs because Saint-Germain offerings were considered anarchist, signing-up a performer for a record contract was a tremendous risk. One of Canetti's first decisions was to take on Les Frères Jacques, a singing-clowning team whose routine foreshadowed Absurdist Theatre. Gréco at first refused to make records. Canetti saw this as a lack of courage which contrasted with the risks she took on stage in singing songs by then unknown composer singers like Serge Gainsbourg and Guy Béart who became stars in the Sixties. She did eventually join him but he could get nowhere with Léo Ferré, who nonetheless agreed to let Canetti use his songs in an album by Catherine Sauvage. Ferré instinctively distrusted Canetti's commercialism, a wariness that seemed justified when Catherine Sauvage collapsed and needed psychiatric treatment during a punishing tour arranged by Canetti.

'I pushed her beyond her limits,' Canetti admitted but she was able to return after nearly a year's rest to sing songs by Boris Vian and Kurt Weill. Later, with Georges Brassens, she took a leading role in anarchist galas that preceded the 1968 student revolt.

Canetti had his own company to arrange tours that either made or broke reputations. They were the only way to overcome the problem of direct communication with a wide public dependent on radio. Eventually, Canetti's discoveries obscured all but the best of the Right Bank singers like Piaf, Montand, Gilbert Bécaud and Charles Aznavour. Some, however, would have disappeared without trace but for Canetti's obstinacy.

The most striking example was Georges Brassens, who won

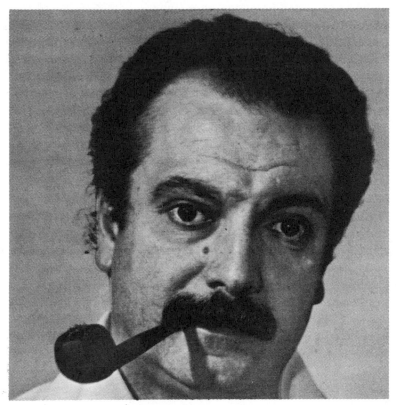

Georges Brassens, like Juliette Gréco, was one of the first singers to introduce 'dirty' words into their songs

the Académie Française poetry prize for his lyrics in 1967. Brassens came to Paris from the Communist-run port of Sète in the South of France and spent much of the war as a forced labourer in Germany. His big, broad face, huge moustache and kindly expression took the sharp edge off songs which attacked every social and moral convention in the French system to the background of an almost monotonous guitar and bass accompaniment. But Brassens, who always lived simply and kept the same childhood friends all his life, was paralysed by stage fright and Canetti had to stand in the wings to encourage him throughout his show. When Canetti gave him a job at Les Trois

Baudets after his downbeat style failed to catch on even in Saint-Germain, Brassens refused to change cabarets despite offers of considerably higher fees.

Canetti also discovered the Belgian singer, Jacques Brel, whom he invited to Paris from Brussels in 1953 on the strength of a trial record. Brel was then working in his father's cardboard factory and left his family behind for what he considered to be a brief visit to Paris. Although he was the most abrasive of new singers because his aggressive voice sharpened his already acid anti-bourgeois lyrics, Brel struck Canetti as 'shy and good-mannered', and he easily persuaded him to stay in Paris, although his rich family reduced his private income.

Brel was a rapid, but not instant success, as his first appearances were badly received by critics, and one journalist told Brel that 'the trains were still running between Paris and Brussels' and advised him to look up the timetable. But the pioneering work of singers like Gréco and Sauvage had increased public demand for lyrics of originality and quality. Brel moved to the Echelle de Jacob in the heart of Saint-Germain and helped make the cabaret into the most popular rendezvous of the late Saint-Germain period.

Canetti had by then developed his ultimate weapon, the mass distribution of micro-groove records which ensured that the forming of taste was neither the monopoly of the broadcasting system nor the exclusiveness of Left Bank performers. The importance of intimate cabaret would be rapidly undermined when it was seen that reputations were made more easily in recording studies.

But the audiences were also much more blasé. The penniless Bohemians seen by *Life* in 1947 were now approaching their thirties and had respectable jobs after graduating from the Left Bank's universities and Grandes Ecoles. There were still many young people like Brigitte Bardot or Françoise Sagan who used Saint-Germain's liberal atmosphere during their struggle to break out of middle-class attitudes as restrictive as those condemned by Simone de Beauvoir. But their lifestyle was considerably less innocent than that of the children of the Forties especially as Saint-Germain's summer annex, Saint Tropez, was already leading the world with a hectic image of its own where sexual freedom was even more pronounced.

What was to be called the Americanisation of Saint-Germain with the introduction of discothèques without cabarets and fashionable tourist-oriented shops to replace craftsmen's workshops was under way. But just as it was being written off as a quartier surviving only on nostalgia, Saint-Germain showed that it had not run out of surprises.

The clubs and cellars of Saint-Germain which had encouraged often bizarre and haphazard partnerships between intellectual dreamers and reckless financial backers had also created a receptive audience for one of the fundamental post-war cultural revolutions – *Le Théâtre de l'absurde*.

8

La Cantatrice chauve

Le Théâtre de l'absurde had four Left Bank evangelists, Arthur Adamov, Samuel Beckett, Jean Genet and Eugène Ionesco. Their backgrounds were so different, their influences so varied and their theatrical ambitions so much at odds that it was a disservice by contemporary critics to lump them all together under a convenient title. There was little or no communication between them and the all-embracing attempt to link their inspiration to Albert Camus's theories on the Absurd in his wartime essay, *Le Mythe de Sysyphe*, was a fanciful piece of analysis that underplayed sympathies for Surrealism and the humorous anarchy of Alfred Jarry.

It is fair to say that the authors themselves were absurd in the strict meaning that they were 'out of harmony' among themselves or in relation to the dominant Saint-Germain currents represented by Sartre and Camus. Both the Armenian-born Russian, Adamov, and the Irish exile, Beckett, used French as their adopted language but there is no record of a conversation between them as Beckett discouraged discussion of his motives even with fellow writers. Ionesco, who considered French his first language as he was educated as a child in France, was born and spent much of his adult life in Romania. He detested Saint-Germain's literary cafés where Adamov and Genet were among the regulars on the fringe of Sartre's entourage. The Romanian-born writer had a brief friendship with Adamov who, at one time, attended every performance of Ionesco's plays but they fell out. As for his contacts with Beckett, Ionesco saw him occasionally at receptions where conversations were limited to brief exchanges on health and weather.

Meanwhile, Genet, whose life became public property through the expression of his personal experiences in his five novels and Sartre's 600-page analysis, *Saint Genet, Comédien et martyr*, was the only Frenchman among the four evangelists but the most foreign in cultural terms as his writing was inspired by revenge on French society in general. The common factor among the four was not their general pessimism at the absurdity of life that was the starting point for Camus's moral exploration, but what Ionesco himself described as 'derision', not merely for bourgeois values but the whole calcified structure of what was known as the *Théâtre de Boulevard*, the normal commercial or state-subsidised stage offerings. Aided by 'fringe theatre' management on the Left Bank, the Absurdists took on a smug establishment, still fat after the wartime boom, and caused a worldwide revolution in stage philosophy.

The turning point was in 1950 when both Ionesco and Adamov produced plays at the Théâtre des Noctambules near the Sorbonne just after Boris Vian's *L'Equarrisage pour tous* which so disgusted critics including Elsa Triolet. The best known chronicler of the Absurdists, Martin Esslin, included Vian in his wide-ranging list along with Britain's Harold Pinter and N. F. Simpson as well as the American Edward Albee and the German, Günter Grass.

All over the Western world at the time, theatre was stuck in conventions firmly dictated by the limits of the proscenium arch and the safety-first attitudes of producers. In France, two leading literary innovators of the post-war period, Sartre and

Camus, were also blamed by the avant-garde for reinforcing conventional moulds in the theatre.

The two writers used the stage more as an orator's tub than a dramatic setting and produced their works on the Right Bank for conservative, middle-class audiences. Of Sartre's plays, only *Huis clos* in 1944 was staged on the Left Bank at Le Vieux Colombier. The rest of his plays presented sound, scholarly polemic but the rigidly-traditional framework was at odds with Sartre's moral, political and philosophical iconoclasm that he preached directly to his Saint-Germain audience.

Apart from their usually political content, Sartre's plays were most noticeable for their technical conventionalism. Even a year after the debate had begun on *Le Théâtre de l'absurde* with its daring innovations, Sartre released a play, *Le Diable et le Bon Dieu*, which was not only a model of conformity but also oddly dated by its content.

The drama was an atheistic response to Paul Claudel's *Le Soulier de Satin* of which one critic said that he was glad that the poet-Ambassador had not described a pair. *Le Diable et le Bon Dieu* was a perfect left-foot match for Claudel's Catholic right-eousness while confirming Sartre's place in the mainstream of Boulevard Theatre.

Sartre, as far as theatre was concerned, had lost his power to shock and was merely the other point of view. Controversy over his search for a moral code to attach to his existential theories had been fought five years before. In 1946, the Christian existentialist playwright, philosopher and theatre critic, Gabriel Marcel, had the acuity to realise that Sartre was looking for a system of ethical values to graft on to his ideas expressed in *L'Etre et le Néant*.

'One could say that Sartre appears to be already installed in a philosophy to which he is trying to annex ethics, rather as one builds a wash-house beside a country house', Marcel wrote. Later, he was to attack *Le Diable et le Bon Dieu* as 'an uncertain mixture of Hegel and Jaspers . . . a Hegel influenced by Nietzscheism dragged down to the level of an evening class in a local café'. As for Camus, Marcel praised him as 'one of the very few consciences in our literature of today' but, despite Camus's experience as a theatre director in Algeria, wrote him off as a poor playwright.

In the general terms of Saint-Germain, where innovation and reform were still the first objectives, Sartre and Camus had become a little boring, more intent on lecturing than inspiring. In theatre terms, they had reinforced rigidity of ideas to the satisfaction of prudent management. All the outlets for change were blocked except for new 'fringe' theatres on the Left Bank, Camus called them '*pissotières*', where young producers and directors were encouraged by the financial success of the clubs of Saint-Germain. The constant renewal of the student population provided the main audiences for the uncomfortable and ephemeral pocket theatres that sprang up in the area which let new playwrights try out their shows at off-peak times. This was the battleground on which, in Ionesco's own words, 'Beckett, Genet and I destroyed Boulevard Theatre.'

The exclusion of his one-time fanatical supporter, Adamov, from the list was deliberate. The Russian emigré was a true pioneer of *Le Théâtre de l'absurde* but was also the first to react against it when his Marxist leanings re-emerged after Bertold Brecht's arrival in Paris in the mid-fifties with his Berliner Ensemble. Adamov then embraced Brecht's 'committed' theatre, repenting publicly for his Absurdist sins in a move which alienated him from Ionesco, Sartre's arch critic.

Because Adamov, Beckett, Genet and Ionesco were such striking individualists, the chronology of the development of Absurdist theatre is one of the most complicated of the period. They were born within six years of each other between 1906 and 1912 but only Adamov's career gives a coherent over-view of French stage history of the time, making it impossible to exclude him from Absurdism on Ionesco's grounds that he reneged. He was the first to try and stage post-war plays out of tune with the contemporary strict frontiers of Boulevard Theatre but his breakthrough did not come until avant-garde producers and directors became impatient at the hold on theatre by established figures in the early Fifties.

Adamov, whose father owned oil wells in Armenia, began his exile in Paris at the age of sixteen in 1924 and was drawn into André Breton's circle of Surrealists, editing the avant-garde periodical *Discontinuité*. He quickly came under the influence of the theatre director, playwright and theorist, Antonin Artaud who founded the Théâtre Alfred Jarry in 1927 and the short-lived Théâtre de la cruauté in 1935, two years before he was confined to a lunatic asylum. Artaud, who died in 1946, was also a strong influence on the actor-director, Roger Blin, who was to launch Samuel Beckett in 1953.

Artaud's theories and mental unbalance were crucial to Adamov's own career. Artaud sought to break out of traditional narrative, dialogue and psychological realism on stage, providing the ground rules, if any existed, for avant-garde theatre. But Adamov lacked the internal stability of other Artaud disciples like Jean-Louis Barrault. After a Surrealist period, Barrault went on to run the Comédie Française and another state-subsidised troupe at the Odéon.

Adamov's own life, while under Artaud's influence, was undergoing inner torment as he tottered from one bout of depression to another made worse by alcoholism. His despair at his sexual problems, including masochism and the 'inability to complete the act of carnal possession' were vividly described in his autobiographical work, *L'Aveu*, written between 1938 and 1943. By then he was already on the fringes of Sartre's group at the Café de Flore, a depressing, badly-dressed figure shuffling about in open-toed sandals. Sartre's existentialism exercised a strong influence and Adamov wrote: 'What is there? I know first of all that I am. But who am I? All I know of myself is that I suffer. And if I suffer it is because, at the origin of myself, there is mutilation and separation.'

As an unorthodox Marxist in the Surrealist tradition, Adamov desperately wanted to be accepted by dominant cultural leaders. His personality conflict was complicated by his natural attraction to the avant-garde while trying to come to terms with the realistic theatre of Sartre and Camus. Adamov's first two plays, on the inability to communicate, were considered too avant-garde to be staged when they were written in 1945. Gradually, he submitted to the broad lines of Sartre's theories and wrote *La Grande et la Petite Manoeuvre*, a half-way house between the 'committed' and Absurdist theatre. It echoed some of the grand arguments of Camus's *Les Justes* and Sartre's *Les Mains sales* on terror and revolution as the play evoked the fall of a totalitarian state whose revolutionaries imposed their triumph through brutality and terrorism.

Surrealist elements in the play, however, indicated Adamov's split cultural personality while providing a glimpse forward to his later reaction to Absurdist Theatre. One of the characters loses his limbs one by one, watched over by a sadistic mistress. The same theme of mutilation was used by Brecht in a play in 1925.

La Grande et la petite manoeuvre was performed at the 'fringe' Théâtre des Noctambules in the Latin Quarter in November 1950. Three days later, the plays he wrote in 1945, *L'Invasion* and *La Parodie* were staged by Jean Vilar at the Right Bank Studio des Champs-Elysées. Vilar was a strictly conventional product of French theatre having studied under the Left Bank's best-known actor-director, Charles Dullin, the man who first staged Sartre's plays. In 1947, Vilar founded the Avignon Festival and, in 1951, after sponsoring Adamov, was appointed to the State-subsidised Théâtre Nationale Populaire where he maintained conventional theatrical output in an attempt to attract working-class audiences.

Adamov was a pillar of the Old Navy bar on the boulevard Saint-Germain where Vilar met him regularly, discovering in him a superb talent for theatrical analysis and a natural generosity that overcame his morose side. As a result, Adamov was the first to create Right Bank interest in progressive stage theories as Vilar praised him for 'abandoning the lacy arguments of dialogue and intrigue and giving back drama its stark purity'. Vilar saw Adamov's plays as the antidote to the theatre of Claudel 'which borrows its effects from the alcohols of faith and the grand word', a statement that might be seen as an implicit side-swipe at Sartre's equally grandiose *Le Diable et le Bon Dieu*.

Before his reconversion to political theatre, Adamov concentrated on Le Théâtre de l'absurde for four years or so, producing his best absurdist play, *Le Ping-Pong*, in which life is an aimless contest on a pinball machine. The theme was directly inspired by Adamov's own fascination with pinball machines in the Old Navy bar and the nearby Mabillon.

The most durable play in Absurdist theatre, however, was *La Cantatrice chauve* by Eugène Ionesco, produced at the Théâtre des Noctambules six months before Adamov made his début. It needed complicated reasoning to attach the play to any political current. More than anything, it proved that Le Théâtre de l'Absurde was a literary jigsaw puzzle in which none of the pieces fitted.

If it had been possible to group the four Absurdist evangelists at a reception in the mid-Fifties, there is little doubt that Ionesco would have been the centre of attention. Beckett, an oversensitive introvert, cut off conversation even with his peers by retreating into banalities. Adamov had the ability to transfer his constant depression to the most optimistic listener. Genet was so much a professional homosexual queen that he surprised even people like the actor-singer Mouloudji who spent his entire life among the entertainment world's eccentrics.

Ionesco, in contrast, was a happily married extrovert who enjoyed being drawn into theatrical analysis and who was buoyed up by one of the great cultural happy ends of the period. A small, mole-like figure who returned to France after the Nazis became too prominent in pre-war Romania, he also made no secret of the fact that he disliked Sartre for several reasons, always a good subject for a rousing discussion. Although Ionesco acknowledged a debt to the 'club life of Saint-Germain and all that', he loathed the 'mentality of Saint-Germain which was in sympathy with the Communists'. He supported the often expressed view that Sartre was a political opportunist 'sometimes Communist, sometimes anti-Communist' but, in the mid-Fifties, Ionesco's main reproach was that the philosopher contributed heavily to immobility in theatre itself.

In the three decades since *La Cantatrice chauve* opened at Les Noctambules on May 11, 1950, Ionesco has had plenty of time to develop theories about his 'Theatre of Derision', as he prefers to call Absurdist theatre. But the play itself still seems more like a remarkable piece of creative intuition than a carefully prepared revolt.

Ionesco wrote the original in Romanian after studying the Assimil method of English, *L'Anglais sans peine*. He was amazed by the ridiculousness of obvious statements such as the ceiling being up and the floor being down. As a publisher's proof-reader, already swamped by words, he was suddenly struck by their pure dramatic quality. He never learnt English and it was his wife, Rodica, who tried to interest theatre directors like Jean-Louis Barrault.

Barrault, no more than any of the other leading theatrical figures she approached, had any faith in a play which begins with a clock striking 17, 'a long minute of English silence' and the announcement by Mrs Smith that it is 'now nine o'clock'. The attack on current French bourgeois values must also have seemed obscure as the setting was English surburbia, reflected in terms irrelevant to an impoverished France of 1950.

Madame Ionesco was, despite the rejections, equally as confident of her husband's genius as he was himself and set about raising 54,000 francs, several times her husband's monthly salary, for a privately financed production. Several pocket theatres had sprung up around Saint-Germain-des-Prés as part of the general enthusiasm for new talent. Les Noctambules, which depended on student audiences, was one of the most daring and lent the auditorium free of charge, although Ionesco met all other expenses.

La Cantatrice Chauve was put on at 6 pm as a 'fringe' offering before the main bill which included Franz Kafka's only play and Bertold Brecht's *L'Exception de la règle*, the first Brecht production in Paris since *L'Opera à quatre sous* before the war.

La Cantatrice Chauve was, according to Ionesco, 'an insane gamble' and he lost his money. The audiences warmed neither to his attack on Boulevard Theatre nor to his attempt to project 'the astonishment I felt when faced with the world'.

'The world seemed banal and unreal to me,' he said. 'This idea of vacuity was not understood by the people who were used to finding a moral message in the theatre. My theatre was a metaphysical theatre, a theatrical structure where characters spoke kindly to each other and then got angry. I liked the sound of words, the unreality of the real. The Leftists were for Socialist Realism. I have always believed that reality is unreal. I am not a realist because I do not know what reality is.'

In retrospect, it was to prove Ionesco's salvation that he had no concept of reality which, as far as *La Cantatrice chauve* was concerned, was bleak. Having invested his last borrowed franc in the production, Ionesco could rarely afford the fare to see how the play was getting on. With his wife, he used up his last two Métro tickets for a ride to the Left Bank from his flat in northern Paris believing he could cadge the return tickets from his director, Nicolas Bataille.

He arrived to find the auditorium empty while Bataille swept out between the seats. The director had no money either so the two men spent the evening walking up and down the boulevard Saint-Michel as sandwich men trying to advertise the play.

Bataille was only twenty-three and one of the play's best assets. An authentic product of the post-war Left Bank obsession with youth, he had won a Ministry of Fine Arts avant-garde prize two years earlier for his adaptation of Rimbaud's *Une Saison en Enfer*. He was closely involved with the one-time Surrealist Art et Action group founded by the film and stage director, Claude Autant-Lara, who would be one of the unjust victims of New Wave cinema which turned the youth cult into a form of fanaticism at the end of the decade.

Bataille's personal progress also reflected the steady disillusionment of young people with Sartre's leadership. Bataille had been influenced by *Huis clos* and still used it as a point of reference. But, by 1953, the young director 'wanted a newer form of theatre, a more aggressive form'.

'Sartre's theatre was intelligent boulevard which everyone could understand, but it was not new,' Bataille said. 'As far as the traditional stage was concerned, Ionesco's writing was like a bomb that scattered the dust.'

Bataille developed *La Cantatrice chauve* in many details but the eventual title was a happy accident. An actor used the phrase when he fluffed his lines in rehearsal but not even that inspiration saved the production from a terrible beating from the critics. *Le Figaro*, by far the most influential paper for general audiences, wrote off Ionesco as 'an idiot and a charlatan' and expressed pity for Nicolas Bataille 'who thinks he has staged a masterpiece which is nothing at all'.

Ionesco, however, had been adopted by some of Saint-Germain's leading influences. Jean Paulhan, whom Ionesco called 'the Pope of French literature', became one of his most ardent supporters when *La Leçon* was staged at another ephemeral Left Bank theatre, Le Théâtre de Poche, two years later. Not only did Paulhan see the play several times but made a point of taking along visiting foreign writers. Raymond Queneau, meanwhile, stood at the door of Gallimard's cocktail parties and told every guest on arriving that Ionesco's work was the most interesting in the city. André Breton conferred honorary membership of the Surrealist group on Ionesco by telling him, after seeing his plays, that 'we should have been doing that'.

The Romanian-born writer was also drawn into the Collège de 'Pataphysique alongside Vian and Queneau. The nihilist group of writers and scientists, inspired by Alfred Jarry, was also a centre of anti-Sartrism, as most of its members were former Ecole Normale Supérieure graduates who rejected 'commitment' and treated life like an undergraduates' rag stunt. It was, Ionesco said, 'anarchy raised to the level of metaphysics'.

As a result of his talent and such formidable sponsorship, Ionesco plays mushroomed everywhere on the Left Bank. *La Cantatrice chauve* reappeared for two months at the 95-seat Caveau de la Huchette, financed by the young film director,

Louis Malle. *Les Chaises* opened at Le Théâtre Nouveau Lancry and *La Leçon* at Le Théâtre de Poche. It was there that Adamov distinguished himself by attending every performance and encouraging the cast with frequent, loud 'bravos'. Another short-lived 'fringe' theatre, Le Quartier Latin, put on *Les Victimes du Devoir* while *Amadée ou comment s'en débarrasser* followed in 1954 at Le Théâtre de Babylone. La Huchette staged *Jacques ou le soumission* but now Ionesco's polemic with the traditional theatre had become a crusade.

L'Impromptu de l'Alma, which ridiculed hostile critics, was staged on the Right Bank. The happy ending to the story came in 1957 when La Huchette again staged *La Cantatrice chauve* under Bataille's direction. More than twenty-seven years later it was still running in a double bill with *La Leçon* making it the longest run of any post-war French production.

With Ionesco's success confirmed, it had taken barely half a decade for the theatre-going public both in France and abroad to change its attitude to the stage. A formidable wave of energy and talent among new theatre directors was released. An ability to shock, even scandalise, was often paramount in the choice of authors. Jean Genet supplied these ingredients both in his plays and life-style.

Most of his work falls outside the period when public tastes were being changed by Adamov and Ionesco and their contemporary, Samuel Beckett, whose *Waiting for Godot* was produced on the Left Bank in 1953. But Genet, who rejoiced in being a homosexual thief, became public property in 1952 with Sartre's flattering study, providing the thrill of audience identification with the author which neither the modest Ionesco nor the timid Beckett supplied.

There is nothing abstract about Genet nor his plays. Real life and personal experience spill over the borders between creation and existence. The excitement of a Genet play is the discomfiting of a bourgeois audience discovering the savagery of the society they defend.

Genet, born in Paris in 1910, knew neither of his parents and grew up in an orphanage. Sent to a children's penitentiary for petty theft at the age of fifteen he vowed to make himself notorious through stealing. After deserting from the Foreign Legion, he made his living from prostitution and theft and started writing in jail at the age of thirty. His novel, *Nôtre Dames des Fleurs*, written in Fresnes prison in 1942, brought him to the notice of Jean Cocteau who pleaded with the Vichy judiciary to release him. From then on, Cocteau was Genet's protector although he was also a prominent member of Sartre's entourage at the Liberation.

Cocteau's patronage ensured Genet's acceptance in literary-minded bourgeois homes but his kleptomania caused many rows. While spending a weekend with friends in the country, he stole several ornaments which were discreetly removed from his luggage just before he left. The writer reacted furiously describing his hosts as 'incorrigible bourgeois' for having dared go through his suitcases. But he was also a compulsive giver. Once, when going out with a racing driver, Genet went round his acquaintances trying to raise money to buy a car for his friend.

Genet said in an interview that the only reason he continued writing was to keep himself out of prison, a belief reinforced when the Socialist President Auriol gave him a general pardon while police were trying to arrest him for theft. By then, Genet had already written his first play, *Les Bonnes*, which was staged at one of the most conservative theatres in Paris, L'Athenée, in 1947 by one of the most conventional directors, Louis Jouvet.

Jouvet was best known for his long collaboration with the playwright Jean Giraudoux and was appalled by some of Genet's ideas. Advised by Cocteau and Sartre, Genet accepted some major changes to the true story of two maids who murder their employers. Many lines were modified while Jouvet refused to have the play performed by men dressed as women. Genet's bare main set on a staircase was also refused and Jouvet set the play in the mistress's bedroom with turn-of-the-century costumes and scenery.

To stage it at all, however, was courageous as the Right Bank audience saw the theme as a challenge to law and order and traditional society in general. It was hissed and booed on the opening night, most of all when the maids decided to murder their mistress. Pressure was put on Jouvet to stop the play which was nevertheless performed ninety-two times. *Les Bonnes* eventually became identified with the Absurdist movement when a less bowdlerised version was produced on the Left Bank in 1954 before a successful run abroad.

In 1949, *Haute Surveillance* was also presented on the Right Bank. Packed with underworld slang, it inverted traditional moral and religious values. The black murderer, Boule de Neige, was the most admired man in a system whereby crime led to a sort of State of Grace. The programme notes themselves were written to shock. Describing the play, Genet said: 'An almost fabulous murderer dominates another, less brilliant one who himself astonishes a thief. This prestige draws its strength from the very origin of seduction.'

Haute Surveillance, with its homosexual transvestite character, Alice, received execrable notices from critics, one of whom described it as 'an intellectual urinal'. Cocteau, Sartre and De Beauvoir led defence of the play while the actor, Robert Hossein, who played the role of the thief, Lefranc, provided a sympathetic portrait of Genet whom, he said, was 'full of the gentle madness of childhood'.

According to Hossein, Genet paid particular attention to the scenery and costumes and took pleasure in shaving the actors' heads himself for their convict roles.

'He was very dandified, very elegant, wrapped up in a camel hair coat tightly drawn in at the waist,' Hossein recalled in his autobiography. 'He laughed at the childish tricks he played on us and went into brief towering rages. His moods were vulnerable to the pains and blessings of this world.'

While Genet was 'sensitive to beauty, luxury, haute cuisine and good wine', in Hossein's words, he lived in the slum working-class areas around the Bastille, choosing his Arab homosexual friends from brutal working-class company. He was also afraid of being arrested for some minor offence and changed his hotel rooms frequently, telling the managers not to give a forwarding address.

Genet, who wrote five books inspired by his experience of homosexuality and criminality by 1950, was staggered by the public attention caused by Sartre's 600-page *Saint Genet* and temporarily gave up writing altogether until *Le Balcon* was performed by a private London theatre club in 1956. Set in a brothel in which characters act out their fantasies, the play could not be performed in France at the time because of censorship, but, only four years later, Peter Brook staged it in Paris. Genet liked neither the staging nor costumes.

A year before that Paris production, Genet's *Les Nègres* was produced on the Left Bank by Roger Blin. An all-black troupe of actors played whites as seen by blacks, an improvisation on Sartre's idea that 'how the Other sees us conditions identity'. Ionesco walked out of the first-night presentation but, in a rare meeting shortly afterwards, Genet asked him why.

'Because the blacks were killing the whites and I did not want to be killed,' Ionesco said.

'Ah, but it's so good to be killed,' Genet replied.

By then, Genet had no need to write to keep out of prison and wrote little for publication until his anti-Extreme Right play, *Les Paravents*, caused a controversy in 1966. But before his semi-retirement, he made it clear that he still hated society.

'Because it has treated me cruelly, odiously, ever since I began to breathe', he said. 'Social order is maintained at the price of an infernal curse which strikes people of whom the vilest is a thousand times closer to me than any virtuous well-off bourgeois. Everybody knows I am a homosexual . . . a man, who by his very nature, refuses to enter the system for which the entire world is organised.'

Genet wrote for revenge, but Samuel Beckett wrote to escape depression. As a loner from both a social and literary viewpoint, the Dublin-born protestant playwright does not fit easily in the legacy of Saint-Germain except by association. He was no youth cult figure, as he was forty-seven when *En attendant Godot* was staged in its original French version in 1953. Age, though, was less relevant than his inability to exploit useful contacts. Hundreds of hopeful writers, singers, actors, cinéastes and poets were attracted to the area because the café life offered direct communication with people of influence. Artistic clans developed like lobby groups who knew where to go and whom to see for a recommendation to someone who mattered. Producers and publishers, including the rapidly growing post-war Editions du Seuil in the rue Jacob, were constantly scouting for new talent, an ideal situation for a self-publicist. The art of making yourself known was to be perfected by the brash young cinema directors of the Nouvelle Vague. This public parading by ambitious, over-confident youngsters was the worst possible scene for the shy, anxiety-ridden Beckett whose conversation has been described as a succession of sighs interrupted by whispers. His belated recognition as a writer, leading to the Nobel prize for literature in 1969, was more like the discovery of an impoverished, misunderstood nineteenth-century Bohemian than a post-war Left Bank success story. Even when he tried to follow the rules, he muffed his chance. Sartre and De Beauvoir took an interest in one of his stories for *Les Temps Modernes*, but Beckett sent only half the manuscript by mistake. That was published but when the Irishman sent the other half, De Beauvoir thought he was trying to pull a fast one. Communications with Saint-Germain's royal couple broke down.

Beckett seemed not so much to be living in Paris as hiding there. In 1928, he taught English at the Ecole Normale Supérieure and became closely associated with James Joyce's circle in Montparnasse which included some influential literary patrons like Nancy Cunard. But his own attempts to establish himself as a writer in the pre-war years were a muddled series of European journeys, visits to Ireland, flashes of poetic genius and a near total inability to sell himself. His first novel, *Murphy*, was published in English in London in 1937, but only after being turned down by forty-two publishers in Britain and the United States whose names Beckett still keeps in a notebook.

Murphy sold poorly but not as badly as the French edition released by Bordas in 1947. Over the next five years the book

A rare photograph of Jean Genet, ex-convict, writer, homosexual. One critic called his play, *Haute Surveillance*, 'an intellectual urinal'

sold only 95 copies out of a 3,000 volume edition. As far as new work was concerned, Beckett was hardly heard of again in a literary sense until 1951 with the publication of *Molloy*, in French, by Les Éditions de Minuit, the avant-garde Saint-Germain publishers who later sponsored the *nouveau roman*. Jean Bruller (Vercors) had unsuccessfully tried to keep the Resistance Press in existence after the war but had to hand over to other interests which were equally adventurous in a literary sense. The company was on the verge of bankruptcy when it accepted *Molloy*, *Malone meurt* and *L'Innomable* for projected simultaneous publication against an advance of 25,000 old francs. Handsome as this sounds, devaluation had brought the franc to such a low ebb that it was barely the equivalent of a labourer's weekly wage. Beckett, who had let his companion, the motherly Suzanne Deschevaux-Dusmesnil to make all the approaches and negotiate the contract, thought the advance would be enough to sink Les Editions de Minuit.

Beckett and Les Editions de Minuit, however, staggered on despite disappointing sales with the writer surviving mainly from translation including work for Unesco. A play, rather than a book, would make him famous, but *En attendant Godot* had a familiar ring of agonising failure about it at first.

During the war, Beckett was active in the Resistance for which he was awarded the Croix de Guerre but was on the run most of the time with his companion, Suzanne Deschevaux-Dusmesnil, who first met Beckett when he was lying on a Paris pavement bleeding from a stab wound inflicted by a petty criminal. Part of the time, the couple hid in the country home of the novelist, Nathalie Sarraute, who gave them the only comfortable bedroom. Beckett returned to Ireland at the Liberation but came back to France with an ambulance unit. From then on he would write first in French.

A visit to his London publishers to collect what he hoped would be substantial royalties from *Murphy* had been a shock as the book sold barely 600 copies in nine years. As a result, he placed his hopes in play-writing as an antidote to depression and lack of self-confidence. His still-to-be performed *Eleuthéria* was completed in 1946.

'Life at that time was too demanding, too terrible and I thought theatre would be a diversion', he told his biographer Deirdre Blair. The experience hardly cheered him up. The manuscript was given to Jean Vilar in 1947 who mislaid it for several months before rejecting it as too long. Beckett refused to cut it although he recognised several years later that it was a bad play with too many characters and an over-complicated plot.

Beckett could not face producers himself. All business arrangements were carried out by his companion, Suzanne Deschevaux-Dumesnil, an intensely practical woman who helped eke out the meagre budget with her needlework.

Suzanne, whom Beckett married in 1961, was seven years older than the writer and was as persistent in trying to sell his work as he was in writing what appeared to be unacceptable

Samuel Beckett, whose first novel, *Murphy*, was turned down by 42
publishers in Britain and the USA

literature. By 1949, at the same time as she was seeing book
publishers, the play's script was turned down by seven mainstream commercial theatre directors, and it was decided to try
the avant-garde circuit. Roger Blin, an actor-director who was
once associated with Antonin Artaud's *Théâtre de la cruauté*, and
with Jean-Louis Barrault during his Surrealist period, was
given both *Eleuthéria* and the recently-finished *En attendant
Godot*.

Eleuthéria had seventeen characters and required a divided stage, elaborate props and complicated lighting. Blin had no money at all of his own and could not think of anyone who owned a theatre suitable enough for such a complex production.

He felt more confident of *Godot* because there were only four characters. 'As they were supposed to be tramps they could wear their own clothes if the worst came to the worst', he said. 'I needed nothing more than a spotlight and a bare branch of a tree for scenery.'

However, not even the adventurous Théâtre des Noctam-bules had any confidence in *Godot* at that time. While Blin's negotiations for other theatres fell through, Suzanne Deschevaux-Dumesnil took Beckett's scripts to more than thirty directors without success. In January 1952, a Ministry of Fine Arts grant enabled *Godot* to make a timid, shortened appearance on radio and it seemed that it might at last be performed publicly at Montparnasse's Théâtre de Poche. When that deal collapsed, Blin obtained the Left Bank Théâtre de Babylone where *Godot* opened in January 1953 in front of a suitably bleak, unheated auditorium in a converted shop where the audience sat on canvas chairs.

Despite a Ministry grant, Blin and Beckett were obliged to make do with a shoe-string budget which indirectly helped a play in which two tramps wait in an atmosphere of stifling boredom for Godot's arrival. Lighting was supplied by three hand-held oil cans with light bulbs inside. The only piece of scenery, a tree, was made of coat hanger wire covered with paper and rooted in a lump of foam rubber which one of the cast had found on a pavement. The actors were Blin's friends but this meant that he could not pick and choose. Three weeks before the opening night, the actor playing Lucky had to be replaced because he was incapable of memorising his part. Everything pointed to a first-night catastrophe when the actors playing Estragon and Vladimir, baffled by an actionless text, frequently mixed up scenes in rehearsal while Beckett watched with increasing dismay.

Unable to stand the strain of opening night, Beckett went to stay in the country at a small house he was building with an inheritance from his mother. The motherly Suzanne Deschevaux-Dusmesnil was left to handle his business affairs and correspondence. He returned to the city a fortnight later, famous at the age of forty-seven.

At first, the play was not so much a success for its literary quality but because of its notoriety. A night out at the Théâtre de Babylone quickly became a 'must' for the fashionable Tout Paris from the Right Bank. But much of the audience came to experience innovation which Adamov and Ionesco had pioneered. Although there was heckling and even fighting, the dominant mood was in favour of the play which was soon to prove that a demand for change was not confined to the Left Bank. At the end of the year, Blin took *Godot* on a triumphant tour of provincial France, Switzerland, Italy and Germany, before an English translation created the same phenomenon in Britain and the United States.

Inevitably, on the Left Bank, differences of opinion on Absurdist Theatre were political as well as cultural. The reaction was inspired by the successes of Brecht's Berliner Ensemble which reinvigorated the Marxist debate on commitment in literature. Adamov was the first to break ranks with the Absurdists even though he had once rejoiced at being part of what he called 'a gang' for the first time in his life. After the success of *Le Ping Pong* in 1955 – the play was well received and was performed 150 times – he returned to his Marxist roots and wrote *Paolo Paoli*. The turn-of-the-century fable used the trade in butterflies as a metaphor for an attack on world capitalism. Avantgarde theatre, he said, was 'deceitful'. Its techniques were 'void and useless if the author does not put himself at the service of an ideology'.

Only one ideology qualified, of course, and the Left Bank's playwrights were identified as Brechtians or non-Brechtians, each with their teams of pro or anti-Marxist critics. *The Observer*'s Kenneth Tynan summed up the conflict as 'the Cold War in little'. The casualties were often accidental. Sartre was attacked for not having brought Brecht to public notice earlier, an allegation that hid an oblique attack on Sartre's reliability as a Marxist. Jean Vilar, director of Le Théâtre Nationale Populaire, was reproached for a lack of purity in a production of *Mother Courage* that had been staged five years before the polemic broke out. Jean-Louis Barrault, who tried for years to put on Brecht plays, was among directors now considered politically untrustworthy by the Communist Party and excluded from bidding for Brecht's performance rights.

The rights were held by Robert Voisin, editor of the *Revue du Théâtre Populaire*, a pro-Marxist publication edited in Saint-Germain's rue Bonaparte. Voisin's decisions on who should produce Brecht amounted to an official accolade of Marxist purity. Other contributors also played an important role, including Bernard Dort, who taught at the Institut d'Etudes Théâtrales at the Sorbonne and trained young students in Brechtian orthodoxy. Eulogistic articles on Brecht, written for the same magazine, enhanced the reputation of an outstanding intellectual, Roland Barthes whose book, *Le degré Zéro de l'écriture*, in 1953, marked a new approach to literary criticism. His influence would be crucial in destroying young people's fascination with Sartre during the Sixties.

But Brecht's success as pure theatre also made an indirect contribution to the decline of pocket 'fringe' productions on the Left Bank. State-subsidised theatre became a fashionable political cause, an attitude which would be accelerated and refined by André Malraux when he became Culture Minister in 1959. The cold, badly-lit theatres of the Left Bank, with their improvised sets and threadbare productions, were gradually boycotted by audiences spoilt for comfort and choice by the liberal distribution of Government money. The reckless, cheap, off-beat theatrical outlets that might have sponsored a creative post-Absurdism disappeared.

The argument between Brechtians and non-Brechtians was a fragment of a much wider political debate over Marxist theory and Left-wing unity in general. In 1956, the Russian invasion of

Hungary and the subsequent Kruschev revelations on Stalinist crimes to the Soviet Congress had a shattering impact on the French Communist Party. Although stronger than ever in Parliament where Proportional Representation in the 1956 general elections had given it more than 150 seats, the Party's intellectual support was scattered by outside events. The upheaval made it impossible to identify the exact leanings of many fellow travellers, notably Simone Signoret and Yves Montand who went to the Soviet Union at the height of the controversy and met Kruschev to explain the dismay of the French Left. Louis Aragon, of course, remained loyal to the Party hardline but was ostracised by many intellectuals who blamed him for deliberately hiding the true nature of Soviet leadership. Non-Party or dissident Marxist opinion-makers in Saint-Germain staked a claim to being the holders of the true faith. They founded a magazine, *Arguments*, published by Les Editions de Minuit, which rallied the young generation of intellectuals whose education at the Grandes Ecoles and Universities was completed at the height of Sartre's fame in the previous decade. Roland Barthes, then thirty-four, was a leading contributor.

For the next six years, the centre of independent Marxist debate shifted from *Les Temps Modernes* to *Arguments*. Sartre was isolated apart from a ferociously loyal entourage led by Simone de Beauvoir.

Just before the Budapest uprising, Sartre seemed to be moving nearer Party membership and had written a play, *Nékrassov*, a satirical comedy, which ridiculed anti-Communist psychosis among the French middle classes. The play was also an intensely personal comment on his self-doubts, which his biographer, Francis Jeanson, summed up as that of 'mongrel, impostor, and traitor – that is intellectual.'

But Sartre's internal crisis at his impotent social and political role was paralleled by more damaging concern for his health. Doctors had advised him that he risked a general breakdown through overwork and drug abuse. As a result, his work rate dropped and he depended increasingly on De Beauvoir for his business arrangements. Writing of the years between 1954 and

1958, De Beauvoir recalled that Sartre was told that if he continued to 'work against the clock' he would die in six months.

'In 1954, death had become an intimate presence', she wrote in her *Mémoires*. 'But, from now on, it possessed me'.

During 1956, a tired, self-doubting Sartre chose what Francis Jeanson called a 'semi-rupture' with the Communist Party. Derided by Party hardliners like Aragon and ignored by the Marxist liberals of *Arguments*, Sartre seemed a spent force. The Left itself was disintegrating across-the-board even though the 1956 general elections had voted in a Socialist administration led by Guy Mollet. Pressured from the extreme Right by a new petit-bourgeois political movement known as Poujadisme, Mollet's Socialist government discredited itself with ultra-conservative initiatives such as the Sucz operation of 1956 and the decision to send young conscripts to fight against Algerian independence as the war intensified.

Over the next six years, France would be as divided as during the Nazi Occupation with cultural movements reflecting a general splintering in national attitudes. In 1959, at the very height of the crisis in the wake of De Gaulle's takeover and a threat of Civil War, attention was concentrated on the arrival of *La Nouvelle Vague* of young film directors. At the Cannes festival of that year, François Truffaut with *Les 400 coups* and Alain Resnais with *Hiroshima mon Amour* both won prizes for their first full-length feature films. The event was followed by a rush of new directors with low-budget films. The fresh approach would be exploited as proof that Gaullism was synonymous with national renewal. The enthusiasm with which the New Wave would be greeted in France contributed to revolutions in technique and production control even inside Hollywood. But the irony of the New Wave's dominant choice of subject was politically significant only inside France.

For the most part, New Wave directors' preoccupations were aseptic and apolitical, concentrating on their own selfish problems and those of well-off middle-class young people. The Algerian war and the return of a military-led government which seemed to echo Pétain's Vichy administration were not even a distant echo in their scripts. The New Wave simply turned its back on France's traumas. In the context of the fifteen years of political debate that had animated the Left Bank since the Liberation, it was a detachment of special significance. La Nouvelle Vague was Saint-Germain's last cultural legacy, shaped and guided by young men and women who had grown up among the post-war political turmoil and debate of the quartier's cellar clubs, cafés and publishing houses.

9

Hiroshima mon amour

Cinema played a powerful role in the legend and reality of Saint-Germain-des-Prés but was the last of the main cultural streams to undergo a Left Bank transformation. By the time the Nouvelle Vague of cinema directors such as François Truffaut, Jean-Luc Godard and Alain Resnais were producing their sensational work at the end of the Fifties, the liberating forces released earlier in the decade had become accepted practice in literature, theatre and popular music. The political, social and moral innovations preached by Jean-Paul Sartre were no longer the reserve of Left Bank discussion but standard reference points for middle-class debate throughout the country.

Painting and classical music, neither of which needed the stimulus of Saint-Germain to continue progress which had started decades before, added their experiments to a climate that made France, culturally at least, Europe's most progressive nation. After De Gaulle's *coup d'état* in May 1958, André Malraux, as Cultural Minister, reinforced this adventurous atmosphere through State subsidies that made Left Bank ideals accessible throughout the provinces and to all classes.

Inevitably, Gaullist administrators seized on a coincidental revolution in cinema technique and subject to make it appear at home and abroad that the Nouvelle Vague was part of a vigorous New France induced by the dynamic forces of Gaullism alone. The claim was true inasmuch as the dominant intellectuals of Saint-Germain never took cinema sufficiently seriously, missing the point that it was the most rapid access to popular audiences.

Sartre's attempts to become a scriptwriter failed several times after commissions to adapt other people's works, and he never tried to use the medium as a method of getting his own ideas across to the proletariat he idealised.

Camus went even further, rejecting films as frivolous and refusing offers to write for the cinema. If the Communist Party's intellectuals had been alert enough to seize opportunities offered by film, they might have stimulated a reply, but Aragon and Triolet were also totally devoted to the power of the written word.

Sartre and his followers did, on the other hand, have enormous indirect influence. It was the children of Existentialism, the middle-class youth who had debated cultural rebellion in Sartre's shadow at Le Tabou in the late Forties, who created the Nouvelle Vague. By 1958 they were men and women in their late twenties and mid-thirties who had emerged from the naïve revolt in the cafés of Saint-Germain to become frustrated creators. A minority remained resolutely Left wing but most had reacted against Sartre's Marxism, not least because his anti-Americanism clashed with their youthful idealism of Hollywood. The Nouvelle Vague directors were observers of the Left Bank's changing values, and their films were to project the mood of Saint-Germain towards the end of its influential period – a sort of *mal de siècle* or disillusioned vision of modern France that still, to a large extent, forms the image of the country abroad.

By the time the Nouvelle Vague emerged, the great ideals of the Liberation or progressive Marxism had long been submerged by the more superficial priorities of a meretricious Parisian middle class who themselves foreshadowed a future section of French society interested mainly by consumerism, egotistical personal relationships and professional success.

From the pre-war days, when Jacques Prévert and his brother, Pierre, had established their *bande* in the Café de Flore, Saint-Germain had been cinema territory. Finance was in the production houses on the Champs Elysées but the ideas and talent were on the Left Bank. Scriptwriters and directors, like the Prévert brothers, grafted naturally on to the huge pool of acting talent at Left Bank schools sponsored by well-known stars and directors. The ambition to be a theatre or cinema actor was an automatic rite of passage into Saint-Germain's youth élite. Among the more literary-minded young regulars at cellar clubs, journalism, particularly as a theatre or film critic, was seen as the natural preparation for directing or scriptwriting.

By the time Simone Signoret first visited the Flore in 1941, just before Sartre's repatriation from a PoW camp, the area was already a vast waiting-room for the stage-struck. Most of the established figures that attracted them, however, were part of a cinema production system which resolutely resisted reforms after the war. These personalities, such as the leading script-writers, Pierre Bost and Jean Aurenche, who dazzled starlets like the young Signoret, later became the targets of the Nouvelle Vague and were demolished mercilessly in critical articles when impatience for a youth-oriented breakthrough began to wear thin in the Fifties.

Although they were rarely directly attacked, Sartre and De Beauvoir were strongly identified with cinema conservatism because of their lack of vision. The attitude of two people so involved with reform for reform's sake was inexplicable as both were passionately fond of films.

During their long cycling tour of the South of France before its occupation by the Nazis, they went as often as possible to the cinema to see American films banned in the Occupied Zone. Hollywood exercised a strong hold on popular imagery, representing hope. In contrast the couple were able to observe the

Simone Signoret, playing in *La Casque d'Or* (1952). She was a key figure in Saint-Germain

formidable use the Nazis made of cinema propaganda, notably with the anti-semitic film, *Le Juif Süss*.

Going secretly to post-curfew showings of Hollywood films in clandestine Left Bank ciné clubs was seen by De Beauvoir and Sartre as an act of intellectual resistance completed by a boycott of all German films, overtly racist or not. Immediately after the war, before the Cold War forced intellectuals to take sides, the couple were acutely aware of the impact of Hollywood and American ideals on their former pupils and disciples in Saint-Germain. For the majority, the living, dynamic vision of contemporary America was always more powerful than the literary promises of a distant, just Marxism.

The French are often said to take cinema more seriously than any other nation, a fact attributable to the origins of the invention and a feeling of guilt at neglect during the First World War when Hollywood overtook the once highly productive French studios to become the world's biggest film factory. By the Second World War some of the damage had been repaired by an eccentric film collector, Henri Langlois, who had founded a Cinémathèque and fanatically gathered all the early film he could lay his hands on.

Langlois reconstituted a national heritage that became part of the cultural stakes during the war.

A heavily built, single-minded man, Langlois established his Cinémathèque on the Right Bank but the preservation of pre-war films was a Left Bank affair.

Alexandre Astruc who later had a strong influence in updating ideas in the cinema as a critic and director, recalls that during the war Langlois recruited his disciples at the Café de Flore, where he would arrive with boxed reels of film. He then sought out young students whose parents lived in the suburbs and asked them to take care of the films.

'There was no doubt in our minds that those films which he wanted to bury in our gardens were the real issue of the war,' Astruc said. As a literature student with a journalist father, Astruc had been attracted to the Flore for the same reasons as Signoret – its cinema connections. He later accepted Camus's invitation to become cinema critic on *Combat* 'because I saw journalism as a way into films'.

In 1943, when Astruc, then twenty, first went to the Flore, cinema had no frontiers provided by opposing generations. The groups of young students who would later watch at least two or three films a day, usually at the Cinémathèque, had not yet been seduced by Hollywood ideals that created the belief that American directors were free to choose their subjects while the French film world revered outdated conventions. But even in 1943, the main actors of the future divisions were already present.

Two of the main reactionaries were scriptwriters, Jean Aurenche and Pierre Bost, both long-established residents of

Saint-Germain and among its most active personalities after the war.

They were indirectly associated with Sartre's entourage through one of the philosopher's unconditional admirers, Jacques-Laurent Bost, Pierre Bost's brother. Aurenche, like the Bost brothers (members of a family of ten) was part of Gallimard's NRF stable. All three were novelists of quality, a factor which made Aurenche and Bost the most sought-after post-war adapters.

They were also among the most highly-paid scenario writers who inspired a stream of followers convinced that a good film was an adaptation of a French literary classic. This worthy approach was well rewarded as a top scriptwriter received up to ten million francs for a script, at least a fifth of overall production costs. Aurenche and Bost became experts at literal adaptations of classics by Stendhal and Colette which rigorously respected the style of dialogue of the original work.

As both Sartre and Camus openly praised their literary skill, Aurenche and Bost were among the demi-gods of Saint-Germain during the late Forties and were particularly admired by Boris Vian.

Despite their wealth and prestige, the scriptwriters mixed just as easily with the famous at the Flore as the struggling bohemians, like Anne-Marie Cazalis and Alexandre Astruc, who pioneered the Montana Hotel bar in the rue Saint Benoît as the headquarters of cinema struck youngsters when the Flore became too well-known.

Film directors like Jean Renoir and Marcel Carné, however, remained remote, almost canonised figures of a distant High Church, whereas Jean Cocteau merged himself wholly into the area's cinematic ambitions. He was struck by the forceful Astruc, one of the most typically hedonist figures of the late Forties before the more serious-minded group of critics from the magazine, *Les Cahiers du Cinéma* introduced a much more sober view of cinema professionals. A tall, red-bearded man, Astruc's drinking ability and fierce hangovers made Vian remark that the future director 'could fillet himself alive'.

It was Astruc who directed the 1949 film, *Ulysses et les mauvaises rencontres*, the 'young people's practical joke' co-authored by Jean Cau and Anne-Marie Cazalis that brought together individuals as diverse as Jean Cocteau and Juliette Gréco. The never-to-be-screened film was one of the earliest indications that a new spring of adventurous film talent was available outside the rigid commercial circuit.

A year before *Ulysses*, Astruc coined the term '*camera stylo*' in an article that was a forerunner of the demands by the *Cahiers* group in the Fifties for a '*cinema d'auteur*' in which, as Astruc put it, films would be 'written like books' – an image that particularly appealed to André Malraux.

Astruc's personal attitude illustrated the increasing apoliticism of the former Tabou group. At the end of the war the young journalist had published a novel at Gallimard's and felt part of the Sartre-Camus cult. By the time *Ulysses* was made he told friends that he was rejecting political commitment, the start of a steady drift back to his bourgeois Right-wing origins.

Astruc was also a pioneer of the arrogantly confident self-publicity that was so important in launching the Nouvelle Vague. He told Boris Vian that he saw himself as having 'a special genius like that of Orson Welles and Shakespeare joined together'. By repeating this message to dozens of producers, he raised enough finance for a low-budget feature film, *Le Rideau cramoisi*, in 1952, a forerunner of the cheap films of the Nouvelle Vague that by-passed the high cost production system.

Le Rideau cramoisi was a middle-class social drama involving two principal actors, one of them the relatively unknown Anouk Aimée, and cost only nine million francs, the salary of one scriptwriter on the normal circuit. Despite the union and distribution obstacles that normally shackled any independent projects, *Le Rideau cramoisi* was shown on the Champs Elysées, inspiring a rush of cinema vocations and concentration on young middle-class priorities that became the hallmark of the Nouvelle Vague.

In the terms of the contemporary cinema industry, Astruc had broken down the doors of the Bastille.

Only about a hundred films were made each year and most of them were entrusted to directors whose reputations had been established two or three decades before. An aspirant director was expected to wait twenty or thirty years before being given his chance after apprenticeship as an assistant. To be entrusted with a film before forty was considered enormous luck.

As post-war governments had been unable to stop the flood of American films whose entry was linked to the distribution of Marshall aid, sponsors in French filming felt in much the same position as during the war when Vichy saw encouragement of traditional culture as the main hope of undermining German influence. Relying on classical literature for their inspiration, serious film-makers shied clear of provocation. Great and divisive issues like the war and colonialism were ignored. The threat of Government censorship or that of a withdrawal of State subsidies ensured conformity, reinforced by the Communist controlled technicians' unions who also discouraged political controversy. Not even the introduction of active pro-Marxist militant stars like Gérard Philipe, who lived in Saint-Germain, or the fellow-travelling Yves Montand disturbed the complacency. Political sterility would last for two decades longer than sexual taboos.

Film historians date the rallying cry of the Nouvelle Vague to 1954 when François Truffaut, then only twenty-two, wrote an attack in the magazine, *Les Cahiers du Cinéma*, on the rigidity of the contemporary production and direction system that summed up a debate going on among the contributors since *Les Cahiers* was founded in 1951. The effect of Truffaut's article took some time to be felt, but in the same year a publishing phenomenon occurred which created public acceptance of the dominant themes of the Nouvelle Vague with its emphasis on the crises of middle-class youth.

In 1954, when Simone de Beauvoir won the Prix Goncourt for *Les Mandarins*, a *roman à clef* which relaunched public interest in Saint-Germain-des-Prés, and Jean-Paul Sartre made his first enthusiastic visit to Moscow, a nineteen-year-old woman caused a sensation by publishing a slim novel, *Bonjour Tristesse*. Françoise Sagan, the author, was an authentic product of the Left Bank, the little sister of a generation that had grown up around Le Tabou. By 1954, the centre of literary discussions had shifted, as far as Sagan was concerned, to the Village bar between the churches of Saint Sulpice and Saint-Germain. When *Bonjour Tristesse* was published, the quartier was already plunged into a new, purely literary argument.

A group of Right-wing writers calling themselves the Hussards was vigorously opposing Sartre's generation, whom they called the Grognards. The philosopher was criticised for imposing unacceptable standards of political commitment on the novel, an attack which preceded the more important emergence of the Nouveau Roman, devoted to a totally new approach to the art of writing novels.

There was nothing political about Sagan's novel but, despite her Press-created image of a reckless teenager driving fast cars in her bare feet, she was one of Sartre's political admirers and her rebellion against her rich middle-class Parisian family was inspired by existentialism. She had just emerged from a particularly intense existentialist phase during which she met both Sartre and De Beauvoir and was a close friend of Juliette Gréco and her circle. Sagan's book, whose title was taken from a poem by Paul Eluard, a Communist and close friend of Louis Aragon, appalled the middle classes which took it as proof that the corrupting forces of Saint-Germain-des-Prés were now being made available to a mass young public. *Le Deuxième Sexe* was already five years old but the novel was considered more damaging as it was easy to read and added to the myth that youthful sexual liberation was an essential element of social and literary success.

Thirty years later, reflecting on the scandal that made her overnight one of the highest paid writers in the country, Françoise Sagan was still puzzled by the affair, particularly as a much more provocative book, published by Jean-Jacques Pauvert, the sado-masochistic *Histoire d'O*, written anonymously by another woman, went unnoticed. Sagan said she felt

Gérard Philipe, pin-up of the 1940s, here playing the lead role in Raymond Radiguet's *Le Diable au Corps* (1948)

at the time she had done nothing more than repeat 'something already in the air' but which had never been expressed in a novel. An attempt to stir up scandal had not been premeditated, she said.

'I suppose I told the story of a young girl who slept with a boy without becoming pregnant and without feeling unhappy afterwards. The book was judged immoral because, at the time, lovemaking was a sin. Now it is different. Lovemaking is compulsory,' she said.

Bonjour Tristesse was among the most successful first novels of all time, quickly selling two million copies in France alone, but Sagan, despite the exaggerations of her personal behaviour, maintained a more responsible attitude than many of her admirers. Far from adopting the apoliticism that was becoming part of the atmosphere of the creative Left Bank, she was closely linked with protests against the Algerian war, identifying with

Sartre. As a result, extreme Right-wing terrorists tried to kill her with a bomb.

Once *Bonjour Tristesse* had established an image in the public mind, the banalisation of the moral iconoclasm of Saint-Germain was taken up by the cinema and accelerated with startling speed. Youth and the power to shock became values in themselves. Sagan's success sent a wave of panic through the over-thirties who had followed traditional creative routes where maturity was supposed to appear near middle age. In the background was a stunningly sterile and uninspiring national political debate. The public was primed for the arrival in 1956 of Roger Vadim's film *Et Dieu créa la Femme*. Vadim was twenty-eight but the star, Brigitte Bardot, was just twenty-one with a career of sixteen films behind her since her debut at eighteen.

Vadim, a society-conscious, former photographer for *Paris Match* can be given the credit for sparking off the Nouvelle Vague with *Et Dieu créa la Femme*, his first film. A vulgarisation of the intellectual and literary messages of *Le Deuxième Sexe* and *Bonjour Tristesse*, the film had a poor plot but its romantic, liberated view of Saint Tropez, Saint-Germain-des-Prés's summer playground, had an enormous impact on popular audiences. The film was cheaply made and was a tremendous commercial success, particularly in the United States. Later Jane Fonda, the American actress who married Vadim, described the film as 'a great leap forward for women's liberation'. In France it was a demonstration to convention-bound producers that quick money could be made from cost-cutting films with a young image.

Middle-class audiences were shocked not so much by the eroticism of the film, in which an overtly pleasure-loving young woman plays off three lovers, all of them brothers, but the statement that a woman had the right to choose her own way of life.

Bardot herself came from a sheltered, bourgeois family in the sixteenth arrondissement of Paris and at fourteen danced in a

Françoise Sagan. Her first novel, *Bonjour Tristesse*, which sold two million copies was one of the most successful of all time

specially written ballet to illustrate an exhibition at her mother's hat shop, a dance which led to her portrait being used in a fashion magazine, *Jardin des Modes*. Soon afterwards the magazine *Elle* featured Bardot on the cover but respected her parents' wishes not to publish her name and identified her only as BB, her French nickname ever since.

Vadim, who was working as the assistant of the director Marc Allégret was chosen to approach Bardot's parents about a possible film career. Despite his charm, Bardot's parents were appalled at the arrival of a young man whom they rejected as a Zazou. As the first meeting was in 1951, their identification of

Vadim with a defunct wartime youth movement showed how dimly the echoes of Saint-Germain's existentialism were heard in the more sheltered areas of Paris's West End.

Bardot was fifteen and more than susceptible to Vadim's glamour, but her film career did not start until eighteen when her reluctant parents agreed to let the couple marry at a lavish ceremony which was as conservatively alien to Saint-Germain as the new hedonism was to the sixteenth arrondissement.

In *Et Dieu créa la Femme*, Bardot looks more sixteen than twenty-one and Vadim said he wanted 'to reconstitute the climate of an era, the psychosis of our generation after the war through Brigitte'. According to opinion polls, Bardot's behaviour in the film was still very much a minority view. Even twenty years later, surveys showed that more than two out of three Frenchwomen still prized virginity and went to the altar without having gone to bed with their future husbands. The proportion was probably much higher in 1956 but moral outcry against the film fell flat. Parliamentarians and Churchmen who railed against the film's moral liberalism were simply ignored. Almost overnight, tolerance seemed to have come into fashion, at least as regards sexual matters. Even the Communist Party could not prevent the working classes from idolising Brigitte Bardot, a product of the accursed bourgeoisie.

Vadim had been inspired in his quest for production backing by the enthusiasm of his close friend, Alexandre Astruc, by then on his second low budget film, *Les Mauvaises Rencontres*. Astruc was the centre of Left Bank admiration for his cheek in squeezing money out of a hide-bound production system. Vadim now became an object of envy as well. The group of critics at *Les Cahiers du Cinéma*, who spent much of their time meeting Left Bank cinéastes in Saint-Germain's Le Nuage bar to attack an unjust production organisation, now had few excuses for delaying their own careers as directors. They had been talking for a long time as the adventure really started in 1940 when Sartre's essay, *L'Imaginaire*, caught the eye of a young journalist, André Bazin, who became the most praised film critic in French history and 'godfather' of the Nouvelle Vague.

Brigitte Bardot. Her film career began at eighteen when her parents reluctantly allowed her to marry Roger Vadim

Bazin's career was also indirectly influenced by Albert Camus who, in 1950, led opposition within Gallimard to the continued publication of *La Revue du Cinéma*, then Paris's most influential film publication. Its demise resulted in the founding of *Cahiers* by Bazin and another Left-wing critic, Jacques Doniol-Valcroze. Ironically, they found a freer atmosphere for their discussions of cinema reforms in the Right Bank offices of the

Brigitte Bardot's film career was launched in Roger Vadim's *Et Dieu créa la femme* (1956) in which she starred with Curt Jurgens and Jean-Louis Trintignant

Cahiers on the Champs Elysées than in their social haunts of Saint-Germain.

Bazin, a Left-wing Catholic, was one of the most loved personalities of Saint-Germain-des-Prés, closely associated with its community of young people whom he helped both by his kindness and his natural ability to inspire a team. While the eccentric Henri Langlois saved the raw material of French film history by his fanaticism at the Cinémathèque, Bazin nurtured its new generation of creators by a combination of generosity and intellectual brilliance.

By the time he died in 1959 at the age of forty-one, he had led the Nouvelle Vague of young directors out of a messy rebellion against old standards into a position of strength where they offered an alternative cinema that caught the mood of a generation moving into the Sixties.

What distinguished Bazin from most other Left Bank intellectuals was his down to earth approach to popularising culture among the working classes. His theories on cinema, which earned him homilies at his death from the world's leading film-makers, were inspired by the reaction from popular audiences he went out to meet on their home ground.

Bazin, who came to Paris before the war from La Rochelle where his father was a bank clerk, studied as a primary school teacher in the suburbs and was associated with Langlois's campaign to preserve the French cinema heritage during the war, founding his own underground cinema club on the Left bank, where Sartre and De Beauvoir often risked arrest during the curfew to attend showings.

A prolific critic, who wrote for most leading magazines with an interest in cinema, Bazin admired Sartre as a theorist. But he had been educated by Christian Brothers and was strongly influenced by writers at *Esprit*, a magazine seen as the liberal conscience of French Catholics. It was published on the third floor of 27 rue Jacob, headquarters of the new Editions du Seuil which moved there in 1945. Although independent of the publishing house, the magazine was such an important rallying point for Left-wing Catholics that it was often rumoured that Seuil itself was financed by the Jesuits. As *Esprit*'s film critic, Bazin was at the centre of meetings between a new generation of progressive writers who proved that atheistic existentialism by no means dominated Saint-Germain.

Bazin's main post-war responsibility was the cinema section of a movement called Travail et Culture in the nearby rue des Beaux Arts. The Left-wing association, with its strong Catholic current, became a refuge and an educational institute for students and young workers in the area. In the broad-minded years after the Liberation, Travail et Culture maintained links with the Communist Party and received government subsidies to enable it to spread a serious cultural message on the factory floor and university campus.

Soon a much-admired critic, Bazin was associated with Jean Cocteau's Objectif '49, the Saint-Germain film club which sponsored Le Festival du film maudit at Biarritz in 1950. The festival, which showed films excluded from the newly-founded Cannes festival, was a turning point in French cinema as it aired divisions between traditionalists and innovators – the precursors of the Nouvelle Vague. On the day the Biarritz festival started, Bazin's son, Florent, was born. But by then Bazin had all but adopted an unruly young man, François Truffaut, in an act of kindness that was to have important repercussions for French cinema.

Truffaut has said that everything good in his life happened after he met Bazin as a sixteen-year-old. At the time the critic was twenty-seven, but he became Truffaut's surrogate father. Truffaut's real father was an architect and his mother a secretary. But he was an unwanted child and had taken refuge in films. He met Bazin during one of the critic's Sunday film club meetings in 1948 when Truffaut was running his own rival Cercle des Cinémanes. Truffaut asked Bazin to change the dates of his meetings but after a day's negotiations, the future Nouvelle Vague director accepted work at Travail et Culture alongside Bazin and his wife.

Despite his poor health, absorbing family life and his often precarious income, Bazin devoted much of the rest of his life to saving Truffaut from the psychological consequences of his Parisian childhood and his own troublesome personality. Truffaut's ciné club had got into such deep debt that his father committed him to a reform school, but Bazin arranged his release. Later, Truffaut volunteered to serve in Indo-China and deserted. He was sent to prison for six months. During this period, his real parents relinquished responsibility to the Bazin couple. The way was open for Truffaut's eventual entry into the *Cahiers du Cinema* alongside its most influential critics and future Nouvelle Vague directors, Jean-Luc Godard, Claude Chabrol, Jacques Rivette and Eric Rohmer.

Les Cahiers du Cinéma is now seen more as a campaign than a magazine, a propaganda sheet for specialists in which the director's role in film-making is all-important. But between its

François Truffaut. After Reformatory and deserting the army in Indo-China, Truffaut became a leading film director of the Nouvelle Vague

creation in 1951 and the emergence of the Nouvelle Vague eight years later, it was also one of the most enlightening focuses in the shift of influence and values between two generations.

After the demise of Gallimard's *La Revue du Cinéma* in 1950, hastened by Camus and Sartre, Cocteau's Festival du Film Maudit inspired the industrialist, Léonid Kiégel, to sponsor a new magazine, *Les Cahiers du Cinéma*. Jacques Doniol-Valcroze, former assistant editor of the Gallimard magazine, was made joint editor with Bazin. Both of them were working at the time as film critics for the pro-Socialist *France Observateur* which had rapidly established itself as the main weckly Press outlet for the non-Communist Left.

The *Cahiers* was published on the Champs-Elysées among

the production houses but the staff still crossed the Seine to mix with the film fanatics at the Montana Hotel and later at the Nuage Bar, near the avant-garde publishing firm, les Editions de Minuit. These casual meetings kept them in touch with the actors who were to form the repertory company of the Nouvelle Vague – Jean-Paul Belmondo, Jean-Claude Brialy, Catherine Deneuve, Anna Karina, Jeanne Moreau, Jean-Pierre Léaud and Bernadette Lafont who emerged from the Left Bank acting schools and cabarets. Links were also maintained with the more political Left Bank group of professional cinéastes, notably Alain Resnais, Agnès Varda and Chris Marker, whose debating headquarters were at Les Editions du Seuil in the rue Jacob.

Doniol-Valcroze was barely thirty when the first edition of *Les Cahiers du Cinéma* was published in April 1951 but was considered another generation by the young contributors.

'I was ten years older than Truffaut, for instance, but I had been in the Resistance,' he said. 'Talking about it pissed off the youngsters who felt it was like papa talking about Verdun. As the boss, I had to resist a drift to the Right as some of them were frankly right wing. Their hero was the American director, Sam Fuller, and they admired the films of the American Right. As there was no question of censorship of political views, we sought a balance by exploiting what might be called the Christian side of Chabrol and Rohmer.

'What joined us together was the immense work needed to have cinema recognised as an art form during this period. This would be impossible to imagine today. The essential thing was to impose the metteur-en-scène,' he said.

The campaign overcame serious personality differences. Jean-Luc Godard, the youngest of the group, was contemptuous of François Truffaut's more limited imagination. Truffaut, whose articulate openness counterbalanced Godard's long silences, eventually fell out with the voluble Chabrol, a Paris chemist's son who was perhaps most typical of the easy-going Saint-Germain generation. Doniol-Valcroze, meanwhile, felt that Rohmer was too arrogant and the couple were often at odds.

The real divisions were based on theories. Rohmer, the same

age as Doniol-Valcroze, considered himself leader of the impatient youngsters made up of Godard, Chabrol and Truffaut who called themselves 'Hitchcocko-Hawksiens', as a tribute to two of their favourite directors.

Bazin, Doniol-Valcroze and another future Nouvelle Vague director, Pierre Kast, who had a respectable series of short films behind him, wanted more thoughtful change that would preserve the quality of tradition but increase what Bazin described as 'the personal touch'. For nearly a year, the prudent reformists delayed publication of François Truffaut's 1954 article 'Une Certaine Tendance du Cinéma Français' with its reckless attack on old values.

Truffaut was twenty-two when it appeared and his real cinema experience had been a brief period in the Ministry of Agriculture's cinematic division which ended in his being sacked.

Truffaut's attack concentrated on demolishing the *cinéma de qualité* represented by the Saint-Germain scriptwriters Jean Aurenche and Pierre Bost. Truffaut demanded the liberation of cinema from literary men – Aurenche and Bost were accused of unfaithfulness, blasphemy and profanity – and encouragement of film authors in the tradition of Jacques Becker, Jean Renoir, Jean Cocteau, Jacques Tati, Robert Bresson and Abel Gance.

In essence the article repeated the more elegant arguments of Astruc, Bazin and Cocteau, but the timing was better. Audiences were becoming bored with the Aurenche–Bost type of adaptation, which had spawned many imitators. Watching these more or less faithful homages to French literary classics had been something of a patriotic duty to balance the influx of Hollywood offerings. By 1954, educated audiences were demanding something more acid.

Had the Nouvelle Vague not emerged, French cinema might have resorted to offerings of commercial sure-fire successes with actors such as Jean Gabin and Fernandel. Truffaut's attack, like all that went before it, was essentially an expression of anger. The money that helped prove that fresh ideas were marketable came from within the *Cahiers*.

The *Cahiers'* contributors thought up several schemes to initiate a breakthrough, including adventurous short productions and 16 mm filming. They considered a cooperative venture with the Left-wing Left Bank group of Resnais, Agnès Varda and Chris Marker. Eventually, the turning point came by chance when Chabrol's wife inherited money from her grandmother and invested 30 million francs in Chabrol's first film, *Le Beau Serge*, which he began shooting at the age of twenty-six.

The film was set in the central French village where Chabrol was sent during the war and where he was known by other young Parisian evacuees for his magic lantern shows. Costs in the village family drama were kept to a minimum using young actors and sparse equipment. With an advance on box-office receipts, he financed his second film, *Les Cousins*, but had to be bailed out by a friendly producer. As a result the two films came out almost simultaneously in 1959. As much interest was shown in how they were made as in the films themselves. Chabrol had no film experience at all apart from writing a brief script for another *Cahiers'* critic-director, Jacques Rivette. Chabrol's other cinema contributions had been writing film biographies for an American company and inventing French titles for American films. He had never handled a camera before and, on his first day's shooting, mistook one of the bolts on the apparatus for an auxiliary lens.

The idea that a journalist could become a full-length feature film director overnight without going through the usual twenty-year apprenticeship as assistant proved *Cahiers'* theories. One after another, like overheated cabs on a rank, the other *Cahiers'* contributors, including the editor Jacques Doniol-Valcroze, found finance for their débuts. Nearly all, though, had to wait until François Truffaut's *400 Coups* made its sensational impact on the 1959 Cannes Festival. Truffaut, then twenty-seven, had married a producer's daughter, Madeleine Morgenstern, which eased problems of raising finance for his autobiographical film.

It was another marginal low-budget production, strongly marked by Truffaut's theories on 'cinema in the first person singular'. Jean Renoir, one of the few old brigade directors the

Nouvelle Vague admired, summed up Truffaut's style by saying it was the product of 'one man alone that looks with an equal eye on the problems of acting, the sound system, the camera. There are no great problems, no small problems'.

Jean-Luc Godard reinforced this personal style in *A bout de Souffle*, released the following year. Among cinéastes the film was less remarkable for the cynical love story between Jean-Paul Belmondo and Jean Seberg than the open mockery of established rules of direction. Godard, feverishly sucking on a cigarette and talking in rapid, sometimes incomprehensible staccato, had to film with available light, including ordinary electric lamps. There was neither enough money to keep rented equipment long enough for normal shooting, nor enough film for careful editing. Godard's own impatience and improvisation surrounded this film with more myth than any other during the Nouvelle Vague. It was said his innovative technique owed much to his anger at being told by his producer that it was too long and that he cut haphazardly when editing, with only length in mind.

The anti-Gaullist magazine, *L'Express*, invented the term 'Nouvelle Vague' and Malraux's Cultural Ministry intensified interest in a new generation that destroyed traditions. Normally cautious producers were swept up in the excitement, sending out scouts in search of virgin talent. Between 1959 and 1961, 65 directors the public had never heard of made their first films.

The hunt concentrated on the young bourgeoisie with a talent for self-publicity. Their inspiration was largely confined to introverted preoccupations of a young, frustrated middle class which had grown up after the austerity period. The favourite subject matter was adolescent disillusion set against the background of Saint-Germain, the Quartier Latin or the chic quartiers around the Champs-Elysées and the sixteenth arrondissement. In the excitement of the Nouvelle Vague the good and the bad of the period were indiscriminately mixed, but the films left a lasting image of a certain type of France that still angers many cultural leaders.

At the time the image was known as 'Saganism', although the novelist Jean Cau said it had neither the grace nor the melancholy of the works of Françoise Sagan. Cau, who split with Sartre in 1957 for political reasons but without bitterness, was one of the first to express dismay at the impact of the Nouvelle Vague. In *L'Express* in 1960 he made an attack on the inheritors of *Les Cahiers'* breakthrough, saying the Nouvelle Vague directors had not fulfilled their promise of the 'lyricism and the storminess of Shakespeare'.

For a decade, he wrote, young critics had demanded cameras and said they were inspired by Stroheim, Griffith, Murnau, Eisenstein, Welles, Rossellini, Renoir and Kazan while their literary 'godfathers' were Shakespeare, Faulkner, Kafka, Joyce, Conrad and Dostoevsky.

'We took them at their word,' Cau wrote. 'What do they tell us? They tell us about Saint Tropez, sports cars, whisky, skiing stations in winter, the whimsical games of love and chance, the doltish empty witticisms of boys and girls who sleep together at the flick of a finger like the salivation of Pavlov's dogs. France has become under the eye of their camera a sort of Monaco, peopled by fashion photographers and Chanel models who drink whisky (never Cognac) and to whom life is a monotonous sequence devoted to amorous libertinage.'

At least twenty of the Nouvelle Vague directors were to rise to the status of major cultural opinion-makers during the following two decades and many of them have reinforced a distorted image of France which still dismays important figures of the Tabou era. In the peak years of the Nouvelle Vague, the frivolous subject matter was tantamount to sacrilege as France was involved in the most desperate stage of the Algerian War. France herself was on the verge of civil war, stirred up by the extreme Right OAS secret army. As melancholy years in modern French history, 1958 and 1960 were as humiliating as the worst times of the Second World War.

The escapism induced by the Nouvelle Vague has its parallels in the Collaborationist bars of the Nazi Occupation, but, in another echo of the war with Germany, art sometimes tri-

umphed. Against the flood of middle-class egotism has to be set
the Alain Resnais–Marguerite Duras film, *Hiroshima mon
Amour*, another lauréat of the Cannes Festival of 1959 that
stands out like Saint-Germain's last great monument before the
area went into decline.

Partly because the most successful Nouvelle Vague director,
François Truffaut, has become the resident spokesman of
modern French cinema, Resnais is too often seen as inaccessible, particularly as his films are rare and he likes to film in an
atmosphere of drawing-room intimacy. In fact he enjoys going
over the long and discouraging period before *Hiroshima mon
Amour* brought him fame with the Critics' Prize at Cannes in
1959.

Much of Resnais's early initiation on the Left Bank has a
familiar ring, a semi-orphan state which accelerated self-
discovery. In 1938, because of asthma and family tension,
Resnais, then sixteen, was sent to Paris from his home in
Brittany to live with his grandfather in the rue de l'Université.
The flat was only a few yards from where he made his perma-
nent home after marrying Florence Malraux, André and Clara
Malraux's daughter, in 1969.

The son of a provincial chemist, Resnais had been given a
movie camera at the age of thirteen. His first films were of girls
leaving the local Catholic Church. But once outside the control
of his strict parents, Resnais's asthma disappeared and he was
able to indulge his 'cinema fanaticism' in Paris. At the time the
Cinéac on the Champs-Elysées specialised in American films in
their original undubbed versions, which Resnais preferred even
though he did not speak English, a preference shared by most
Nouvelle Vague directors for whom technique was all-
important.

'There were only about four French films a year worth
seeing – the Carné, the Renoir, the Duvivier, the Clair', he said.
'My own world was really American. The sight of a tricolor
stirred nothing in me but I would stand up for the Stars and
Stripes.'

Resnais's fascination with films continued during the clan-destine showings on the Left Bank during the war when he helped André Bazin, but the Saint-Germain intellectual atmos-phere intimidated him, particularly as he did not even have the baccalauréat, a distinction he shared with his future father-in-law, André Malraux.

'I was too shy to become part of the regulars at the Flore although I can claim to have seen Sartre and De Beauvoir writing calmly at their corner tables,' he said. 'After *La Nausée*, Sartre was a god for me. Gréco, Vian and the others I watched from afar. They were too intelligent for me – they seemed to be another generation.' (Gréco was, in fact, five years younger and Vian only two years older.)

In the immediate post-war period, Resnais trained at the Institut d'Hautes Etudes du Cinéma, IDHEC, at the Palais de Chaillot on the Right Bank. The Institute had been recently transferred from Nice but did not have enough equipment and staff to give proper training to students who later made up the support battalions of the revived film industry.

As a film editor with a highly original talent, Resnais might have become an influential director much earlier if he had used the Saint-Germain network properly. At one time, he lived in the same block of flats in the rue du Dragon as Gérard Philipe. They went drinking and shopping together, but lost touch when Philipe's career, as the most praised of post-war actors, took off.

Philipe was an active Left-wing militant. Resnais's main Marxist contacts were among the cinema technicians in the production houses on the Champs-Elysées, but his 'sentimen-tal' attachment to the Left was not enough to earn encourage-ment from the Communist Party. He made it too clear that he was not ready to follow Party rules 'such as sacrificing little pleasures and stopping listening to Stravinsky'. He also became too strongly identified with the writers at Les Editions du Seuil at the time when rumours that they were sponsored by the Vatican had to be denied.

After making a series of short films about painters at work, on

Alain Resnais, film director – the intellectual atmosphere of Saint-Germain
intimidated him and he felt too shy to join in

his own initiative, Resnais received financial backing for
documentaries, one of which illustrated the absurd state of
French censorship in 1954. With his friend Chris Marker,
another habitué of the Seuil discussion groups, he made a film
on African art called *Les Statues meurent aussi* in which he
praised indigenous culture, and implied that it was as worthy of
a place in the Louvre as Greek art. The film was banned as
subversive, an attack on French colonial policy.

'It was censored simply because the political line was different from the official government one,' he said. 'In fact it was what I would call a Unesco style film, a sort of boyscout image of Africa. All the same, it seemed to be the end of my career. No producer approached me for two years and I had to make ends meet by grabbing any freelance work going, like taking publicity shots for a provincial bank.'

Resnais's contacts with the Left Bank group and his friends at Seuil kept his name circulating, however, and in 1956 a Polish-born industrialist, Anatole Dauman, who was three years younger than Resnais, asked him to make a film on the concentration camps. The documentary was released as *Nuit et Brouillard* and its impact ended a French cinema boycott of the realities of the Second World War. The politically-committed Dauman, fascinated by Resnais's meticulous direction, which owed so much to his professional training as an editor, asked him to film a documentary on the nuclear bomb.

In 1954, when he was twenty-seven, Dauman had financed Astruc's *Le Rideau cramoisi* and was a friend of most of the new cinéastes. He recalled that after asking Resnais to consider the bomb documentary, the director researched the project for six months before backing out, saying he preferred to make a feature film on a woman's view of Japan.

Dauman said Resnais suggested Sagan or De Beauvoir as scenario writer. Sagan was chosen but did not turn up for the first meeting. Resnais then suggested Marguerite Duras, 'a writer I had hardly heard of', Dauman said, and whom the director had not even met.

Resnais agreed to meet Duras in her flat in the rue St Benoît, where they talked for an entire afternoon. 'She had an idea about a love story with the atomic bomb as background', the director said. 'We were both anti-bomb but I don't believe that cinema can give a political message. What we wanted to show was the effect of the bomb on ordinary lives.'

Finance for the film depended on finding Japanese money to back up a sum held by French interests but blocked in Japan. To persuade the Japanese producers to participate, Duras recorded the script outline on a tape which Resnais took to

Marguerite Duras: her films *Hiroshima mon Amour* and *Moderato Cantabile* quickly became classics

Hiroshima. Even the tape itself was to play an important part in the inventive direction techniques that made *Hiroshima mon Amour* one of the most influential productions in cinema history, alongside acknowledged masterpieces such as *The Battleship Potemkin* and *Citizen Kane*. The rhythm of Duras's voice inspired Resnais to give the sound track its distinctive radiophonic pace.

Nowadays the film is discussed and analysed for its cinematic innovation and its relation to the Nouveau Roman group to which Marguerite Duras, with her elliptical style, was inevitably allied by association. The later use of Alain Robbe-Grillet, leading theorist of the new novel, for Resnais's *L'Année dernière à Marienbad* increased these links. Resnais's unexpected success also helped the career of the Belgian born director, Agnès Varda, a member of the Seuil-linked Left Bank group, who made the enigmatic *Cléo de 5 à 7*. In turn she launched another literary filmmaker, her husband Jacques Demy.

Resnais recalled that the artistic success of *Hiroshima mon Amour* had a considerable effect on relaxing censorship throughout Europe and North America. The most spectacular success was in Canada where *Hiroshima mon Amour* was banned. In the outcry that followed, the censorship committee was dismantled. The film also added to the complicated relationships between committed and unorthodox Marxists in Saint-Germain as the Soviet Union was angered by the political content. Resnais and Duras received an official reprimand from the Soviet Writers' Union, somewhat ironical in the case of Marguerite Duras, who had quit the Party nine years earlier in protest against its authoritarianism, after the failure of her attempts to change the Party's structure from the inside.

Resnais's close association with writers at Seuil identified him indirectly with a literary struggle to break Sartre's influence on the novel. Although he had failed to finish *Les Chemins de la Liberté* by abandoning the promised fourth volume, Sartre had considerable success in persuading writers that novel writing must have social and political commitment.

Seuil, with its Catholic links, often felt itself the centre of opposition to Sartre, a role confirmed in the Sixties when it sponsored the literary magazine, *Tel Quel*. The founder was Philippe Sollers, who at the age of twenty-three published his first novel, *Une Curieuse Solitude*, at Seuil in 1959 on the recommendation of François Mauriac. Sollers moved to Paris from Bordeaux and gathered around him a new generation of authors whose contributions to *Tel Quel* eclipsed Sartre's *Les Temps Modernes* as a focal point for literary debate, just as *Arguments*, published by Les Editions de Minuit, took over leadership of Marxist-linked philosophical discussion.

With *Hiroshima Mon Amour*, Resnais was brought into close contact with Marguerite Duras's publishers, Les Editions de Minuit, operating from grubby, cramped ground-floor offices that evoked its Resistance beginnings. Even its policy of publishing difficult, often outrageous, authors and its encouragement of the Nouveau Roman seemed like a tribute to its original subversive vocation.

Its 1942 founder, Vercors (Jean Bruller) used up much of the money he made out of his bestseller, *Le Silence de la Mer*, to keep the company afloat after the war. But his daring publishing policy in releasing 'unknown' or unacceptable authors like Dylan Thomas, Georges Bataille, Karl Jaspers and Arthur Miller accelerated the company's shaky financial position. In 1948, he handed over the business to a friend, Jerôme Linden. Three years later, Linden moved the offices to the rue Bernard-Palissy, a street named after the sixteenth-century ceramic artist whose statue stands in the grounds of Saint-Germain Abbey. The presence of this highly adventurous firm encouraged new literary meeting places such as the Village bar and Le Nuage.

Linden pursued what seemed like a suicidal course, choosing authors who had been rejected by everyone else. His association with Beckett threatened the firm with extinction until the success of *En Attendant Godot* changed the company's fortunes. In 1957, four years after the play's success, Les Editions de Minuit had become the powerhouse of the New Novel, publishing in the same year, Alain Robbe-Grillet's *La Jalousie*, Claude Simon's *Le Vent*, Michel Butor's *La Modification* and a revised version of Nathalie Sarraute's *Tropismes*, first released in 1938 by Robert Denoël. The following year, Les Editions de Minuit published Marguerite Duras's *Moderato Cantabile*, her first real success, opening the way to her script-writing role for Alain Resnais.

The Nouveau Roman was to create more literary controversy than any other cultural argument during the Fifties. Most of the debate was devoted to writing off the movement altogether.

Nearly thirty years later, it is still described as being on the verge of extinction or as never having existed. But, of contemporary French writers, the new novelists are among a handful of authors whose works are automatically translated into English as soon as they appear, selling particularly well in the United States.

As the authors have a fanatical, scientific devotion to seeking new forms for the novel their books would have found a limited audience whatever the atmosphere in the book industry. But it is hard to believe that the Nouveau Roman would have unified as a movement without the special circumstances of Saint-Germain-des-Prés where an adventurous small publisher, born out of the Resistance, had immediate access to an enclosed critical debate where authors themselves recommended new books on the strength of literary café discussions. It meant that even isolated authors, like Nathalie Sarraute, who lived on the Right Bank and who had suffered a dismally discouraging response to her literary experiments, were to have international influence quite late in life.

Sarraute, a small, engaging woman, who hides an attractive personality behind a somewhat stern appearance, was born in Russia and first came to Paris at the age of two when her father, an industrial chemist and factory owner, separated from her mother. Much of her early childhood was divided between France and Tsarist Russia where her mother wrote books under a man's name. Her adolescent education was at a Left Bank lycée and she later went to Oxford before qualifying as a lawyer. In 1923, she married another lawyer and had three children. Her husband has always been the first to read her manuscripts, encouraging her to give up Law for literature.

Her stable family life, most of it spent in the sixteenth arrondissement, contrasts with the more turbulent emotional lives of her contemporaries like De Beauvoir, Duras and Yourcenar with whom she has little or no contact. Her first book, *Tropismes*, was begun in 1932. It is a very personal fascination with multiple layers of thoughts and reflections which underlie normal conversations. It took seven years before acceptance by

Nathalie Sarraute, a Russian Jew by origin, became one of the leading exponents of the Nouveau Roman

Robert Denoël who discovered Raymond Queneau and Céline and published Elsa Triolet during the war.

Because she is a Jewess, Sarraute took refuge in the country with her children during the Occupation, an exile memorable for a brief stay by Samuel Beckett when he was on the run from the Nazis in 1942. She turned out her children from the only habitable bedroom to give it to Beckett and his companion and again gave him refuge at the Liberation when he returned to Paris. Beckett's version of these events, in which he said that he was put up in an attic alongside Sarraute's dying father, has not endeared the Irishman to Sarraute and she has not seen him since the war.

'Frankly, his metaphysical despair disturbs me,' she said. 'What his characters say doesn't interest me. He is always snivelling and I don't like his lack of decency.'

Tropismes hardly caused a sensation either before or during the war. After the Liberation, a disappointed Sarraute sent a copy to Sartre along with her latest book, *Portrait d'un Inconnu*. Although deluged with manuscripts at the time, Sartre prefaced *Portrait d'un Inconnu* but it was a publishing disaster, selling only 400 copies. The rest of the run was shredded.

'It was painful to be rejected everywhere,' Sarraute said. 'I had the impression of showing something that had never been shown before. No one understood anything.'

Sarraute considered Sartre 'very generous' but sympathy stopped there partly because she could not stand De Beauvoir's work. As for Sartre's output, Sarraute liked *La Nausée* but much preferred Céline's *Voyage au bout de la Nuit*. She was particularly influenced by Proust and to a lesser extent by Virginia Woolf, but was advised not to mention Proust when contacting Sartre. The philosopher disliked Proust, who was unpopular among Left-wing intellectuals after the war. Sartre considered that a homosexual was incapable of describing the thoughts and feelings of a heterosexual.

'Proust was the bête noire after the Liberation,' she said. 'The aristocracy he described no longer existed. Sartre believed that a workman could not feel what Swann felt. Personally, I believe we all feel the same things at a certain emotional level, proletariat and bourgeois alike. But Sartre idealised the proletariat and believed that a bourgeois could not write about them because the proletariat was distinctively proletarian.'

She saw neither Sartre nor De Beauvoir after publication of *Portrait d'un Inconnu* because 'Sartre considered new forms of the novel as curiosities, as odd little monsters.'

'His theory of the roman engagé was the opposite of my ideas. Anyway, he and De Beauvoir had an unbearable hierarchical attitude. They surrounded themselves with people who formed a sort of court.'

Increasingly frustrated at lack of recognition, Sarraute wrote 'L'Ere du Soupçon', an essay in which she described her ideas about novel writing. She argued that the central character, 'believed in' by both writer and reader, could no longer be the 'centre of gravity' in a fictional work. The essay was sent to *Les Temps Modernes* and would probably have been refused by Sartre. But in February 1950, he was absent and Merleau-Ponty accepted it. When Sartre returned, a second essay, 'Conversation et sous-conversation' was refused by the review.

The essay was an indirect challenge to Sartre's ideas of 'committed novels' and had no place in *Les Temps Modernes*. Sartre's censorship of ideas that ran contrary to his own caused considerable resentment among intellectuals and it was not until 1956 that a wider public heard of Sarraute's theories when a collection of essays, again called *L'Ere du Soupcon*, was published by Gallimard. Sarraute was then fifty-six, and was to become the oldest of any of the intellectual opinion-makers of the Saint-Germain period to make a wide impact. Even Beckett had been only forty-seven when *En Attendant Godot* was performed for the first time.

Just as Ionesco had needed the enthusiasm of the young Nicolas Bataille to launch his career with *La Cantatrice Chauve*, Sarraute was to benefit from an intellectual partnership with a much younger writer, Alain Robbe-Grillet. At the time Gallimard's released *L'Ere du Soupcon*, Robbe-Grillet was only twenty-four but had the talent for self-publicity and the naïve crusading spirit that had launched so many young cultural personalities.

Robbe-Grillet, who had studied agriculture, wrote his first book, *Les Gommes*, when twenty-one. In 1956, he reviewed *L'Ere du Soupcon* in a magazine called *Critique*, published by Les Editions de Minuit, and invited Sarraute to take part in a conference about new ideas on novel writing.

'Alain Robbe-Grillet argued that we must form a movement to struggle against critics who were still imposing eighteenth-

and nineteenth-century forms on the novel,' Sarraute said. 'I was also convinced that novel writing had to be transformed in order to remain an art.'

The group had no title until an angry critic in the influential review, *Arts*, attacked Robbe-Grillet's 1957 book, *La Jalousie*, under the headline, 'Le Nouveau Roman est Mort', rubbishing the work of Les Editions de Minuit's experimental authors.

'The Nouveau Roman title stuck and helped me enormously,' Sarraute said. 'Suddenly my books were published abroad and I was invited to give lectures.'

Sarraute, who wrote her books in long-hand in a café near her sixteenth arrondissement flat, stayed out of the quarrels of Saint-Germain-des-Prés. Robbe-Grillet, a broad extrovert who is now as popular in the United States as in France, was confident enough to fight alone. He had been a member of Les Editions de Minuit's *comité de lecture* since 1954 and was awarded the Prix des Critiques for his 1955 novel, *Le Voyeur*, a year after Françoise Sagan received the prize for *Bonjour Tristesse*.

In addition to publishing ten novels, he gave a large number of interviews, organised conferences and published dozens of critical articles that made the Nouveau Roman one of the most talked about literary movements in history. It was an attitude that did no harm to his sales. *La Jalousie* sold only 600 copies at first but it has since been translated into fifteen languages and is a favourite subject for university theses, particularly in the United States.

'The latest books by Claude Simon, Nathalie Sarraute and myself attract real public interest,' he said. 'We have several dozen thousand sales for each work. The Nouveau Roman is still alive because the books we published in the Fifties are still being bought and read. Our public in the United States is as big as that in France.'

He admits that the Nouveau Roman's writers were brought together 'somewhat artificially by me and some critics'.

'What stirs up the media, what makes literary conscious move, is the power of groups,' he added.

The power of groups was the essence of Saint-Germain. Since

the area's influence dispersed, French culture has had a much lower impact internationally. In France, new authors, playwrights and cinéastes sometimes complain that they have been intimidated by the innovations of the era, that there is no new ground to break in a country that has now absorbed all the cultural, social and moral experiments into its way of life.

There does seem to have been a faltering in self-confidence after the decline of Saint-Germain-des-Prés but this seems mainly due to a fragmentation rather than a lack of talent. A strong central figure like Sartre with the power to excite reaction and counter-reaction will probably have to emerge before a new movement is created. When a revival does come, it is unlikely to settle again in Saint-Germain-des-Prés whose central place in French culture ended as suddenly as it began.

Many elements contributed, not least the changing attitude of French society as it emerged from years of austerity and political instability into a more prosperous television age. More liberal moral attitudes nationally made it difficult for innovators to gain attention through cultural scandal.

As for the major personalities of Saint-Germain, particularly the singers and the film directors, they became national or international property rather than villagers. Even Juliette Gréco temporarily abandoned the Left Bank for a film career in Hollywood. Death, age and illness broke up groups of friends who had been influential since the war years while Saint-Germain itself was to undergo a material transformation of its own that changed its Bohemian image. The cafés that had been at the centre of so many new ideas came to depend more and more on tourists.

The end of the Saint-Germain period can be safely dated to 1962 when Jean-Paul Sartre left for good. The three years before, as France went through the final convulsions of the Algerian War, were the saddest of Saint-Germain's two decades of fame.

10

La Nostalgie n'est plus
ce qu'elle était

Three days before Boris Vian died, Jean Cau chatted to him during one of their frequent casual meetings in the Village bar on the corner of the rue Bonaparte and the rue Gozlin. He was, as usual, extravagantly pale, 'a white clown with sad horse's eyes', according to Cau. Vian often used an Auvergne accent, picked up from the proprietor of the Flore, to overcome his awkwardness. All Cau can recall of that last meeting was Vian's routine greeting: 'Alorrrs, ça va, coco?'

On June 23, 1959, Vian died watching the poor film adaptation of his book, *J'irai cracher sur vos tombes*. There was no censorship of the publicity posters, as there had been for the play adaptation, and no public outcry at the content. Vian himself had slipped from public interest since *Le Déserteur*, but his public disclaimer of the film at least reminded people that he was still working.

The shock of his death at thirty-nine was the signal for the first wave of reminiscences on the great post-war period of Saint-Germain. Like Cau, many people would regret that they had not made notes of conversations with Vian or jotted down some memories of the high days at Le Tabou. Middle age had overtaken Saint-Germain without warning.

There were several other sad occasions between 1959 and 1961 that signalled the end of an era. André Bazin, inspiration of the cinema Nouvelle Vague, died at forty-one, just as his protégé, François Truffaut, filmed the first sequences of *Les 400 Coups*. Gérard Philipe whose stage and film career began with Camus's *Caligula* died of cancer. He was thirty-seven. In 1961, Maurice Merleau-Ponty died at the age of fifty-three. By the time of his death, the brief reign of Existentialism had been eclipsed by an upsurge of Structuralism, a philosophy which seemed intent on belittling and demobilising mankind, in contrast to the often naïvely uplifting ambitions of the Marxist-linked message preached by Merleau-Ponty and Sartre.

For all the sadness or shock of these deaths, none caused the emotion or dismay that followed that of Albert Camus who made frequent nostalgic visits to Saint-Germain and particularly the Flore. The author died in circumstances as ironic and poignant as any novel; a passenger in a car driven by his editor, Michel Gallimard, the nephew of Gaston Gallimard. In Camus's briefcase were the closely-written 160 opening pages of his last, uncompleted book, *Premier Homme*. The author had reached a new phase in a long, self-questioning period begun with *L'Homme revolté* and continued more enigmatically with *La Chute. Premier Homme* was, in his own words, 'very auto-biographical', a determined attempt to set his mind at rest by judging life through events that had affected him personally. Everything indicated an important watershed in the life of a forty-six-year-old man coming to terms with his own genius.

The accident that killed him occurred at exactly 1.54 pm on January 4, 1960 at the village of Villeblevin in the flat, open Yonne department south of Paris. Camus had spent the last few months at his new country home at Loumarin north-west of Avignon, writing the first draft of *Premier Homme* and making plans for his own Paris-based theatre. Michel Gallimard had collected him at the village to return to the capital. The publisher drove a French-built Facel-Véga sports car but

Camus disliked being driven fast and the journey was split in two with an overnight stop. On the second day, the car slid off a long stretch of the RN5, hit two roadside trees and turned over into a field. The brief-case containing the last manuscript was thrown out of the car into the mud. Camus, whose skull was fractured, died before the car overturned. Michel Gallimard lived for another six days.

There was considerable morbid reflection after the accident, particularly as Camus had a return rail ticket to Paris in his pocket. His friends remembered a series of premonitions of Camus's death, some by the author himself. The actress, Maria Casares, recalled that Camus had once said that there was nothing so stupid as death in a car accident. Other friends claimed that Camus, beset by self-doubt about his talent, had morosely wished to die young like Gérard Philipe.

Perhaps the only good thing that came out of the crash was a post-mortem reconciliation with Sartre. The philosopher wrote a moving tribute to his old friend, saying of Camus: 'In this century, and against history, he represented the current inheritor of a long line of moralists whose works make up what is most original in French literature.' A year later, Sartre also wrote a fine eulogy for his estranged comrade, Merleau-Ponty.

In some ways, though, the crash was timely. It removed Camus from a new controversy. The Left, both Communist and non-Communist, had accelerated its campaign in favour of Algerian independence. Those who refused a clear-cut commitment to the Algerian FLN movement were treated with the contempt once reserved for Vichy supporters. Camus's attitude was disturbing. He campaigned against French Army torture alongside Sartre and Malraux but become increasingly identified with the Pieds-Noirs, the white settlers. He was again searching for a middle-way solution reminiscent of past political vacillation. Much was made of his remark, when he received the Nobel Prize, that he believed in Justice, but if he had to choose between Justice and his mother, he would choose his mother.

Even to be obliquely in favour of a French role in Algeria was considered reactionary. The Left had gone back to its anticolonial sources of the Thirties, reawakening the campaigns of André Gide. This time, though, they had to count without André Malraux, a man who had exercised an increasing influence on Camus during his last years.

Sartre's unorthodox followers in Saint-Germain-des-Prés had seen their worst predictions proved when André Malraux joined De Gaulle's government as Information Minister in 1958 before starting a ten-year career as Cultural Minister. Secretly, he had campaigned to be Interior Minister, a sinister job in a barely legitimate government backed by conservatives and upheld by the Army.

He explained his ambitions by his determination to play a role in resolving the Algerian problem, which, at the time, meant a militarily-imposed French solution. As in so many decisions made by French intellectuals, his association with De Gaulle's government was not free of personal rivalries.

Malraux said he would prefer to seek a solution for Algeria inside the government 'rather than at the Flore', an image still linked to Sartre's Marxist entourage. But it was outdated imagery, evoking 1944 and 1945 rather than the reality of 1958. Even Camus's irregular, nostalgic visits to the café had nothing to do with politics. He went there to fulfil a compulsive search for new women companions.

As the debate on Algeria became more complex, with De Gaulle turning against his own generals and campaigning for Arab-run independence, Malraux seemed more and more as if he were acting out his role of being De Gaulle's best-known Minister rather than making any contribution other than superbly-weighed speeches that continued to develop a mystic veil around the general.

Malraux needed something to grasp at to avoid being overwhelmed by the tragedies of his private life. In 1961, his two sons, Gautier, twenty-one and Vincent, eighteen, were killed in a car crash not far from the village where Camus died a year before. The boys were buried next to their mother, Josette Clotis.

Malraux's attitude until his death in 1975 was always puzzling and interpretations were not helped by his semi-fictional life story, *Antimémoires*. But at least there were no significant political changes to match his still unexplained switch to Gaullism from Communism somewhere in the Maquis in 1943. Louis Aragon, on the other hand, made a very personal change in his life-style when Elsa Triolet died in 1970 after more than forty years of companionship and marriage. It was a change that made him one of the most despised intellectuals of the post-war period.

In 1965, he had written *La Mise à mort*, an autobiographically-based analysis of a love-hate relationship that could lead to madness and murder. Two years later there was another novel, *Blanche ou l'oubli* which spoke of the destructiveness of passion. No one doubted that he was referring to Elsa, possibly the subject of more love poems by a husband than any woman in history.

When Elsa died, Aragon installed a shrine at the entrance of his flat dominated by a ten-foot-high portrait of Elsa, her mouth drawn, her eyes stern. During the twelve years he survived her, he remained the Communist Party's favourite star, turned out on the platform for the annual *Humanité* gatherings in Paris which attract up to a million people. But it was considered treachery in the Party to refer to Aragon's night-time activities, which destroyed the ennobling image of the elegant poet's love story with the novelist from Moscow.

Aragon's white hair was distinguishable from afar and Parisian gossips soon became tired of tales that the poet was now seen regularly in the city's homosexual haunts. A few re-membered that Aragon had been attracted by homosexuality before he met Elsa and had told his friends that he liked to think it shocked his Surrealist mentor, André Breton, who was disgusted by male love affairs.

In the last few years, when Aragon was often surrounded by flocks of beautiful young men, there was amusement that after the gay scene had shifted to Saint-Germain-des-Prés, he went to the area he had so often cursed to seek out 'conquests'.

However, he still avoided the Flore which became an evening meeting place for homosexuals but which still liked to show off Sartrian relics including the philosopher's favourite table and De Beauvoir's teapot. Aragon almost certainly avoided the rue Saint-Benoît as well. Marguerite Duras still reigned over the street and was among those never afraid to express her contempt for the Communist poet. Once she recalled how she had been nauseated by a television appearance by Aragon in the late Seventies when he claimed to have condemned undemocratic methods in foreign Communist parties.

'His face had become a mask, but a living one,' she said. 'It was horrifying. He lied all the time. I despise him – a dustbin hero.'

By the time Aragon gave in to his homosexuality, metaphorically spitting on Elsa Triolet's giant portrait, there was nothing at all left of his brief understanding with Sartre before the mid-Fifties. The Hungarian revolt and the Kruschev revelations on Stalin's crimes had reopened the personality and ideological gap. From then on, both men were to treat the other as a hypocrite.

Sartre's 'semi-rupture' with the Party coincided with disintegrating health. Few people expected him to survive the decade. His self-esteem could hardly have been helped by the decision to award Camus the Nobel Prize in 1957, although he consistently denied any jealousy. Seven years later he refused the Nobel Prize for his work.

A much more staggering blow than Camus's success was the ease with which the Right re-established itself with De Gaulle's coup d'état. Sartre was obliged to confront a bleak assessment of the uselessness of his political commitment decided eighteen years before during the Phony War. He had done nothing with his reputation except divide the Left more deeply and allow the Right to creep back through the chaos.

Many of his friends felt that De Gaulle's return to power, with its overtones of a Vichy renaissance, would kill Sartre. Instead, it acted like a shock treatment. He feverishly threw himself into writing *La Critique de la raison dialectique*, rushing through its 600 pages with hardly a halt to make corrections. It was an exercise strikingly familiar to his dedication to *l'Etre et le Néant* during the war. The vestiges of the little boy who wanted to be admired for his brilliant mind had again triumphed inside the besieged middle-aged man.

La Critique was intended to provide the moral and political code left largely unanswered in *L'Etre et le Néant* and botched in the hasty *Existentialisme est-il un humanisme?* The new book not only gave him a new lease of life at the age of fifty-two, but seemed to serve as a lesson in humility. His editor, Robert Gallimard, recalled that Sartre hardly behaved like the vindicated philosopher, triumphant at his new insight into modern man, when he turned up at the Gallimard offices in the rue Sébastien-Bottin.

Instead of pushing his way into Robert Gallimard's office, as a star author was entitled to do, Sartre took his place in the foyer alongside unpublished hopefuls and waited to be invited in. When Robert Gallimard greeted him, Sartre handed over his manuscript and said: 'I wonder if this would interest you?'

The work was too late to renew his widespread influence, particularly as 1960 was hardly the time for political reflection but for militant action. His waning stature however recovered among his admiring circle who dutifully followed him in his ferocious attacks on French policy in Algeria. He even took the risk of being imprisoned when he publicly defended his biographer, Francis Jeanson, who had established an Algerian independence movement logistical network in France. Hatred for Sartre among his Press and political enemies flared to heights not seen since the Liberation years. It was implied that Sartre was the mastermind of a traitorous pro-Arab underground movement.

The physical threat he had failed to confront when the Nazis occupied France, caught up with him in Saint-Germain-des-Prés in 1962. Right-wing extremists of the OAS Secret Army tried to kill him with a bomb outside his flat. Sartre had to leave the area and take a small studio flat in Montparnasse, leading a

A reunion of *Les Temps Modernes* in 1978. Sartre was almost blind, Simone de Beauvoir seated next to him remained a pillar of strength throughout his life

semi-clandestine life that completed a circle started at the Hotel Mistral in 1941.

From then until his death, Jean-Paul Sartre's influence was part of a pattern of Left-wing alliances that was finally to oust the Right from power in 1981. As he took up so many marginal causes, his role was not always clear but he rallied a dispersed, intellectual conscience group, holding together the Left's extreme flanks that always threatened to disintegrate into pointless anarchism.

Opposition to the Algerian War provided an identity of views on the Left unknown since the Nazi Occupation. Uneasy links, inspired by contempt for De Gaulle, survived the new peace. In 1965, Mitterrand, playing on his visceral rivalry with the General, was given the support of the entire Left, including the

Communists, in his first bid for the Presidency. Mitterrand rallied a surprising 45 per cent forcing De Gaulle to undergo a humiliating run-off vote. In 1974, Communists and the extreme-left again endorsed Mitterrand who came within a few thousand votes of defeating Valéry Giscard d'Estaing. That election signalled a historic decline of the Communist Party, now a tame, neutered element of Mitterrand's Socialist administration.

Although Sartre's multitude of causes as an all-purpose agitator meant that he was rarely out of the news for more than a week or two, his hold over middle-class Parisian youth was never renewed. In May 1968, when the whole of the Left Bank was aflame, he tried to assemble rioting students under his banner. The effort was greeted with derisory humour and calls of: 'Go home to bed, grandpa.' For that generation, the Saint-Germain figure who really counted was Boris Vian, by then the best-selling author of the decade and the inspiration of Left Bank slogans that echoed the cynicism of the lavatory wall in the Bar Vert.

'Be reasonable. Ask for the impossible' was pure Vian. For all the supposed extreme-left leadership of the student riots, the flare-up was not a political outcry in the terms of Sartrian commitment. It was 'Ras l'bol', the cry of a youth movement fed up with strictures and regulations handed down from their convention-bound parents and professeurs. In 1968, Vian's Saint-Germain was alive and well and living in the Quartier Latin. The spirit of Le Tabou had outlived that of the Flore.

As for Saint-Germain itself, some of the personalities who made it famous still live there. Marguerite Duras still rules over the rue Saint-Benoît. Jean Cau lives in the rue de Seine while Alain Vian, who was so close to his brother, Boris, throughout his life, has a music shop in the rue Grégoire-de-Tours. Few have moved much further than walking distance from the parish. Astruc, Cazalis, Gréco, De Beauvoir, Ionesco, Montand, Signoret, Resnais and Vercors-Bruller are among them.

Most are still very active, even though the post-Saint-Germain period, for some, was harrowing either emotionally or for health reasons. Those who showed exceptional courage in their youth, like Vercors, still play an energetic role in crusades of conscience. On the Right Bank, Claude Bourdet, as striking as when he was young, campaigns against nuclear weapons. Not far from him, Nathalie Sarraute, at the age of eighty-three, scored a triumph in 1983 with her childhood memories, *Enfance*, which was also presented as a play at Jean-Louis Barrault's new Rond Point theatre off the Champs Elysées the following year. In an adjoining auditorium, Duras was presenting her much-acclaimed *Savannah Bay*, confirming her as one of the most productive and influential of contemporary French writers.

Signoret, still the most-admired of French actresses, started a vogue for reflections on the post-war period with her 1975 autobiography, *La Nostalgie n'est plus ce qu'elle était*. Soon afterwards, Juliette Gréco, who abandoned her Hollywood career to continue singing, brought out her own memories. In 1984, Françoise Sagan followed suit, bringing home the fact that the *enfant prodige* was now approaching fifty. Her contacts with Sartre had been formal when she was young, but in old age she was his last confidante. In the last year of his life, they dined regularly together in Montparnasse. He refused to give in to his blindness although he told her that when he lost his sight in 1976 and realised that he could write no more he thought of committing suicide.

'I didn't even try', he told her. 'I just continued to be happy through habit.'

Of his death – Sagan was among the few friends who went to the second ceremony after the tumultuous funeral – Sagan said she would never get over it or forget Sartre's 'voice, intelligence, courage and generosity'.

There were other indications of passing time including the 1984 award of a special Grand Prix by the government to Jean Genet, a benign grey-haired old man held in as much esteem as the other surviving Absurdists, Ionesco and Beckett, poor, haunted Adamov having committed suicide in 1970. As for Saint-Germain's singing poets, Catherine Sauvage, Léo Ferré and Juliette Gréco still attract large followings, but Jacques Brel died in 1978 and Georges Brassens in 1981.

Most of the Nouvelle Vague of directors have been eclipsed or settled into routine commercial productions whose quality makes many of the films they attacked in the Fifties look like masterpieces. Astruc, the pioneer, now concentrates on novels. Jacques Doniol-Valcroze, former editor of *Les Cahiers du Cinéma*, makes only television films. None of the big three, Truffaut, Chabrol and Godard has anything flattering to say about the others. Only Godard has retained links with New Wave experimentation. Resnais, meanwhile, readily talks about his technical skill, but shies from any analysis about subjects in case he has to admit, in his own words, 'that it's only a film'. Cocteau, the showman, died in 1963, but muffed his exit by quitting the stage in the same week as Edith Piaf who stole all the headlines. French cinema has not found a replacement for Brigitte Bardot who retired at forty. Only Catherine Deneuve, of the New Wave women stars, is a guaranteed box-office success.

Saint-Germain's personalities seem unable to provoke controversy any more in a France fascinated by consumerism and technology.

Yves Montand, however, has become one of the most written about men of his generation since he turned savagely on the Communist Party, producing a popular centre-Right blend of politics that has put pressure on him to try a Reagan-style bid for the Presidency.

From a literary point of view, De Beauvoir stands alone as a subject of criticism. Her concentration on a posthumous Sartre cult, of which she is high priestess and sole arbitrator, has caused considerable bitterness, coupled with accusations from Sartre's old friends that she is censoring his unpublished material to boost her own role and belittle that of others.

The novelist and former editor of *L'Express*, Olivier Todd, who was once an intimate part of the philosopher's 'Family' before accusing him of 'ruining an entire generation' said De Beauvoir was acting like a *'veuve abusive'*. Since *La Cérémonie des adieux* there has been a public chill between De Beauvoir and Sartre's adopted daughter, Arlette El Kaim-Sartre, who strongly influenced him in his marginal campaigns of the last years. She has accused De Beauvoir of making her look like a fool and of implying that Sartre was manipulated by his young entourage when he was all but senile.

Some of Sartre's friends from the Saint-Germain days felt squeezed out in the later years by a new generation with new causes. To put it crudely, in a remark made by one of his first disciples who for charity's sake will remain anonymous, 'Sartre was all right until he fell into the hands of the Jews.'

As a semi-recluse, De Beauvoir rejects all pressures to defend herself against accusations that she is falsifying Sartre's arguments and his view of his friends. She knows that Sartre left her enough unpublished works, particularly letters, to give her the last word.

Except for the traffic and the tourists, Saint-Germain's outward appearance has not changed much. Most of the monuments – the Flore, Le Tabou, Les Deux Magots – are intact. On a quiet morning it is easy to reconstruct the casual intellectual life and youthful dreams of the post-war period. The Algerian War, however, produced another side-effect as important as the departure of Sartre from his flat overlooking the Place Saint-Germain. An influx of returning Pieds-Noirs bought out the old artisan class, replacing their ateliers with antique shops and up-market kitsch. Speculation turned most of the damp, barely inhabitable medieval buildings into 'desirable property'. The area now has residents who would not have considered living there thirty years ago, including several Right-wing politicians. Property values have resisted the downward trend of much of the capital, a proof being the sale of the Café de Flore for nearly two million dollars in 1984, although Paul Boubal keeps a table there under a special sale clause which respects its historical décor. Saint-Germain is now a very chic place to live. A square metre of living space sells for as much as a similar area in the bourgeois sixteenth arrondissement whose smugness so appalled its most famous son, Jean-Paul Sartre, that he took refuge on the Left Bank to save his liberal soul.

Recommended Reading

(Where translations are available, the English publisher is given in square brackets)

ARTHUR ADAMOV *L'Aveu* (Gallimard) [Calder] 1942
— *Ici et Maintenant* (Gallimard) [Calder] 1964
— *L'Homme et l'enfant* (Gallimard) [Calder] 1967
HENRI AMOUROUX *La Vie des Français sous l'Occupation* (Fayard) 1961
RAYMOND ARON *Mémoires* (Julliard) 1983
LOUIS ARAGON *Aurélien* (Gallimard) 1945
— *Le Roman inachevé* (Gallimard) 1956
ODETTE ASLAN *Jean Genet* (Seghers) 1973
SIMONE DE BEAUVOIR *L'Invitée* (Gallimard) [Fontana] 1943
— *Les Mandarins* (Gallimard) [Fontana] 1954
— *Mémoires d'une fille bien rangée* (Gallimard) [Penguin] 1958
— *La Force de l'Age* (Gallimard) [Penguin] 1960
— *La Force des Choses* (Gallimard) [Penguin] 1963
— *Le Deuxième Sexe* (Gallimard) [Penguin] 1949
SAMUEL BECKETT *En Attendant Godot* (Editions de Minuit) [Faber] 1953
DIERDRE BLAIR *Samuel Beckett* (Picador) 1978
NICOLE BOTHOREL, FRANCINE DUGAST, JEAN THORAVAL *Les Nouveaux Romanciers* (Bordas) 1976
CLAUDE BOURDET *L'Aventure Incertaine* (Stock) 1975
PIERRE BERRUER *Jacques Brel va bien. Il dort aux Iles Marquises* (Presses de la Cité) 1983
CHANTAL BRUNSCHWIG, LOUIS-JEAN CALVET, JEAN-CLAUDE KLEIN *Cent ans de Chanson Française* (Seuil) 1981

ROBERT BRASILLACH *Poèmes de Fresnes* (Plon) 1983
JEAN-MICHEL BRIAL *Georges Brassens* (Editions PAC) 1981
ALBERT CAMUS *L'Etranger* (Gallimard) [Penguin] 1942
— *La Peste* (Gallimard) [Penguin] 1947
— *L'Homme Révolté* (Gallimard) [Penguin] 1951
— *La Chute* (Gallimard) [H. Hamilton] 1956
— *Carnets* (Gallimard) 1964
— *Caligula* (theatre) (Gallimard) 1945
— *Le Malentendu* (theatre) (Gallimard) 1944
— *Les Justes* (theatre) (Gallimard) [Penguin] 1950
— *Actuelles: Ecrits Politiques* (Gallimard) 1950
NADINE BERTHE CASTRO *Le Théâtre de Michel de Ghelderode* (Editions l'Age de l'Homme) 1976
ANNE-MARIE CAZALIS *Les Mémoires d'une Anne* (Stock) 1976
JACQUES CANETTI *On cherche jeune homme aimant la musique* (Calmann-Lévy) 1978
GEORGES COULONGES *La Chanson en son Temps* (Les Editeurs Français Réunis) 1969
MARGARET CROSLAND *Women of Iron and Velvet* (Constable) 1976
TONY CRAWLEY *Bardot* (Henri Veyrier) 1979
JEAN CAU *Une Nuit à Saint-Germain-des-Prés* (Julliard) 1977
DOMINIQUE DESANTI *Drieu la Rochelle* (Flammarion) 1978
— *Les Clés d'Elsa* (Ramsay) 1983
JACQUES DUCHATEAU *Boris Vian* (La Table Ronde) 1982
MARTIN ESSLIN *The Theatre of the Absurd* (Pelican) 1968
CHARLES FORD *Histoire du Cinema Français Contemporain* (Editions France Empire) 1977
RENÉ GAUDY *Arthur Adamov* (Stock) 1971
FRANZ-OLIVIER GIESBERT *François Mitterrand* (Seuil) 1977
JULIETTE GRÉCO *Jujube* (Stock) 1982
JEAN GENET *Les Bonnes* (Jean Jacques Pauvert) [Faber] 1947
— *Haute Surveillance* (Gallimard) [Faber] 1949
— *Oeuvres Complètes IV vols* (Gallimard) 1951
— *Le Balcon* (l'Arbalète) [Faber] 1956
— *Les Nègres* (l'Arbalète) [Faber] 1956
— *Les Paravents* (l'Arbalète) [Faber] 1966
ROBERT HOSSEIN *La Sentinelle Aveugle* (Grasset) 1978
— *Nomade sans Tribu* (Fayard) 1981
ANDRÉ HALIMI *On Connait la Chanson!* (Table Ronde) 1959
— *Chantons Sous l'Occupation* (Marabout) 1976
IAN HAMILTON *Koestler* (Secker and Warburg) 1982
EUGENE IONESCO *La Cantatrice Chauve* (Gallimard) [Calder] 1950
— *Les Chaises* (Gallimard) [Calder] 1952
— *La Leçon* (Gallimard) [Calder] 1954

— *L'Impromptu d'Alma* (Gallimard) [Calder] 1956
FRANCIS JEANSON *Sartre* (Seuil) 1974
JEAN LACOUTURE *Malraux* (Seuil) 1973
GUY LECLERC *Le TNP de Jean Vilar* (IO/I8) 1971
HERBERT LOTTMAN *La Rive Gauche* (Seuil) 1981
— *Albert Camus* (Seuil) 1978
JOHN MACQUARRIE *Existentialism* (Pelican) 1973
ANDRÉ MALRAUX *Antimémoires* (Gallimard) 1967
GABRIEL MARCEL *L'Heure Théâtrale* (Plon) 1959
— *Théâtre et Religion* (Emmanuel Vitte) 1958
HENRI MICHEL *Paris Allemand* (Albin Michel) 1981
— *Paris Résistant* (Albin Michel) 1982
JOËLLE MONSERRAT *Jacques Brel* (Editions PAC) 1982
IRIS MURDOCH *Sartre* (Harvester Press) 1979
CÉCILE PHILIPPE, PATRICE TOURENNE *Les Frères Jacques* (Balland)
    1981
GAËTAN PICON *Panorama de la nouvelle littérature française* (Gallimard)
    1976
RAYMOND QUENEAU *Exercises de style* (Gallimard) [Calder] 1947
FRANÇOISE RENAUDOT *Il était une fois Boris Vian* (Seghers) 1973
JEAN RICARDOU *Le Nouveau Roman* (Seuil) 1973
ALAIN ROBBE-GRILLET *Pour un Nouveau Roman* (Editions de Minuit)
    [Calder] 1963
— *Les Gommes* (Editions de Minuit) [Calder] 1953
— *La Jalousie* (Editions de Minuit) [Calder] 1957
DRIEU LA ROCHELLE *Gilles* (Gallimard) 1939
J-P ROUX *La France de la Quatrième République* (Seuil) 1980
GEORGES SADOUL *Le Cinéma Français* (Flammarion) 1962
FRANÇOISE SAGAN *Bonjour Tristesse* (Julliard) [Murray] 1954
— *Avec mon meilleur souvenir* (Gallimard) [Murray] 1984
NATHALIE SARRAUTE *Tropismes* (Editions de Minuit) [Calder] 1957
— *L'Ere du Soupçon* (Gallimard) [Calder] 1956
— *Portrait d'un Inconnu* (Robert Marin) [Calder] 1948
JEAN-PAUL SARTRE *La Nausée* (Gallimard) [Penguin] 1938
— *L'Etre et le Néant* (Gallimard) [Methuen] 1943
— *L'Age de Raison Les Chemins de la Liberté* (Gallimard) [Penguin]
    1945
— *Le Sursis Les Chemins de la Liberté* (Gallimard) [Penguin] 1945
— *La Mort dans l'âme Les Chemins de la Liberté* (Gallimard) [Penguin]
    1949
— *Les Mouches* (Gallimard) [Harrap] 1943
— *Huis Clos* (Gallimard) [Methuen] 1944
— *Le Diable et le Bon Dieu* (Gallimard) [Penguin] 1951
— *Saint Genet Comédien et Martyr* (Gallimard) 1952

— *Critique de la Raison Dialectique* (Gallimard) [New Left Books] 1960
— *Les Mots* (Gallimard) [H. Hamilton] 1964
— *Situations I–VII* (Gallimard) 1947–64
— *Les Carnets de la Drôle de Guerre* (Gallimard) 1983
— *Lettres au Castor* (Gallimard) 1983
PIERRE SEGHERS *La Résistance et ses poètes* (Marabout-université) 1953
GENEVIÈVE SERREAU *Histoire du "Nouveau Théâtre"* (Gallimard) 1966
ANDRÉ SEVE *Brassens* (Editions du Centurion) 1975
SIMONE SIGNORET *La Nostalgie n'est plus ce qu'elle était* (Seuil) 1975
ALFRED SIMON *Samuel Beckett* (Les Dossiers Belfond) 1983
ELSA TRIOLET *Les Amants d'Avignon* (Denoël) 1943
— *Le Premier Accroc coûte Deux Cents Francs* (Denoël) 1944
— *Le Cheval Roux* (Gallimard) 1953
VERCORS *Le Silence de la Mer* (Livre de Poche) [Macmillan] 1942
FRANCE VERNILLAT, JACQUES CHARPENTREAU *Dictionnaire de la Chanson Française* (Larousse) 1968
— *La Chanson Française* (Presses Universitaires de France) 1971
BORIS VIAN *l'Ecume des Jours* (IO/18) [Penguin] 1946
— *La Belle Epoque* (Christian Bourgois) 1982
— *Textes et Chansons* (IO/18) 1966
— *Manuel de Saint-Germain-des-Prés* (Chêne) 1974
— *Théâtre* (IO/18) 1965
— *J'irai cracher sur vos tombes* (IO/18) 1946
— *Automne à Pékin* (IO/18) 1956
JEANNINE VERDES-LEROUX *Les Intellectuels au Service du Parti* (Flammarion) 1983

Index

Numbers in italic refer to illustrations